25

THE MAD HATTER OF LONDON

THE MAD POET OF LONDON

A NOVEL IN PROSE SONNETS
AND TRADITIONAL VERSE

MARK LASKY

Troubador Publishing Ltd
Unit E2 Airfield Business Park,
Harrison Road, Market Harborough,
Leicestershire LE16 7UL
Tel: 0116 279 2299
Email: books@troubador.co.uk
Web: www.troubador.co.uk

ISBN 978-1-80514-397-0

British Library Cataloguing in Publication Data.
A catalogue record for this book is available from the British Library.

Typeset in 10pt Minion Pro by Troubador Publishing Ltd, Leicester, UK

For Ian Leigh, Mummzie, Zion and my brother Carl.
Karen 'Knuckles' Sibley, Kelly Dolan and especially Damien Wallace.

ABOUT THE AUTHOR

Mark Lasky has lived an unconventional life and has spent nearly seventeen years in prisons and secure hospitals. He's gained a BA in Creative Writing, a MA in Screenwriting and has had poems published in literary magazines. He now works as a screenwriter.

KRAM SKYAL'S POETRY
COLLECTION

PROLOGUE

i-1

2016, February the fourteenth
The night's wind howls outside,
To the moon's bequeath
An eeriness for ghosts to hide.
A shadow of a man stands,
In black, to the night he commands.
An owl hoo-hoos,
As the wind to the night, brews.
As Mr and Mrs Stapleton sleep
A loud smash comes to their surprise,
The car alarm to night defies,
Mr Stapleton from his bed, makes a leap.
He stares out of the bedroom window,
As a mist of rain sweeps in a neon glow.

1

i-2

'Emma, I'm sure it's him!'
As car lights in orange flashes.
'I feel his circling fin.'
Then, out of the bedroom, he dashes.
He puts on a sweater and slips on boats,
As fear to anger dilutes.
'Dean, be careful; he'll be armed!'
'But not with a gun, so don't be alarmed.'
He picks up a long-handled axe,
And walks outside in a violent show,
In shouts, beckoning his foe,
As night's cold hand to him smacks.
'Is that all you can do,' Dean lashes,
As rage and anger within him crashes.

i-3

He quickly becomes incredibly spooked,
Like a rabbit caught in a snare
His stomach churned and looped,
Noticing a cloud, a breath of air.
He grips his axe handle tight,
And steps further into the night.
Suddenly, a crossbow bolt enters his chest,
And he falls, dying, nearing death's rest.
The hooded figure stands in eerie pose,
As Emma's screams from window drown,
He drops a letter to shock the town,
Then, into night's blanket, he quickly goes.
Dean's eyes close, as death embraces,
Still, Emma screams, as terror chases.

i-4

Emma grabs her mobile and calls,
To alert the police
And against the window, she falls,
Still screaming to release.
'He's just struck seconds ago,
I live at fifteen Elm Lane, Walthamstow.
The Mad Poet of London struck again,
He must still be in North East's domain.'
The phone rings, 'Sir, Rhys, it's him!
He struck minutes ago,
In the heart of Walthamstow.
I've called all patrol cars to circle within.'
'Good, Rhys, thanks for letting me know,
Whereabouts in Walthamstow?'

i-5

The area has been cordoned off,
With a taped barrier in blue and white
As Chief Forensic Officer Adrian Goff,
Controls the scene, keeping it tight.
Dressed in a white paper suit,
He places in a bag some half-eaten fruit.
Then another investigator, enthusiastic,
Hands DCI Wallace a letter, in plastic.
'I'm sure it's him, it's him alright!
The Mad Poet of London,
This poem makes it a dozen,'
As Wallace holds it up to morning's light.
With latex gloves, he opens it,
And reads aloud with awe and grit.

The Jagged Edge of Night

The jagged edge of the night
Where dark souls take flight
I kill boredom dead with fright,
Society's hypocrisy, I happily fight.

But hold tight, hold fast,
I realise my reign won't last.
As I hold tight to soul's mast
Through stormy seas, I blast.

The warring grey/brown stormy sky
Hit me hard with rain's cry.
As I cursed aloud in God's eye
With clenched fist, I held high.

I have no peace nor no reason,
My future's bleak on cold horizon.
It's where my soul had first arisen,
In your cold, dank, unyielding prison.

But what else can I do?
Vengeance grabbed me like the flu.
Blood and death are my crew,
I'm off chaps now; enjoy the view!

Yours sincerely,
The Mad Poet of London

CANTO 1

1-1

Kram, in '96, sits under a bridge,
As the rain crashes down
His emotions are on a ridge,
Above insanity's beckoning town.
A rat scurries past,
He looks on aghast.
He feels his youth wilting,
And feels the ridge tilting.
'*I agree with Camus, the world's absurd.*'
Kram gazes into the past
Wondering why he's an outcast,
As painful memories recurred.
He gets up in poetic grace,
And walks through rain at a stoic pace.

1-2

Kram, in '77, aged 4, sat in silence,
No company or stimulation, just a wall.
His mother sleeps in flatulence,
As his father, to his mother, does call.
'I'm home, get up, you lazy cow –
I'm hungry, get to cooking now!'
Finally, she awoke,
To a cough and a smoke.
His father in bedroom then snaps,
With a menacing smirk,
'Come on, woman, get to work!'
And on her bottom, he slaps.
'Alright, alright, I'm up now –
And stop calling me a fucking cow.'

1-3

In the bedroom, Kram stands alone,
Watching rain through the window
As tree branches are blown
By the rain and wind in accelerando.
The road outside, like a river,
In a boat, he imagines sailing forever.
He pushes his forehead upon the glass,
Then spots a fox dart across the grass.
A haze of condensation grows
Upon a view of cold and wet
His mother calls, in a threat,
'Get your food, Kram! Now!' He froze.
Kram feels his soul yanked by chain,
'Kram! I won't fucking call again.'

1-4

Kram sits ravenous at the table,
Storming through his meagre rations
Listening to parents' monotonous babble
In cyclic waves between mastication's.
'Ruth, let's get smashed tonight.'
'I'm up for it, Leon; I feel like shite.'
As Kram's thoughts drift to the fox
'Oh, that Anna's gone on a detox.'
Kram envies his cunning fox friend,
Going wherever he wanted, no chain,
No fucking rules, no fucking pain
Wondering when this nightmare will end.
Suddenly, a bottle hit Kram's head,
His mother laughs as his head bled.

1-5

That evening, Kram watches television,
Lying motionless upon the bare floor
His fantasies and the film are in fine elision,
As enemy soldiers get killed in score.
Kram imagines shooting his parents,
Whilst firing guns with such flamboyance.
As the western sun rises proud,
Producing a fine bronze-lit cloud.
The credits rise against the horizon,
Returning Kram to his dispirited theme
As ruminations became less extreme
Back again to his earthly prison.
Upstairs, he creeps in gentle tread,
Then, he gets quietly into his dirty bed.

1-6

Night's arc is ending by the rocks,
As Kram, in fear, curls
Then, suddenly transforming into a fox
Across rocks, he jumps and twirls.
He escapes deadly shadows with ease,
And with fangs, he kills two geese.
But then he hears a demonic shout,
And in fear, he tries escaping echoes out.
He finds nothing or nowhere to hide,
Only a land of desolation
In a gripping fist of terrorisation,
Unable to scream as his mouth has dried.
The shouts occur again and again,
His rapid heart races, unable to regain.

1-7

'Kram! Kram!' his mother bellows,
'You left the fucking TV on,'
As Kram lay in bed, curls
'I'll get your fucking dad, Leon!
Leon! Leon! Kram's playing up –
You're so stupid; I'm fucking fed up.'
'What, Ruth? Is he fucking around?
K-R-A-M!' his father screams, like hell's hound.
Then grabs Kram by the hair.
'He's no fucking son of mine –
Look, he's trembling, no spine,'
As Kram looks on at his evil glare.
Both parents laugh, like devilish imps,
As Kram, to hell's depths, does glimpse.

Kram awakes to the morning light,
At the bottom of the stairs
He looks a dreadful bloody sight,
With blurred vision, he stares.
'You better not be there still –
For when I come back, I will kill.
Ruth, clean this fucker up.'
'I will, Leon, but I'm so fed up.'
Later, near the garden's gate
Kram sits upon the wet grass,
Wishing for the pain to pass,
As he curses at his feeble state.
At evening time, in his bedroom's tomb,
He eats bread within the gloom.

Will I sleep and will I dream –
Or will I live, or will I die?
Kram thinks, too scared to scream,
So, he closes his eyes to cry.
Suddenly, his father bursts in,
Kram jolts up in a spin.
His father breathes deeply and glares,
As Kram braces himself and prepares.
But his father leaves, closing the door,
As the beam of light beneath, glows
As the shadowy feet, after a pause goes,
Kram then sighs and untenses jaw.
And before long, he falls asleep,
And in dream's vortex, he goes deep.

Back along the road in '96
Kram is now screaming in the rain,
Memories and reality intermix,
To passing traffic, he looks insane.
Kram's completely soaked thro',
As he stands crying, in flashing blue.
A police car approaches, stopping near,
As Kram looks on in growing fear.
Intending to warn and investigate,
The officer approaches him on fate's cue,
As Kram seethes self-hatred like a Nazi-Jew
As haunting nightmares grate.
He asks Kram politely, for his name,
But Kram couldn't speak; nothing came.

1-11

He studies Kram very carefully,
His long, wet, unkempt hair
Simply upset or suffering insanity
With a dark-eyed pain, etched stare.
'Can I have your name, please, sir?'
Kram continues staring before muttering, 'Er.'
'Can you tell me your name, please?'
'Kram Skyal,' he finally says with ease.
'What's your date of birth?'
'Thirtieth, September, seventy-two –
I'm not going back ever, thank you.'
'Please, sir, come back to Earth!'
Then a lightning bolt strikes its glory,
As the officer asks, 'What's your story?'

1-12

The question strikes Kram with fear,
As he studies the dark cloudscape,
Like being stabbed with a spear
His instinct urges him to escape.
Then suddenly, he let go and bolts,
Across road barriers, he vaults.
The radio goes, as the officer gives chase,
Both, dodging cars in haste.
They were sprinting both at full pace,
But Kram is tired, in no fit state,
With rapid breathing and heart rate
He is so defenceless; no carapace.
But he is outwitted, outfoxed,
As he's quickly caged and boxed.

I-13

Cuffed and panting in the car,
Cold and wet within the mire
Cuffed and panting, looking far,
Cold and wet within mind's fire.
The officer shows annoyance and charm,
Without intending to do any harm.
Kram's breathing slows, but still a wreck,
As the officer on radio does a PNC check.
Kram sits there still, a man of mystery,
But the officer chills at what he's heard,
That this crazed man has done some bird
A long time for, 'Christ, what a history!
Did you really do that at eleven?
Did you really do a sentence of seven?'

1-14

The police car starts and drives away,
As Kram's dark thoughts trail off.
He gazes out the window, far away,
As Kram loudly starts to cough.
'You a smoker?' the officer does ask,
And Kram nods with stoic mask.
The rain, for some, tinged world in life,
Beckoning flowers and wildlife.
But for Kram, he only saw window's plight
As raindrops down its visceral plane
As he wonders of how much pain
He could take from the world's spite.
The windows pane, mirrors his soul's fight,
As raindrop fingers cling him tight.

1-15

Kram, in '84, gazes through the window
With a bloody, bruised face, he does stare,
As his parents play music slow
What a fucking horrible evil pair.
He growls aloud with venom,
Dressed in a jacket of dark blue denim.
He cuts open a carton of milk,
It flows down his throat like silk.
Kram thinks back to yesterday,
When topping cider bottles with antifreeze
That should take them away with ease,
Surely, they must drink those today.
Suddenly, he hears his parents gasp,
And Kram smiles, with knife in fist's clasp.

Kram goes down the stairs to gloat,
To a cacophony of syncopated groans
He cuts open his mother's throat,
And jumps upon his father, breaking bones.
Then, with his knife, he does slice,
Whilst shouting, 'This is the price! –
For years and years of fucking pain –
And now you cunts, I have slain.'
He lies on the dirty, stained sofa,
Starring happily at his work
In contentment, he does smirk
Gently sipping an ice-cold cola.
I'm finally free from you bastards,
My parents, my ex-slave masters.

1-17

So Kram, in '96, tells his story to the officer,
'My mother especially was a cunt –
That's why I only got manslaughter –
Times two. Called Old Bill, no manhunt.'
'Your father sounds like a right bastard!'
(pause) 'Chance of a hotdog and mustard?'
'Once booked in, I'll get you food to eat,
Followed by a warm cell. I'm Pete.'
'Thanks. For months, I've been sleeping rough –
Salvation Army helps. I beg, too.
Christ, Pete, I'd kill also for a brew!'
Pete laughs. 'Haven't you done enough?'
'Enough what, Pete?' 'Killing!'
Kram throws his head back, laughing.

1-18

Seated in the bright interview room,
Kram gently sips a can of pop,
Then says aloud, 'Cognito ergo sum,'
To the hugely amused suited cop.
'I think therefore I am. Right?'
'Right, for a copper, you're bright.'
'Anyway, I want to be charged.' 'Why?
You need a bed?' Kram gives a sigh.
'Your record is incredibly long,
Manslaughter and car theft convictions.
And motorbikes! Do you have any addictions?'
'No! Drugs are for the weak; I'm strong.'
'We have here a mental health nurse.'
'No. I'm not mad! My memories are my curse.'

1-19

The pleasant Indian doctor asks,
'Do you know why you've been sectioned?'
'I'm a suffering man.' Kram gasps.
'From bad memories in retrospection.'
'Kram, you're held under a Number Three Section…'
'Look! I don't want meds or a fucking injection.
I'm just having flashbacks; I'm not mental,
Nor violent, dangerous, I'm gentle.'
'Sorry, Kram, I'm writing you up for…'
'No, Doc, no!' Kram bolts from the room
And through the ward's sterilised gloom
Then attempts to exit the ward's door.
But the white metal door is firmly shut,
As a mass of burly nurses inject his butt.

After the injection, he feels dejected,
As they carry him off to seclusion,
He is humiliated and not respected,
As he lies in a dazed confusion.
His vision's a blur as he dribbles from mouth,
And before long, his mind goes south.
Hours later, a dazzling ray of light shone,
As a name echoes in his ear, 'Leon.'
'No. No. Not you, Dad, please go away,
I killed you, Dad, and that bitch,
You're a fucking cunt, and that witch,
Fuck off. Go away. Go away!'
Kram's temper flares as his heart does race,
'I sent yous down for the devil to chase.'

Kram paces slowly in the small room,
Not knowing how long has passed,
Feeling dragged through a narrow flume,
Not knowing what hand fate has cast.
Suddenly, at his door, the flap opens,
But as the nurse speaks, his rage deepens.
He shouts his thoughts as they unbound,
As only air exhales, he hears no sound.
His rage surges as he kicks the door,
Then, he punches the flap with his fist,
On seeing the proverbial red mist.
What biased law keeps me in devil's claw?
This ship is a one-way ride,
With no beach to escape at low tide.

1-22

Kram, in '84, sits in an office,
Opposite a blue-eyed, grey-haired man
Within an impenetrable built edifice,
Listening to a rickety old fan.
'Kram, this isn't a prison, as you know,
It's a secure children's home where you'll grow.'
Kram looks thro' him, to that night,
As a smile grows. 'You're bright –
Your psychologist notes in a note.
Your IQ registers at one-three-five,
You'll do well in our educational hive,
You've got great potential, he wrote.
You're one of our youngest here, aged eleven,
And quite a shock you got a sentence of seven.'

1-23

Hopelessness drifts across Kram's mind.
'I feel lost without a future!'
'Kram, I'm not just pretending to be kind,
But you definitely have a future!
Christ, with your intelligence, wow!
You've got everything going for you, holy cow.
I'd like to view this place as a school,
Nothing more, nothing less than a school.
Everyone here is doing education and therapy,
I've read your case file; I feel for you,
Your parents belonged in a zoo!
The judge and jury need a lobotomy!'
Suddenly, an alarm. The sirens scream,
As Kram's thoughts ran in a ghostly dream.

1-24

'So, what do you intend?
With your intelligence, I mean, Kram,
Contribute to society, work, re-offend?'
'This isn't a fucking school; it's a sham!'
'Sham? What's that you say –
Every place is what you make it, okay?
It's your chance to change and learn,
And all that shite in your past, burn!
Be in the pursuit of the new you,
Don't be a victim of your past!
And let it become, your ship's mast.
Direct your life's journey to a better view.'
His words uplift Kram to new schemes,
And fills Kram with new dreams.

1-25

In '96, Kram lies on the floor with a smile,
Then, through the flap, a patient utters,
'I'll help you escape, but it'll take a while.'
As those words to Kram's stomach flutters.
'All you must do is play the game,
Until you get leave, just act tame.'
The patient walks off muttering,
With a bedsheet cape, strutting.
After some thought, Kram presses the buzzer,
A nurse appears to Kram's new charm,
And Kram apologises, whilst acting calm,
'I'll take the meds; I'm thro' being a nutter.'
Presenting himself as a character in good mood
He fools them all, despite thoughts skewed.

1-26

Kram approaches a male nurse.
'I'm burning my candle at both ends,
Mental illness is a terrible curse.
I need normality and friends.
I have many dreams and desires,
But medication to brain, it requires.
I apologise for before; I needed sleep,
I should've asked for liquid sheep.'
'We saw you sleeping upon the floor.'
'Yes, I can sleep anywhere. I was homeless,
A bumbling idiot, completely aimless.
But now I'm away from torment's claw.'
'Well, I see to treatment, you're devout
And you'll improve; I have no doubt.'

1-27

'Mental illness, Kram, such as schizophrenia
To this place does beckon,
Anxiety, depression, and mania,
Come a close second.
It's mostly due to illegal drugs,
Cannabis, especially, to insanity tugs.
And, of course, Ecstasy, that dreaded pill,
As it can, unfortunately, literally kill.'
'Do meds have side effects?'
'Well, Kram, meds do cure mental torment,
But their negative side effects can lie dormant,
Nothing's risk-free; some do cause defects.
Besides, you can leave hospital today,
Get hit by a car and drift far away!'

A woman with nicotine-stained nails
And a pungent, sweaty odour, sits near
And opposite two obese men like whales
As Kram feels along his cheek, a tear.
He tries staring at the TV hard
To push out from his heart, life's shard.
Feeling down, horrified, and morbid, like in
Some horror movie, slowly etching within.
A man with a furious purple expression
Sits next to him, staring at him in silence.
Uneasy at the constant surveillance,
Kram leaves without causing a commotion.
Muttering sarcastic comments under his breath
As all Kram thinks about is his death.

1-29

A crusty cigarette-smelling mouth awoke
As clouds of smoke from each nostril flare
Leaving Kram's eyes in a veil of smoke
Is he, my future? Kram's thoughts scare.
He has a low, know-it-all laugh,
As Kram stares at his striped scarf.
One-man grunts and barks like a dog,
Then grabs his crotch, saying, 'I need the bog!'
The smoker's room is full of smoke,
A windowless, hopeless, drab land
As he sits still, unable to understand,
Just listening as he starts to choke.
A woman sits with head hanging on chest,
Her stiff grey hair lay across her breast.

At day's end, Kram crawls into bed
Feeling like a dirty letter in an envelope
In white fresh sheets upon the bed
As he needs the dream world to elope.
He threads his way through the days,
Stopping to engage, then by bed, he prays.
Praying the doctor grants his freedom,
Away from hospital's hell in Needham.
Kram notices his tan has faded,
But is now wise and cynical as all hell,
Learning how to manipulate, lie and gel,
Despite feeling completely jaded.
But from a distant light, he recites,
Ballads and sonnets, his brain ignites.

In '84, Kram sits with the rest,
A pupil, like on any other day,
Mrs Glenn teaches with such zest,
Teaching Britain's most dangerous, they say.
She seems full of hope and kindness,
With an undisrupted calmness.
As to who or why they're there,
But acts normal without a stare.
'Who here has heard of Oscar Wilde?'
No one puts their hand up. 'Okay –
Well, you're in for a treat today,'
She says in a voice so mild.
'This is the "Ballad of Reading Gaol".'
Her words then blow Kram's slack sail.

Kram's brain to knowledge devours,
Prose and poetry he began to love.
Studying and reciting poetry for hours,
For Kram, it was like hand to glove.
Awful memories go as poetry took,
By John Keats to Rupert Brooke.
He makes full use of his time,
Studying form, rhythm, and rhyme.
Then, in class one day, Kram read out,
A poem he wrote, in gentle tone,
Not a nerve in sight; he was in the zone.
The class fell silent; no one dared to shout,
They all sat listening and were smitten,
At every word, Kram had written.

I'm Not a Crème Brûlée

I'm not a crème brûlée,
All jiggly and jolly
Nor a savoury souffle
No layers of folly.

I'm not sirloin steak,
In a tender, sweet glaze
Nor a red velvet cake
In heavenly creamy craze.

I'm not at all foie gras
A texture smooth and soft
Nor some salt-cured caviar
Helpless roe, borne aloft.

I'm pizza in a fireball,
Cooked in a blaze of flames,
Melted cheese in a downfall,
Dashings of chilli defames.

Upon a base of blood red,
Cut olives grandiosity.
Lashed toppings and crusty bread,
Lays my colourful monstrosity.

1-34

The class erupts, as they applaud,
As Kram fills up with pride.
The recognition strikes a chord,
As he beams deep from inside.
No longer alone on an island
Poetry brings him safe in hand.
No more dodging round sharp rocks
He is now a smart, resourceful fox.
Kram feels a purposeful intensity,
Through centuries of poetry, he does crack,
From Homer, Keats, and Jack Kerouac,
Poetry was his calling, his virtuosity.
Feeling warmth within the Bible's Psalms,
To feeling love within the sonnets' charms.

Kram, in '96, watches the ward's TV,
Whilst greeting staff changing shift
Politeness is his *dernier cri*.
Trying mentally to stay adrift.
Suddenly, his doctor approaches him,
As his desperation nears its brim.
'Hi, Kram, I've decided to grant you leave,'
As Kram wipes his forehead with his sleeve.
'Wow, Doc, thanks, I do feel better,'
As Kram suppresses his inner gleam
Not wanting to act overly keen,
As a warmth radiates to his loosening fetter.
He holds back tears to the beckoning wild,
Soon to his freedom, he'll be reconciled.

1-36

Kram's imagination takes flight like a raven
Escaping from a flock of unkindness
Flying free across the blue haven
Flying free over mankind's blindness.
Is freedom a hallucination of the mind,
With thoughts and soul's passion intertwined.
Kram's thoughts hang on freedom's thrill,
As he swallows his morning medication pill.
The world trembles under sky's thunder
Scaring all but the very brave
Scaring all in hiding within society's cave
But I won't let laws bury me under.
Kram's mind soars the distant horizon,
Towards the red sky of the setting sun.

CANTO 2

2-1

The large white door, the nurse unlocks,
As Kram feels a surge of electricity
Swallowing saliva like little rocks
It opens out with such simplicity.
Kram steps into the corridor
'Thank you so much, Isadore.'
'Kram, be back by two,
Or we'll phone the boys in blue!'
She locks the door behind him,
As reality to Kram's mind does slap
With anxiety, it might be a trap
I'm ready, world; in your arms, I swim.
He shrinks back worry with a smile,
And walks off in a casual style.

When two o'clock came and went
Everyone fretted with worry,
Whilst Kram was on a train to Kent
His stressed mental state was a flurry.
In an agitative and desperate domain,
And without cash, he bunks the train.
But the ticket inspector comes along,
'Without a ticket, you don't belong.'
Kram panics and punches him quick,
But the passengers hold onto him,
Unable to escape, he cries out a hymn,
And in anger, he lashes out with a kick.
Back at hospital, cleaners find a letter,
Lying on Kram's bed under a sweater.

I Burn My Candle

I burn my candle,
At both ends
By being very naughty.

And Christ, my friends
And Christ, my foes
I won't live to see forty.

2-4

Kram's held on the floor feeling hellish,
And notices a boot in cracked blue leather,
Quite new, with a fresh polish
As Kram drifts in mind altogether.
The train's floor feels wonderfully cool,
It comforts him, reminding him of school.
The great Mrs Glenn, full of passions,
As he feels cared for, he imagines.
The slight rocking feels calming and nice,
As people around him seem to hover.
Suddenly, reality hits, as he can't recover,
And feels his blood turn to ice.
Anxiety turns his mouth to sand,
As he loses feelings in his right hand.

2-5

Kram struggles to breathe,
As his face turns a fierce red
He tightly grits his teeth,
And prepares for death's bed.
But then he sees a strange look,
Like some searching Boobook.
Hidden in its tree hollow, it spies,
Before its envelopes into loud cries.
'He can't breathe – get off him!
His face is turning purple.'
As others to Kram trample
'Get off him. This is getting grim!'
Suddenly, Kram coughs in spluttering gasps,
As to reality, he clearly grasps.

2-6

Kram is pulled up by the arm,
Then, seated by a door, feeling peculiar,
Whilst held by his forearm
He's struck down by melancholia.
That face again, surrounded by blonde hair,
Like a golden halo, Kram does stare.
Having escaped from that heavy heap
Like waking from some deep sleep.
Kram sees around him dead people, bloated,
With a strong, sickly, putrid smell
Feeling he's heading for hell,
On a silver bullet train, in air it floated.
Soon, the train slowed to a stop,
The police enter, and Kram they shop.

2-7

Everyone around eyes Kram curiously
As the silver handcuffs clasp upon
Clicking around his wrists furiously
And within the crowd, that face shone.
They escort Kram out to a cheer,
And that face remains in a silent sphere.
With a straight back, Kram walks proud,
As police thread him through the crowd.
Before an unnecessary push,
Into a waiting police van
Kram gave Freedom a final scan,
Before diving in with a whoosh.
He envisages that beautiful face's smile,
Who he feels, admires his gallant walk in style.

2-8

Staying free isn't Kram's forte,
As he feels his passions run wild
In reception, he dances a jeté
'Stop fucking behaving like a child.'
The desk sergeant snapped aloud,
As Kram imagines dancing on a cloud.
His thoughts fly free like a bird,
But Kram barely speaks a word.
Suddenly, an officer grabs him with force,
To stop Kram from mentally yo-yoing,
Before fingerprinting and photoing,
And when asked, he expressed no remorse.
Then, into a cell, the door slams behind
And then he starts cursing, all mankind.

2-9

As he sits within the cell,
Feeling like a specimen
In some Petri dishes swell
With observations upon him.
He heard the walls laughing,
At his wasted years passing.
Panic arises as thoughts run wild,
And knows his sentence won't be mild.
He feels the walls declaring him insane,
As he loses his concentration,
And he's unable to mentally function,
And shouts at walls for echoing his pain.
Thoughts of hope hang by a thread,
As he shouts aloud what's in his head.

'I'm locked within this hateful cell,
Encircled by suffering.
The depths of hell,
Grip me.
Help.'

2-10

In '88, Kram sits in the office,
With the same rickety old fan
With a lady from the social service
Drinking pop from a can.
'Kram, you've done extremely well!
Pleased to meet you. I'm Danielle.'
She laughs. 'You've not caused any havoc,
Therefore, there's a place for you in Suffolk.
You'll finish your GCSEs there,
And you'll attend St. Benedict's upper.'
'Kram,' says Mr Glenn, 'fancy a cuppa?'
'No thanks, I'm good, I swear.
I know I'll really miss this place,
As everyone here has been ace!'

2-11

The conversation goes on and on
As Kram tells the unvarnished truth
Regarding his feelings for killing Leon
And that evil bitch witch Ruth.
Danielle's voice is gentle and soft,
And calms Kram down, as her words waft.
He feels comfortable and at ease,
And from the fan, he feels a breeze.
After the pleasant meeting ends
He soon loads up her car with his belongings,
Plus, watercolours and biro drawings
And bids farewell to his friends.
Kram and Danielle drive away
And at the road, Kram's thoughts stray.

2-12

As they fly along on highway's song
Dancing between metal bodies
Mileage gone, distance long,
Freedom in speed, the road embodies.
Shooting past unmemorable places,
Shooting past a haze of faces.
As they both laugh and talk
Feeling the power of engine's torque.
He hears the wind, flood his ears.
Through the window, it gushes,
And through his hair, it brushes
As positive thoughts to mind, steers.
Hours pass until journey's end,
To home in Suffolk, they both descend.

2-13

The children's home was bustling,
As a hawk-nose Northerner speaks
Kram looks around him, puzzling,
At all the simple-minded freaks.
The rules were laid out plain,
As outside it starts to rain.
'You can't smoke nor drink,
You must use your head and think.'
Finally, he gets to sign his name,
And then is asked if he wants a tea.
Before staring out at garden's beauty,
Bordered by a white window frame.
He bids farewell to fair Danielle,
And smiles to himself, as freedom fell.

2-14

Two months later, he awoke,
To a care worker entering his bed
To his head, he does stroke
Then sexually assaults, whilst grabbing his head.
Kram fights hard and struggles,
As the care worker strikes with bare knuckles.
'Welcome, Kram, to your new home,
And remember here; you're on your own.'
On each night, he lays in wait
At the awful reality, he does face
A hellish world where demons chase
Was it me, did I do something to create?
As months of terror pass by slow
Pass by slow as rage does grow.

2-15

During the days he goes to school
He became unruly and rebels,
He plans his plan whilst playing the fool,
And shouts to God, in highest decibel.
With a knife in hand, he stabs a tree,
And again, revenge is his *dernier cri.*
In his room at night, he lays in wait,
Holding his knife whilst full of hate.
Then, two care workers enter late,
As Kram threatens and cuts
They panic as Kram erupts.
'Well, you cunts, this is your fate!'
But they escape, and the house they left,
As Kram feels like a man possessed.

2-16

Kram leaves his room via the window,
And through the streets running free
As his emotions reach a crescendo,
And burgles a house for a car key.
A trick he learnt from his mates,
At the secure home, behind locked gates.
He speeds around, feeling free,
Happy and alive in Suffolk's grand prix.
Then, one night, he lit a fire,
The car burnt in its fiery storm,
As flames to thoughts, calm and warm
And fan words in a poetic desire.
Then, in a notebook, he quickly writes,
As the vivid flames to mind ignites.

The Arsonist

The car catches fire instantly,
It burns quick, slowly changing,
Into a deformed mangled shell.

In the morning, the arsonist stands,
Near the wreckage, under the clear,
Autumn sky. Watching clouds float by.

He remembers the car, like a
Dying dragon, bellowing fire and
Smoke, towards the night's emptiness.

This is how the earth will die,
He thought, *a moment of beauty,*
Before transforming into a lonely rock in space.

2-18

Next day, he puts it through the letterbox,
Of the victim's house, whose car he burnt.
And in his mind, his poetry rocks,
And in his mind, he has learnt.
At poetry, I am truly great
And crime in rhyme is my fate.
The owner contacts the police and newspaper,
To highlight this arsonist's latest caper.
And Kram recites that poem repeatedly,
As it made him feel powerful and strong
And at times, when alone walking along,
He shouts the poem aloud, heatedly.
The local paper publishes it outright,
As people feel that poem ignite.

2-19

Nights later, he walks deep in thought,
Replaying over his failed murder plot.
Knowing that attacking them, it means court,
Feeling tense, sweaty, and hot.
Crouching down by the carer's car
He looks above at the Northern star.
Gripping tight with a brick in hand
Swallowing hard with mouth like sand.
Then suddenly, Kram smashes the car window,
As adrenalin shot through his body,
Then wraps a scarf tight around his hoodie,
As the car alarm at night, echoes through.
Suddenly, his target comes running out,
And Kram hit him with the brick, clean out.

2-20

Over and over, he smashes his face,
As anger throws like thunder
People came out to give chase,
As Kram looks down in wonder
But Kram is fast and takes off,
Wishing he had a Kalashnikov.
Then, across gardens like an urban fox
As an epidemic of people grew like smallpox
Then, under a car, he does hide.
As the morning comes on birdsong,
Feeling happy to right that wrong
Whilst crawling out, beaming with pride.
He tidies himself, and walks away,
Content at last night's violent display.

2-21

A firework of ideas storms his brain,
As he walks the early morning road.
No longer does Kram feel his pain,
Now, he is in full rebellious mode.
No looking back, now only forward
No more pain or feeling awkward.
By midday, he burgled and stole
And took a car, which filled his soul.
But now the police, chase and sirens shout
So down his foot, the accelerator goes,
Weaving through traffic as people froze,
Then, into a park, where he bails out.
Running desperately in a bid to escape,
Before crawling under a car, to hide his shape.

2-22

Little over an hour, Kram slides away,
No police in sight, the danger's gone,
Exhausted and needing a place to stay,
He removes his top and walks on.
Along the road, he approaches a house
Then, round the back like a quiet mouse.
Down the garden, he opens a shed
He closes the door, the floor his bed.
Hours pass, and through day he sleeps,
His wilted energy restores in full,
And bolts up, like a raging bull,
Then, out the shed, to the house, he creeps.
With steely stares through the window,
He sees people sitting, playing a Nintendo.

2-23

Kram sits still and patiently waits.
As hours pass, lost in thought
Thinking of all the people he hates
Understanding what each one taught.
He knows himself more than anyone,
And knows life is no trial run.
Each minute of each day matters,
And with determination in crime, he smashes.
The sense of achievement gained in crime,
Each crime, with each a headline
He feels his confidence shine,
As he creates in mind, another dark rhyme.
The downstairs light, suddenly goes off,
And hand to mouth, Kram silences a cough.

2-24

Kram carefully manages to break in,
With screwdriver in the patio lock
Adrenalin and anger make his head spin,
As fear of capture does flock.
The night for Kram grows dense,
And his feelings become intense.
But soon, anxiety starts to dispel,
As he wonders if he's destined for hell.
His progression in life is little,
Knowing one mistake sends him down.
And one mistake will see him drown,
And so, his grasp on freedom is brittle.
Sorrows do lie within his scope,
But a successful crime gives him hope.

2-25

He puts on the kitchen light,
And rummages the cupboard for food.
Finally, the fridge offers delight,
And eating rapidly, lifts his mood.
He gulps down some fizzy pop,
Like a kid running wild in a shop.
Then made a cheese and pickle sarnie,
Then, microwaving some chilli con carne.
He has a strip wash by the sink,
To refresh himself from the chase
To near normality, he does embrace,
As finally now he manages to clearly think.
No muddled thoughts etched with blood,
Or anger crashing deep, with a thud.

2-26

Combing his fingers through his hair
Kram studies his clothes.
And to his complete despair
He sees blood like dotted holes.
So, his tracksuit he bags tight,
Standing in boxers and T-shirt, white
Searching downstairs, high and low
Around the rooms, he does go.
Then, in the hallway, a sports bag
By football boats caked in dirt.
He pulls out shorts and striped shirt,
Emblazoned with a school's flag.
Hours have passed, it's time to go,
Another debt to society, he does owe.

2-27

Car keys in hand, he looks around,
With all his bags, he now boots
As upstairs, they're still silent, not a sound,
As their goods and food, he loots.
He gives himself a private smile,
Driving back fear of capture for a while.
Feeling fragile and lost for many years,
A life he feels is shrouded in tears.
He knows when they get up tomorrow,
And find their items gone.
Feeling violated and angry upon,
To him, the burglar, who gave them sorrow.
But Kram wishes for them to know,
He had no choice in sinking so low.

2-28

In the car throughout the night
As dawn pushes against the dark lagoon
Eagerly, he drives into that light,
And away from the cloud-covered moon.
The darkness like a moving blockade
From night's grim clouded parade.
Kram's thoughts and mood twirl about
As he heads to Essex, from Suffolk out.
He has no guilt, doubt, or qualm,
Needing to satisfy himself for good.
Some bold robberies like Robin Hood
Whilst keeping focused, keeping calm.
Thefts and arsons trail in my wake,
To a greater glory for my future's sake.

2-29

Kram feels his soul burn bright,
Like a comet or shining star
And with clothes within, bagged tight.
He sets fire to the car.
And without police causing fuss
He calmly catches the morning bus.
To Basildon town centre, he does go
As he pulls his baseball cap, down low.
The town centre Kram does explore,
Then sees a woman at a cash machine.
He ran over psyching himself mean,
And with knife in pocket, he goes to war.
He approaches up close and in her face,
He shows the knife, as his thought's race.

2-30

'This is no fucking joke!'
He growls as anger transcends,
Then, with knife, he does poke,
Acting menacingly, he pretends.
To passing people, he cautiously eyes,
When suddenly, she collapses and cries.
Kram recoils in total shock,
As buried feelings take stock.
He drops the knife and runs away,
Finally, hiding in a public library,
Feeling lost and derisory,
Then falls to the floor, in total dismay.
'I tried to rob, I tried to fleece,
Go on, go 'ed, call the police.'

2-31

A small group surrounds Kram
As he cries upon the floor.
In his mind, his emotions jam,
'I must surrender to the law –
Oh, Christ, I need fucking help! –
I need beating, beating to pulp.'
Kram tells all, what he'd done,
As a librarian, on hearing, her head spun.
Armed police soon swept the scene,
And Kram is cuffed.
Whilst people rebuffed.
As he's escorted out to words obscene.
'Oh, that poor woman, why did I do?'
As they drive him off, to the human zoo.

2-32

On remand at a young offenders'
In shock at the various sights.
Maddening screams and drug vendors
With cuts and bruised faces from fights.
Within weeks, his views are skewed,
And permanently in a depressed mood.
At night, he finds it hard to sleep,
As stress and anxiety run deep.
He knew turning himself in was an error,
As some fights he won, most he lost,
At what price, feeling empathy had cost,
And now lives with scum in terror.
Months pass slow before going to court,
What is my future? His feelings distort.

2-33

The day of sentencing slowly arrives,
As Kram walks into the dock.
Courtroom's eyes like little knives,
As prison's memories flock.
He pleads guilty, so no trial,
As he sits in an upside-down smile.
No brave words or acting tough,
For days without sleep, he feels rough.
Kram's victim stands up in the box,
To read aloud her impact statement
As Kram feels now total resentment,
Towards all, while the judge takes stock.
Kram lowers his head in false shame,
As that dreaded moment now came.

2-34

The court is in a ghostly silence,
As the judge to Kram does speak
Detailing the crime's shocking violence
As Kram feels the courtroom's heat.
The judge gives him a sentence of eight,
Eight years behind, the blood-soaked gate.
As Kram feels his world destroyed,
As now, he's entering a birthless void.
A birthless void where prison stands alone,
No longer human, no longer alive
Where many years span, fighting to survive,
Where tormenting souls, swirl in a cyclone.
Swirling around as their thoughts blacken,
As empathy, remorse and humanity flatten.

2-35

A year gone and a half,
As Kram lives in bloody hell.
Bullied by all and prison staff,
As vestiges of humanity fell.
But this has been mankind's craze,
Sending all down to prison's haze.
Knowing it makes bad men worse,
This, for sure, is society's curse.
'Dear Christ, can you help us?'
Kram cries aloud in his screams,
I'm even haunted within my dreams,
If you exist, show yourself, Jesus!
But nothing came, no white dove,
So, violence he joins, like hand to glove.

Fists fly, and razors slash,
In a violent, fiery radiation
People fall, people crash,
A monster born, a creation.
Down the block, where badness grew,
Not taking stock, as thoughts skew.
This is the fate of many men,
Where God forgot or ignored, Amen.
But in the distance, a flame flickers
Of hope, peace, and true love
But without help from God above,
Bad memories to madness, triggers.
Kram lay on the floor, as his nose bled,
As he manically laughs, his face red.

CANTO 3

3-1

Back in '96, Kram knows the law,
Back to prison, it is for him,
As he lies motionless upon the floor
Back to evading guards' circling fin.
Kram knows the game, the red tape,
And needs to think fast, in order to escape.
The large cell door opens out,
Metaphorically to noose and rope's route.
With a vexed look of disgust
A police officer calls him, as fear grips,
Kram's heartbeat leaps and skips,
As his eyes tries to adjust.
'You're off, Skyal, to the magistrates,'
In a vexing tone that castigates.

3-2

Kram stands up with a darting gaze,
Bouncing a curled knuckle against mouth
With desperate thoughts now ablaze
Feeling his dreams and life drop south.
He surrenders his wrists, as cuffs snap on,
Surrendering his life as time ticks on.
Stomach churns, and with a false smile,
He's escorted to the van, the green mile.
He breathes deep, in fear of losing control,
And into the prison van, he goes
Into a sealed cubicle, his soul froze,
To another monstrous dream to unfold.
He soothes himself by stroking his hair,
As he breathes in deep, the stifling air.

3-3

Before long, the van drives off.
He stares out of the plastic window,
To the world, he does openly scoff
As he fantasises, he's in a white limo.
He regains the ability to focus,
As he plans his magnum opus.
A work of art through crime
In criminal status, he'll climb.
From theft, burglary, then robbery
To importing wholesale drugs,
Throughout the country he floods
To higher ranks of criminal snobbery.
From killing rivals, in armed gangs
To laughing like a devil with bloody fangs.

3-4

Then, touching his temples with closed eyes
In attempt to hold back emotion
He must put on a false face in disguise,
As stress embodies him like a lotion.
He lets out an uncontrollable scream,
As sweet covers him like a cream.
He pulls his knees up to his chest,
As he ruminates over his arrest.
Who was that girl who stared?
Another beautiful face to remember.
Especially on a cold night in December,
She saved me on that train, she cared!
The cubicle door opens out,
Alerting Kram, as his eyes cast about.

3-5

The guard cuffs Kram's right wrist
Then escorts him out the van,
He goes calmly and doesn't resist,
Desperately thinking of a plan.
Into the magistrate court he goes,
Into a cell, full of graffitied prose.
He sits down and stares at the wall,
Reading graffiti in prisoner's sprawl.
I got twenty moons. K.Y.
Blah. Blah. Blah. Fuck the judge.
The grass is dead! I love divinity fudge.
Blah. Blah. Blah. Twelve moons. Si.
Then reality and his dreams juxtapose,
As bad memories strike, in violent throws.

3-6

With a furrowing brow, muscles tightened,
As he's led uncuffed into the court,
His thoughts and feelings were heightened,
As the court and law, he wants to thwart.
But in the dock, to his surprise
He stands in shock at court's demise.
A door to his left is swinging open,
As people enter and exit unspoken.
Suddenly, he hits a guard in the throat,
And leaps the dock, the barrier he vaults.
Storming through the doors, he bolts,
As his desperation and fantasies revolt.
Then, onto the streets, Kram explodes,
As exhilaration to fear, and doubt erodes.

3-7

After a mile, he slows, feeling safe,
As he focuses hard on artful cunning
His feet and thighs began to chafe,
But knew the police were out gunning.
Through town, he walks in strong posture,
As serious crimes to mind foster.
Then, into a clothes shop, he goes,
To change his appearance, in new clothes.
And in a suit, he had no doubt,
New trousers, shoes, and shirt
Not looking nervous as to alert,
Feeling confident, he calmly walks out.
Kram feels happy, free, and alive,
And steals not to survive but thrive.

3-8

Kram clearly strategises his next move,
And steals a knife, then robs some shops,
His criminal record he aims to improve,
As fear of doing a long sentence drops.
He robs people in a flamboyant array,
Then hijacks a car, to take him far away.
From criminal obscurity to fame, he rose,
In newspapers and TV, his name grows.
Finally reaching London, he takes flight,
Then sits in a café near the Strand,
Looking for victims, the street he scanned
Before robbing four people that night.
Then, into a nearby park, he creeps.
And under the moonlit night, he sleeps.

3-9

At last, he realises it's finally time,
A replica gun he excitedly buys.
For a more planned and glamourous crime
And harder to catch in disguise.
The bank, he stands, from days of planning,
On a crowded London street, spanning.
Kram walks casually in and queues,
Patiently waiting with thoughts skewed.
Then, approaching calmly, the female cashier
He pushes under a demanding note.
Full of threats and violence, he wrote.
As he shows his gun, to her fear,
A bundle of cash, she pushes through,
In fifties and twenties, crisp and new.

3-10

On exiting the bank, the alarm blares,
But still, he continues walking,
Keeping his nerve from suspicious glares
He starts removing his outer clothing.
Kram took off his jacket of navy blue,
Then, into a pub to use the loo.
So, the scanning police lose their scent,
As he hears the police sirens' descent.
He pulls out a large duffle bag,
And removes his grey tracksuit,
Revealing his clean-pressed suit,
To consciously wave normality's flag.
He walks calmly out, without a sigh,
And metaphorically waves police goodbye.

3-11

Kram repeated this many times,
His quick-change technique
As he escaped from many crimes
Gaining confidence each week.
Sometimes, he changes in the public loo,
Or toilets in pubs, restaurants, and cafés, too.
Sometimes, on public transport,
And sometimes in alleyways short.
He rents a flat with stolen ID,
In Kent, not far from the raging sea.
But far from his robbing spree,
In London, as he's hitting year three.
Three blissful years of robbing banks,
And to other criminals, he outranks.

3-12

Walking on a beach, he covers a distance,
On bare feet against the pebbly sand
Feeling he's winning his fight with existence,
Every day in luck and in fate's hand.
Kram feels a strong sense of destiny,
And knows there's more to life than money.
But feels the more his life improves,
The more he fears he might lose.
But there in the near distance
Something he didn't foresee,
A beautiful girl walking by the sea,
As he tries to build resistance.
But his heart won out, and he approaches,
Beyond his shyness, passion encroaches.

3-13

'Good morning,' Kram says and smiles,
'Good morning,' she replies.
As Kram's hand through hair, styles,
As she mirrors his moves and sighs.
The conversation grows in-depth,
As Kram's soul grows in breadth.
Feeling great chasms spread within,
As great desire makes his heart spin.
So, against the grain, he asks her out,
Nothing formal, just a casual date
She agrees, and Kram feels great,
As passion dances, from desert's drought.
He walks off with her number,
And walks off in love's jumper.

3-14

Back home in his tidy flat
He excitedly dances and clowns,
Love and happiness, he spat,
Engulfed in feelings, he drowns.
Feelings he has never explored,
Feelings through his soul roared.
He had money to last awhile,
And now he can live in style.
His first date goes well,
Then more dates follow fast
As each to mind will last,
Forever in memory's protective shell.
For memories of great joy endure,
And in troubled times, they cure.

3-15

With a display of engagement
Their conversation is witty and fast,
Laughing at each other's statement
In each other's lives, they have a blast.
Kram sheds bad habits to appease,
And with Kram, she feels more at ease.
As fingers ache in need to touch,
With thoughts of sonnets and such.
Each day, he grew in stature,
Almost insane with love
To dizzy heights from above
And in love's hand, catches her.
In strong eye contact, and lips parting,
They feel their restraints departing.

3-16

They kiss and kiss wildly.
With arms wrapped around each other,
In the streets, he dismisses blindly
As his feelings of joy smother.
He pulls back hard to breathe,
With storms of emotions, underneath.
Then holds her tight in his arms,
Entrapped within her charms.
Speaking less, they passionately kiss.
As the gentle breeze blew
Welcoming Love's debut.
Then, back home, to perfect bliss.
But Kram now feels, a fluttering in chest,
As now, he really fears an arrest.

3-17

Kram makes love to her in bed,
With skin flushing with tension
No more words were said,
As he gives her his full attention.
Hands clench briefly, then release,
As excitement and eroticism increase.
With eyes shining, glossy, then softening,
As he gives her his future, in offering.
He didn't want to ever lose her,
The tension was just right.
As he wishes to his past a rewrite,
In ecstasy, he came in her.
They then lay in each other's arms,
As the rain plays, the windows charms.

3-18

Kram couldn't contain his smile,
As he grabs her, squealing.
Tickling her again with style,
Tickling her as she's screaming.
Her face turns to the morning sun,
As Kram realises, she's the one.
In an 'I can't believe it' gesture,
He stretches to love's venture.
With hugs and displays of affection,
Warmth radiates from their bodies,
As love in morning light embodies
And in their eye's sun's reflection.
Thank you God and the hand of fate,
As I realise now, love's never too late.

3-19

With a high chin and exposed neck
Kram kisses her passionately,
And she, in return, does peck,
As she says, 'You fascinate me.'
On morning song, time flies fast,
And to his occupation, she does ask.
He feels uneasy to lie first time,
How can I tell her I'm into crime?
He evades the question cleverly,
By tickling, before finally he addressed,
'I write prose and won a poetry contest,'
But this lie, weighs on him heavily.
As he wanted her to know his story,
In all its darkness, pain, and glory.

3-20

Kram holds her tight in fading euphoria,
Trying to find words he can't express,
As his growing thoughts of losing Gloria
His low finances cause great stress.
For months with her, he's been crime-free,
Crime like a distant vision on stormy sea.
But he feels alone, on a trail to jail,
As tormenting winds blow his sail.
He sees dark clouds hide the sun,
Holding back in grey, a rain deluge
And unable to hide or take refuge,
Entrapped in a boat, unable to run.
Facing probable capture, the inevitable fire,
As he feels the devil and fate conspire.

3-21

After a picnic on the sandy beach
In the reeds, they try making love,
But Kram's passion is unable to reach,
Wondering when to prison, fate will shove.
Gulping desperately at the air,
Questioning why life is so unfair.
Gloria senses also, something is wrong,
Something she's sensed, for time long.
Kram grips her hand tight,
As they get up and walk
As nearby birds squawk
Walking in the evening's dying light.
In distant sky, oblique clouds in red,
Then he passes out, on pavement's bed.

3-22

Gloria panics and then phones
As Kram was knocked clean out
But within minutes, he groans
And panics on hearing sirens shout.
He staggers to his feet,
As he hears approaching heat.
'Sit down, love, the ambulance is here.'
As Kram realises, he's nothing to fear.
With a fake name and details, he does lie,
As to hospital, they sped,
In precaution to scan his head
As Gloria sits worriedly beside.
Then, feeling blood trickling down,
From his unkempt black-haired crown.

3-23

They arrive at hospital's scurry,
And escort him out the ambulance
Into hospital's A & E flurry
He staggers, trying to keep balance.
Police officers pass him in pairs,
As Kram to them, blankly stares.
The paramedics to nurses, relate,
To a nearby drunk the nurses berate.
Kram strangely feels he's in a dream,
Feeling slightly faint at the knees
And in a vision, of fields and trees,
He hears a distant scream.
With the sight of police, he feels taxed,
And to the floor, Kram collapsed.

3-24

Kram is wheeled into theatre,
On noticing blood on brain swell
In moans, he tries to utter
Imagining himself in a prison cell.
Neurosurgeons get to work quick,
And Gloria waits, watching clock tick.
A hole in his skull they then made,
Letting the fluid and pressure fade.
Then, on ward many hours later
Kram lies in a white-sheeted bed,
Lying still with bandages on head
As a nurse came round like a waiter.
Delivering food on plastic trays,
As Gloria, by Kram's bed, prays.

3-25

Days pass, and Kram thanks fate,
With Gloria visiting him regularly
He laughs with her over his metal plate,
Whilst eating smuggled in food, discretely.
'I've been told I'm leaving today,
I'm so glad to finally get away.
What an idiot you must think!'
Kram laughs at Gloria with a wink.
'But about your ID?' she questions him.
'Is your name Kram or Graeme?
Your address isn't either the same!
Tell me the truth, I'm not dim!'
Kram lowers his eyes and sighs,
'I'm Kram Skyal not Graeme Schweiz.'

3-26

But Kram couldn't tell her the truth,
He knows it will be the end.
For being locked up throughout his youth
So, he says, 'Graeme is his friend.
He is using his friend's ID, whilst he's away,
Just for a lark, it started one day.'
Gloria looks at him with relief,
And has no idea he is a thief.
But Kram senses the end is near,
As he needs money like air
Asking for luck within each prayer
As he wants this to be his year.
Then, after a chat with the doc,
This near miss really takes stock.

3-27

Looking at Gloria's pale, slender face,
Could she ever understand?
Or condone my crimes, in violent pace,
In a spree upon this land.
Leaving people in fear and terror,
And the risk of fucking up in error.
I suppose I could make money other ways,
But not when wanted in hunted haze.
So, robbing banks is my duty,
Especially when it aids love,
Something I've been starved ov.
Through years in life's turbulent sea.
I must fight with all my might,
To keep my love and bask in light.

3-28

Walking back home, Kram is quiet,
As Gloria starts to query
With a heartbeat racing in a riot,
At another theory.
That Kram is a criminal of a sort,
And probably, he'll end up in court.
And convicted and taken away,
A locked soul, in prison's decay.
She questions Kram no further,
As ignorance is bliss
From reality's abyss
But suspicion still nags in murmur.
For now, though, within their love,
Bad thoughts to both; they do shove.

3-29

By the window, within the dark
He stares up at the stars,
Knowing to crime, he must embark,
As next night there might be bars.
He knows tomorrow might be the end,
And to hell, he might descend.
As to love, he does grieve,
As in tomorrow, he might leave.
He knows there'll be no happy ever after
Within a barred cell, with only death to see,
Amongst scum and druggies running free
No moments of beauty, love, or laughter.
Like an old tiger sensing his end,
Realising love's memory is his only friend.

3-30

The time has come, the day he plans,
Realising this day, he could die.
Carrying two bags to car, she scans
And to Gloria, he kisses her goodbye.
Kram is cold, as he has to maintain,
A stoic defence through fear's reign.
Then, in his car, she runs for more kisses,
Poor girl, she already misses.
But I'd rather die, than be alone,
Maybe if caught, she'd visit,
I had to lie, so she wasn't complicit.
Gloria shouts, 'After work, please phone!'
At a final glance, he drives away,
As he desperately wishes he could stay.

3-31

He imagines himself getting shot,
As he questions fate's path
With a striking headache, hot
Feeling society's encroaching wrath.
He soon calms to the radio's college choir,
"Ave Maria" by Biebl's creative spire.
He is now focused on the task ahead,
No more imagining himself lying dead.
He parks on the outskirts of London,
Doubt, like a whispering flame, humming,
Doubt, through winter's darkness, coming,
Now in disguise with gun in bag, done.
Walking London's crowded grey river,
As fear and adrenalin make him shiver.

3-32

As Kram nears his usual bank target
A jewellery shop tramples his mind,
Tomfoolery in underworld argot
Second-hand jewellery, he pined.
Tens of thousands in necklaces and rings,
It'll free me from crime, his heart sings.
The taste and style poke his interest,
But pulling this job, will be a huge test.
I'll have to come down hard, with force,
And shout, causing attraction,
And to cope with people's reaction,
It's this, or life and Gloria, I'll divorce.
Oh God and fate, grant me this,
And let me live with Gloria in bliss.

3-33

With pulse speeding he feels tense
Heat flushing throughout his body,
Feeling the world is against
'Jesus, help me,' he cries, feeling groggy.
Give me strength, give me courage,
Don't hold against me a grudge.
To church, I'll promise to go.
As he drinks back Cointreau.
As, this time, Dutch courage is needed
Due to knowing the risks are high,
To spirited alcohol, he drinks dry,
In drink and prayer, he pleaded.
I promise this is my last job,
No more, God, will I rob.

3-34

With sunglasses on to cover his eyes
And to humanity, he does withdraw
He enters in with determined strides,
As he stands blocking the glass door.
In a sudden explosion of his voice,
He feels his hands go moist.
'Fill this bag with fucking jewellery,
And don't anyone attempt any foolery.'
He throws a bag across the counter,
Pointing a gun at a woman's head
'All the jewellery,' he shouts to face red,
As fear and terror surround her.
The woman moves quick, to window's display,
As he bellows, 'Quick, quick, don't delay!'

3-35

Each second feels like an hour
As time seems to slow down
He then feels a surge of power,
As sweat pours from his frown.
Then from an office door, two men came,
Kram panics with thoughts aflame.
Kram hit them wildly with his gun,
Then the alarm blares, he knows he's done.
Suddenly, Kram feels a sharp pain,
As he realises, he's been sliced,
A knife! Dear Christ!!!!!
Then, in terror, he feels it again.
His disguise slips off, in the scuffle,
As he bares face to CCTV's trouble.

Kram glares at the CCTV camera
As he gets kicked and punched about
Then one of the men shouts, 'Pamela! –
Help us out.' As she looks in doubt.
But Kram manages to wriggle free,
As the man shouts, 'Pamela, we need three!'
Then Pamela joins in the fray,
But Kram knocks both men out, to her dismay.
Both men's bodies, block the door,
So Kram quickly drags them away,
As crowds grow outside shop's display,
Which Kram notices and senses the law.
He bolts like a bull, from the shop,
With anger and rage, no one could stop.

CANTO 4

4-1

Kram runs past the gathering crowd,
In a panic, tired and disoriented,
The curious crowd cries aloud
As Kram knows, his love story has ended.
No more romance, as his soul rants
A stark prison cell, to mind implants.
The angry crowd in shouts give chase,
Knowing the newspapers, will have his face.
Together with the Crimestoppers appeal,
He's engulfed in loss and agitation,
And to his intelligence, he does question,
As he pulls out a knife, six inches of steel.
If fate and God won't let me love, I'm done,
If the world wants a villain, I'll be that one.

4-2

With wide eyes and furrowed brow
He finally enters his car,
I'll get my revenge, I bloody vow,
Stifling in thick sweat, like tar.
Suddenly, the crowd, round corner he sees,
And in gloved hands, he fumbles keys.
But manages to start the car's engine,
As the nearing crowd causes attention.
He drives off, and shouts at his misfortune,
As a nearing police car blares its siren,
As blackness engulfs his mind's horizon,
And his vision twitches in distortion.
Kram bails out, for his quick-change escape,
And to this nightmare, he prays to awake.

4-3

Kram sits on the underground train,
Panting as anxiety covers him, like a lotion,
He notices people eyeing him strange,
Can they see my pain, my heart broken?
He reaches the station of London Victoria,
Eager to get to Kent and his Gloria.
Just a final meeting to explain,
Before embarking on his campaign.
A campaign of terror and fire
To burn London to the ground
And to historians, he'll astound
On waging war in London's mire.
He boards a train, for beautiful Kent,
In fantasies deep, of Gloria, he dreamt.

4-4

He wakes after a quick nap,
As he dreamt of a final embrace
Wondering if he's heading for a trap,
As colour drains from his face.
His mouth opens, but no words come,
Is it paranoia? As he feels himself go numb.
A painful tightness comes in his throat,
And thinks of writing instead a note.
But the train slows down to his station,
He leaps up, feeling his knees weaken,
And in uneven steps, his fears deepen,
He steps off train, in crowded formation.
He follows people out in a daze,
And out through, the station's maze.

4-5

He sits in one of Kent's many cafés,
Sipping tea in a pensive mood
Staring at nothing, with eyes fixed glaze
As his racing thoughts stewed.
He inhales deeply through his nose,
And through mouth, exhalation flows.
He gets up after leaving money,
Including a huge tip, due to feeling funny.
Funny in the sense of strange
As if his life and dreams have met,
And in each step, he feels regret,
And wished his entire life, he could change.
To change every one of his negative actions,
So, he could love without distractions.

4-6

He buys a hat and large sunglasses,
A basic disguise for beady eyes
As beady eyes are full of grasses,
As he nears his flat, he gently cries.
He stands quietly in a phone box,
As he has to be careful to outfox.
Then dials Gloria up, to get a feel,
To see if the law has broken love's seal.
Suddenly, she answers in a flash,
Sounding flat without emotion,
Calm, without love or devotion
As dreams of a final embrace, crash.
He senses the police have invaded their zone!
'I'm sorry, I love you,' he says in a dulcet tone.

4-7

He walks fast from the phone box,
And walks hard until his feet bled,
Then sits by the coast on cold rocks,
Wondering if the situation he misread.
The seagulls glide upon the breeze,
As he feels calm and strangely at ease.
He bought some chips, whilst deep in thought,
Those fucking bastards must be taught!
He purchases a screwdriver and lighter fuel,
Latex gloves and lined A4 paper
As his plans for that night, did taper,
While crafting a poem, like cutting a jewel.
Smoking a cigarette with pen aflame,
Poetic words touch soul's game.

Lost Innocence

I walked through the woods,
As the night neared dawn
An eeriness embraced me.

The tree branches were outstretched,
Lifeless without leaves
The world seemed cast in frost.

My breath scorched the air,
Expanding out into nothingness
As the cold bit my skin.

I walked into a field,
The grass crunched beneath my feet,
As out-of-place objects caught my eye.

Ahhh! I realised as I neared,
Cows like still boulders
Huddling the Earth for dear life.

One of them stood slowly,
Looking huge in dense brown
The others soon followed.

They made no sound or moans,
I only heard their gentle feet.
Like bony fragments crunching glass.

The cows hung their gentle heads,
Patiently awaiting the horizon
Living day by day in ignorance.

A tear ran down my face as I thought,
If only they knew their fate
That their world would one day erupt.

I was once very much like them,
Innocent, gentle and carefree
Before being engulfed in hellfire.

As this day continues to roll on,
I wander the crowded streets,
Remembering what I'm fighting for.

4-9

On finishing his poem, he removes gloves,
And finishes off his cold chips,
Large, greasy, and fat, he shoves,
Into his mouth, whilst licking lips.
He notices people walking and laughing,
Seagulls huoh – huohing, and dogs barking.
But then two lovers kissing near,
And by his cheek, he feels a tear.
He gloves himself, and folds his poem,
Slipping it carefully into an envelope,
Addressing it in bold for all to scope,
As he imagines the newsroom in low hum.
And shocked detectives, with faces red,
And public's reaction, of fear and dread.

4-10

The night comes cold and still,
Resonating with Kram's deepening mood
And with determination and will
He walks the streets, alert and shrewd.
On hearing a car, he hides behind a wall,
And when clear, he feels the urge call.
With a screwdriver, he brakes a car's lock,
And set fire to the seat, as smoke takes stock.
The poem he leaves, by the front door,
Then targets cars on repeat,
They burn fast, as flames beat
As Kram ran off, to escape the law.
The fire reflected his soul projections,
As he hears sirens, in all directions.

4-11

Under a caravan, he falls asleep
Beyond the destruction and the grief
And to the netherworld, he falls deep
To the neighbouring peace, he is a thief.
The fire engines put out the fires,
To the night in smoky spires.
Throughout the streets, police do search,
For a suspect with a suspicious lurch.
When morning comes, the letter is found
As the owner reads it aloud and far
But his voice quivers on seeing his car,
And tears it up, upon the ground.
By midday, Kram in stiffness, awakes,
And under caravan, he moves and snakes.

4-12

From crawling out from shadowy under
And to the streets, he walks
Staring at burnt-out cars in wonder
And potential victims he stalks.
To a corner shop, he does enter,
Away from the crowded town centre.
With hat pulled down low,
As not to put himself on show.
Through the rack of newspapers, he scours,
No mention of a poem, not a hint
Just a headline and columns in print
As anger and annoyance devours.
That was a good poem of note,
And not even a line or quote.

4-13

Did the police hold this back,
Is this how those pigs react,
I've gotta do another attack,
My thoughts and feelings I must extract.
With another poem of fury and passion,
To a greater night in a fiery fashion.
So, more lighter fuel he buys
And at fear of arrest he sighs.
Kram thinks hard with pen and plans,
With latex gloves, he frantically writes,
As mystery surrounds him and bites
And cautiously along the streets, he scans.
And into an envelope to newspaper's address,
A new poem for history to caress.

4-14

As hours fly into a ghostly night
He waits in a local graveyard,
Posting his letter when bright
While anxiety and doubts are on guard.
He sits by a tree, near a grave,
As his mortality hits him in a wave.
But manages to focus on the game,
And to the night, he will reclaim.
Once again, he walks the streets,
Alert like the night before
Feeling like he's waging war,
And through his chest, heavy heartbeats.
And once again, with his screwdriver,
He breaks open a car and starts a fire.

4-15

Again and again and again
Burning cars one after the other
Doubling last night's fiery chain
As to the streets, flames smother.
Like being in a war zone,
His thoughts twirl in a cyclone.
No more will I feel victimised,
No longer will I feel ostracised.
As fire epitomises, his soul's rise
As he feels he doesn't need love
As he feels a higher purpose, than love
A goal of infamy in history's eyes.
And on finishing, he hides in a shed,
Tired and worn out, his feet like lead.

4-16

The building of the local gazette
Reporters line up, for the days start,
Oliver Pratt smokes his first cigarette,
As to his night out, his thoughts part.
Then, into the building, with heavy feet,
And to his co-workers, he does greet.
And at his desk, he pulls off his sweater,
And on sipping coffee, feels much better.
A pile of mail on his desk arrives,
He scans each one quickly,
On reading Kram's poem, he feels prickly,
Like being poked by a thousand knives.
'Look here, Dave, read this quick,
Stop yapping and being a prick.'

4-17

My Mind's Dancing

The lioness of vengeance
How it grows.

Blood pumping with venom
In violent throws.

Black eyes like thunder
Teeth clenched tight.

Angrily storming my oven
Echoing soul's plight.

As dew of madness
Passes into red.

Thoughts melt the walls,
Fists have bled.

Mind burns with passion,
In night's arc.

Twisting like barbed wire,
Within the dark.

P.S. I was behind those arson attacks,
Print this in the paper, and I'll stop.
If not, I promise I won't relax,
And burn down a house or kill a cop!

4-18

'Oliver, is this for real or a con?
A madman, student, or crank?'
Dave, 'Relax, mate, don't dwell upon,
It's obvious some idiot's prank!'
Oliver laughs, stands, and reads aloud,
Finishing to cheers and laughs, he bows.
He pins it up, for all to read,
And gets back to work to write the lead.
A story of a man, murdered last night,
Shot through the window of his car,
And two witnesses saw the killer run far.
Before disappearing in a building site.
By midday, Oliver finishes the report,
And gives it to the editor, Mr Davenport.

The arsons appear on page three,
But no mention of the poem he wrote.
Kram knew he must continue his spree,
As he imagines cutting a reporter's throat.
To the public toilets to refresh,
As Kram plans, and fantasies mesh.
Into the shops to buy something flammable,
Something to really fuel, the fiery animal.
Nail polish remover came to mind,
As he buys three bottles from Boots,
Three large to feed flames' flutes
As thoughts of a dream, rhymed.
He composed a poem of some depth,
A poem of beauty and of breadth.

The Next Day

Early morning
The country's wet freshness
Seeped through from the night,
Slowly evaporates in sun,
Like the end of a sweet dream.

Midmorning
A mirage along the grey
Rainswept road flickering
Flickering of hope and rebirth
As it echoed through my soul.

Afternoon mace
From heated polluted roads
Dragging multicolours of cars
Like fast metal zombies
I coughed as they passed.

Early evening
Through the bustling town streets
The muggy rain soon hit,
Clothes clung tight, I couldn't…
I just couldn't fucking…

Midnight
The darkness engulfed my bedroom,
Like a black hole swallowing all
I soon fell asleep,
Preparing for the next day.

P.S. Good luck in the hunt!

4-21

Ten miles away, in a back garden
Cunningly in wait like an urban fox
Behind trees and bushes, he lies hidden
As he feels the beckoning letterbox.
Kram's watch reads almost three,
And gets up and takes a pee.
Then, brushes himself down in preparation,
To unleash his friend, his fiery creation.
He puts gloves on, and runs to the front,
Then places his letter by the door.
And now, for sure, no one could ignore,
Writing 'police' upon it, to ignite the hunt.
But police are lazy and rely on science,
No copper's instinct or gut reliance.

4-22

The nail polish remover in letterbox flows,
As he hears the liquid trickle inside
Following with a lit match, he throws
As flames roar, he feels pride.
But without pausing to stand and admire,
He moves on to start another fire.
Then another, before running away hard,
As sirens encroach and bombard.
And under a van, he does hide
And tries dosing off to another land,
Another land he knew first-hand,
Much more appealing than reality's ride.
As he hears in distant, shouts and screams,
Kram soon drifts off to fiery dreams.

4-23

At one house, ladders go to the windows,
As people gasp out through smoke
Whilst some jump to the garden below
As others call for help, as they choke.
In one house, a fireman got inside,
But the man they found has died.
They discover he was a D-day vet,
A frail old man, who posed no threat.
A recipient of the Military Cross
And also, had been a prisoner of war,
A law-abiding man, who followed the law,
A war hero and a great loss.
All other victims suffer smoke inhalation,
But receive immediate help on location.

4-24

When early morning comes, Kram walks off,
As fear of capture on thoughts drop
He lit a cigarette to a smoker's cough,
As he heads to a nearby bus stop.
CID and forensics follow the routine,
And they discover the letter at a scene.
The poem and message really struck,
And the gall of wishing them luck.
Kram's fear of capture and his demise,
Grows from his night of revenge
Feeling society's need, to avenge,
Thoughts of life imprisonment arise,
Kram catches the bus and heads away,
In normality and calm, he tries to portray.

4-25

Covering his face with one hand
Whilst the other crunches the newspaper
Christ, someone died! I hadn't planned,
I've stepped too far, against my nature.
With a feeling of hopelessness and dread,
Wishing to God that he was dead.
Oh, Christ, God help me, I'm going to hell,
I only wanted to cause havoc and rebel!
Looking around in shock and confusion
He hears a voice, but then it goes quiet,
His thoughts and feelings within him riot,
Together with a paranoid delusion.
That he's being spied on, and followed,
And to his shock, guilt, he's swallowed.

4-26

With a hunched posture against the world
He walks off with a heavy sigh,
Biting his bottom lip, he curled
Not daring to look anyone in the eye.
He wanders around town, in and out of cafés,
Staring at the pavement, as eyes glaze.
In and out of his thoughts and dreams,
Then suddenly, in a café, he screams.
Everyone looks at him in total shock,
He pays the bill quick, with a fumbling hand,
Knowing that his nerves, can't withstand,
He quickly runs out, a laughingstock.
With an onset of nausea, he runs away,
From people's gaze, his emotions play.

4-27

Berating himself and wallowing in drink
He sits aboard a train to London,
And after a deep and focused think
He feels his time on Earth is done.
His face goes slack, and pales slightly,
At this realisation, with fists tensed tightly.
There is no backup plan, or any options,
As a poem, he works on, with mind's eruptions.
This poem's my last; no more will I offend.
He writes, and pauses and thinks,
Then wrote more as his world shrinks,
My last poem, with just myself to send.
He finally reaches London's station,
And for his suicide, he gives an explanation.

4-28

My End, I Dream

This world I lived, homeless,
Under the starry night sky
Then, in moon's light, I spy,
As I drown in eternal loneliness.

Silent I remain for the end,
Where memory's signposts point
As curled fingers poise at joint
The cold blade I thee befriend.

In life's conspiracy, no soul does hide,
In stoic mask to disguise lost love
As the knife slides into heart's glove
I go now. Goodbye. Now I've died.

4-29

He buys a kitchen knife of three inches,
Plus, two bottles of malt whisky
Every time he touches the knife, he flinches,
As he drinks down whisky like cold tea.
He sits in a cubicle of a public loo,
With a knife ready to ram through.
And guzzles down whisky for courage,
And thinks of the dead man to encourage.
But he's unable to stab himself, as fear grows,
And drops the knife and staggers out,
And wanders the streets, no planned route,
The note in rucksack, to pavement he throws.
To a London bridge, he stands still,
As he feels throughout his body, a chill.

4-30

He climbs the side, to attempt to jump,
But passers-by, grab him down.
On the pavement held in a slump
'I need to die; it's best to drown.'
Kram has no fight, and starts to cry,
They held him tight, or otherwise, he'll die.
The calls go out, and towards them police chase
On discovering his name, the cuffs they lace.
Then, into the patrol car, he's taken in
Then to a cell, in mumbles and cries,
And with deep, quivering breaths, he sighs,
'I'm useless. I'm rubbish. I belong in a bin.'
He's interviewed, by a psychiatrist of note,
'I'm drowning in misery, but my sanity's afloat.'

4-31

Kram screams aloud, to the cold grey,
So finally, I'm in law's clenched fist,
As guilt of the dead man does weigh
And in depression, his mind does drift.
He sits in a cell, as thoughts decay,
In poetic words, his mind does play.
But then a solicitor to him does visit,
As Kram's advised, as his emotions pivot.
The solicitor talks of the jewellery shop,
And the knife used upon him.
A knife used to mark his sin,
As his DNA matches from a blood drop.
He's advised when interviewed, the way to go,
And save arguments for courtroom's show.

4-32

He goes 'no comment' in the interview,
And of the Jewellery shop they question.
With other various crimes in the queue,
As he grabs his hair, on feeling the tension.
Finally by the desk sergeant, he is charged
As Kram burst out laughing, with eyes enlarged.
The police look at him, if he were mad,
As he cries, then laughs, acts happy, then sad.
Why, to my life, did God create?
Why on this planet within this space?
And why am I part of this human race?
As Kram's thoughts to mind vibrate.
Have I lost, or have I won?
Like darkened clouds occlude the sun.

Sent to hospital for assessment,
Locked tight on a secure ward's fight.
He acts vexed with resentment,
To other patients, he ignores outright.
He passes assessment with flying colours,
To great guilt and loss, he only suffers.
So, back to prison on remand,
And into a cell, the devil's hand.
No greeting on meeting other cons
They act staunch and complete,
But underneath, they've panicking feet,
As they glide around like swans.
A pen and paper he buys from canteen,
Then, in a poem, he writes as routine.

4-34

The House of Whispering Hate

The house of whispering hate
Locked doors against painted brick
All behind a twisted metal gate,
Time without a sundial stick.

At seven minutes to half-eight
Whilst finishing off my cold supper
In a desolate mind, I do recreate
As I slowly stir my hot cuppa.

Thankfully, I have no cellmate,
As I'm deemed too high a risk
So luckily, I can stay up late.
As my thoughts ran devilishly brisk.

Myself I've heard rumours of
A new prisoner on near E-wing
A right cunt and fucking toff
Killed his wife, who dared to sing.

The rumour mill endlessly rolling.
As prisoners slowly roll on – roll off,
Nattering nannies, secretly whispering
Moving through wings on – off, on – off.

Some people like inventing rumours
As it passes the time away
But me, I see them like tumours,
Cancerous entities in every way.

The syncopated beats of voices
Nattering in the lunch or phone queue
Humming with various news, rejoices
Whether stories are false or true.

Once, some old bloke got slashed
Due to a rumour, he did rape,
And to a little girl, he had flashed
And before he raped, he tied with tape.

It turns out he only stole scholarships!
So, me, I like being on my own,
Without joining in prisoners' politics
No friends or family to phone.

Endless rumours I can't stand,
Endless shite within the twisted gate
In this house, whilst on remand
In this house of whispering hate.

A month before his trial date
Where he knows he's looking at life
Years inside is his fate,
An ocean of time, an ocean of strife.
God, why have you betrayed me,
I was in love, happy and free.
As he sits in his cell watching the rain,
Tapping against the window's plastic pane.
He feels like one of the living dead,
Feeling almost invisible
To courts, he's divisible
With a heavy heart like lead.
He leans on a book, on his scruffy bed,
Writing a poem, as his feelings shed.

Drowning in Prison's Sea

Sunlight shone through the cell window,
But still, I lay motionless, feeling cold.
Shadowed bars stretched across the floor,
As prison held me in its stranglehold.

Within the concrete cage of light
The dusty cell floor compels upon it,
Darts of freedom stab at my mind
My once-ordinary thoughts begin to split.

My mind burnt and shined with pain,
My skin grew paler through lost years,
As I start to forget who I was
My dark eyes enlarge with tears.

Suicide soon appears as freedom,
Imagining myself hanging bravely free
But if I did, they would have won,
So, I went on, drowning in prison's sea.

CANTO 5

5-1

The day of the trial comes
As Kram stands in the dock,
No public fanfare drums
He stands still like a rock.
'I'm sentencing you to life imprisonment,
For such a violent and horrid event.
And with a tariff of six years.'
As Kram strains to withhold his tears.
The court staff then take him away,
From all society and mankind
No Gloria in court, to remind,
And now, it's time for him to pay,
As they say, the justice mob,
As Kram's temples start to throb.

5-2

Kram lies in his cell after the trial,
At night, without a light on
No one to speak to, no one to dial,
He gets up with thoughts upon,
And sits on a chair, by the table
With head in hands, feeling unstable.
He puts the TV on, with volume low,
For company, a flickering friend, a bro.
He finally switches on the light,
And pulls out a pad,
As uncertainties clad.
As night's coldness wraps him tight.
He picks up a pen and quickly writes,
With Gloria in mind, his lip he bites.

5-3

Death Becomes My Bride

I'm in a parked car,
On a crowded street
And I see my love,
Dancing on little feet.

My thread is slipping,
Insanity, I hear,
Fingers gripping knife.
Voices, I fear.

To see her like this
With another man
On a darkened winter's day
My lovely Marianne.

Oh, my love,
Why are you cheating,
I'm drowning in anger,
My thoughts twisting.

I stormed out the car.
Marched down the street.
As I quickly approached
I felt my heartbeat.

I stabbed her thrice,
Love to me is cyanide.
Bloods gone everywhere.
Death becomes my bride.

5-4

After writing the poem, he cries
Then sets it alight, to a smoky haze,
Then sits on toilet with deep sighs,
As his thoughts, and heart betrays.
The next day bursts into light,
As noises blare prisoners' plight.
But Kram stays in bed, wrapped tight,
Not wanting the world to fight.
Suddenly, in his cell, two men convey,
In violence to Kram, whilst in bed
As they punch hard with fists of lead
'In future, you pay us, to keep us away.'
Kram knew the game and how to play,
'Okay, alright. I'll pay on canteen day.'

Perhaps Kram ought to have bought,
As the bullies did say
But as he's from trial and overwrought
He prefers a melee.
On canteen day, they enter his cell,
Kram is prepared and gives them hell.
His fists connect to their jaws,
As he doesn't, for a second, take pause.
He jumps wildly upon their bodies,
Until they're fucked thro' and thro'.
And within his soul, he feels anew
And prays to God, in hope he sees.
'There you are, God, you want a villain,
Well, here I am, a villain on a mission.'

5-6

Alarms go off, and guards come in,
As Kram backs up slowly
They grab Kram up, as he does grin,
'It's thanks to God, I'm not holy.'
They give him a crazed, furious glare,
'To these cunts, the fight was fair!'
But they took him away, to the block,
A bleak, barren world, where demons knock.
'You'll see the governor in the morning.'
Says the harmonious, disparaging voice,
'Listen, Skyal, the fight was your choice.'
'I'll bend over next time,' Kram says, scorning.
The cell is cold, dirty, and drab,
As he gives the air, a victorious jab.

Kram's yo-yoing from wing to block,
With each year, he compels to be.
Nothing more could scare or shock,
As he surfs through year three.
'Bang up! Workshops! Bang up!
Bang up! Association! Bang up!'
Like being stuck in Groundhog Day,
As he judges time through hair grey.
'To my behaviour, I don't apologise,'
He shouts to himself, aloud in his cell,
His concrete shell, a manmade hell
As pain to his soul does colonise.
Kram sits at his table and writes,
As new poem to his mind, fights.

5-8

Prison's Cycle

Across the yard in prison morn,
A slight mist settles from devil's scorn.

The clusters of curled barbed wire,
Like frost on top of fence's spire.

Round and round the prisoner's go,
Eager to escape, eager to go.

This is the garden of the loving lord,
Keeping devil's children, the banished horde.

As I'm in my cell on autumn's fall,
Watching through window, behind wall.

Then, a suited governor with his sullen frown,
Came through the gate, in prison's town.

Suddenly, some doors bang open, feet scurry past,
The voice of cleaners in synchronised blast.

Then, at my flap, a little grey head,
'Spare any burn?' The old man said.

With a look of sadness, and of shame,
Across his little face, it came.

My nobler nature from me stirred,
But I shook my head – no, without a word.

I gave a yawn and put on the kettle,
As I stood still until it growled on metal.

A cup of coffee with a splash of milk,
As I drank it down, it felt like silk.

And then I lay and smoke some draw,
And thought of ways to outsmart the law.

And on and on, this cycle goes,
As anyone who's been in prison knows.

5-9

Faith comes in slow for year four,
As Kram joins Alpha for a break
A Christian group with an open door
Tempting prisoners in with cake.
Kram laughs to himself, at their belief,
But it's a relaxing time, with food and relief.
Relief of speaking to people who care,
Rather than an unfriendly, stoic guard's stare.
'I'm not a Christian; I make no apology,'
Kram tells the charismatic speaker,
'As I'm no longer human, but a creature,
I'm more entwined with demonology.'
Kram stuffs his face with food,
As he explains his thoughts and mood.

5-10

'But why does God allow suffering?
It doesn't make sense, that it's a test?
And have us accept on discovering,
His kingdom where we're blessed.
I've prayed so hard throughout my life,
In dark times, through trouble and strife.
And in my darkness, he never helped,
And in disaster, I screamed and yelped.
But no white doves or angels in sight
No feelings of love or of peace
Just sirens, alarms, and police
Only tormenting moments in cell at night.
I'm desperate for help, happiness, and love,
But God doesn't help from way up above.'

'I understand, Kram, you've had troubles,
But maybe these troubles, help you grow.'
As Kram slowly cracks his scarred knuckles,
As images of Gloria, make peace flow.
'This is the path God planned for you,
Like meeting us in this human zoo.'
Kram eyes glaze over with his words,
As he picks more food, his thirds!
'I heard a diamond, needs friction to sparkle,
As troubles build a man's character
As I was told by my barrister.
But my troubles have been a debacle,
As in the law, my soul suffered defeat,
Feeling myself sink, in quick-drying concrete.'

5-12

'Okay, Kram, let's forget religion for now,
What are you interested in?'
'I love poetry; I know it's a bit highbrow,
But years ago, it got under my skin.
The library here has none,
I was pissed! My head spun.
I wanted something deep, something magic,
Like Wilde's "Ballad of Reading Gaol" – classic.'
'I've got that at home, Kram; I'll photocopy it.'
Kram glows with widening eyes,
'Thanks,' he says in surprise.
'Prisoners are stupid, no one to talk to and shit.'
'I'll photocopy it for you, and post it in.'
'I'll give you my details,' Kram says with a grin.

In his cell, a few weeks later,
With fantasies of murder in overkill
Fantasies of crime form a crater,
This country will bend at my will!
Kram laughs and feels manic,
Imagining the police in a panic.
Suddenly, something slides under his door,
As he nears the envelope upon the floor.
He opens it up, and to his surprise,
Photocopies of poetry at its best
As Kram holds it close to his chest
As he then reads with watery eyes.
Gripping tightly Wilde's creative spire,
As the poem to Kram does inspire.

Released (Another Name For Nothing Else to Lose)

'Twas the end of prison time
On a morning, calm and cool
And three and twenty ex-cons
Were released from prison rule,
There were some who ran, and others leapt,
Like children home from school.

Away they ran with wicked minds,
With souls drenched in pain
To a higher level of criminality
With thoughts on a higher plain
But still no part in beloved society
As some boarded a London train.

One stole a car and raced around,
Like a demented spiced-up flea
He shouted at the smirking police,
Skidding through town's Grand Prix
But crashed his car then got nicked,
As he murmured, 'C'est la vie.'

Another scored drugs, the illegal type
And with a needle, he did play
The heroin scorched through his veins,
And his head went far away.
But his heart had stopped, due to
Too much purity, after such a prison stay.

Like homing pigeons, they coursed about,
And laughed as they ran.
Their futures were predetermined,
As they stole in predator's scan.
But the killer stands, remote from all,
He was such a melancholy man.

For he did his time, for the killing of
His greedy, unfaithful wife
Over twenty years inside, he spent,
For ending her short life.
But the man who screwed her
Is still about, and now he needs a knife.

'I must kill that bastard, who behind
My back, did it with my wife
I know where he lives and his name,
I must stab him with a knife.
Then, escape back home, to Eastern Scotland
To the beautiful kingdom of Fife.'

There are many stories of such men,
That prison hadn't helped at all,
The mad got madder, and the
Bad got badder, in the huge, bricked brawl.
One day, I hope the prison wall,
Be smashed by a wrecking ball.

5-15

Kram continues going to Alpha,
As he grows friends with all
As peace grows from nostalgia
From little time, outside the wall.
He eats less cake and speaks in rhyme,
About poetry, life, and time.
There is no antagonistic rival,
No fighting for survival.
Then, one day, he's told he's moving,
To transfer to another jail
And at the news, he goes pale,
In anger, he's all-consuming.
He packs his bags, into the trolley,
As he falls back, to his usual folly.

5-16

Kram is two'd up in a cell,
Sharing time with another con
His cellmate is doing life as well,
His name is Ron.
For many hours a day, they do talk,
And round the yard, they do walk.
Then, one day, Ron speaks of his crime,
And talks of robbery as being sublime.
They talk and plan for nearly a year,
As Ron says, he can supply real guns
And Kram, in joy, almost speaks in tongues,
At the thought of doing jobs using serious gear.
Kram's fantasies were becoming true,
And extreme wealth he does view.

5-17

Then, one day, when having a shower,
Men burst in and attack Ron.
As towards Kram, they overpower,
Telling Kram, 'Ron's a wrong 'un.'
'He's a fucking armed robber like me,
Well-connected to the highest degree.'
'No, Kram, he isn't, he did over a girl.'
Kram goes limp, as thoughts twirl.
'I got the details from a reliable screw,
She was just eleven, to whom he raped,
And beat her up, before he escaped.
And my missus checked the details too.'
Kram dressed and left, as Ron gets battered,
Feeling down, as his dreams are shattered.

5-18

Hills tinged red in distant fade,
Surrounded by green fields and flowers,
As a waterfall sparkles in a light cascade
As a huge nearby tree, towers.
Ron runs up to him, screaming, 'Why?'
As Kram covers his ears in reply.
Kram stutters and stammers to hide,
Making excuses for not taking his side.
Kram holds himself tight,
Eyes widening before control is asserted.
As he can't muster a reason, he deserted,
Suddenly, it becomes night.
Kram wakes up from darkest hell,
Crying uncomfortably in his cold, dark cell.

5-19

His bare feet slap the cell floor in echo,
As a far sea breathes in his ear
A year of planning and dreaming, let go,
As he wishes he could disappear.
He stands staring blankly at the wall,
As he hears Ron screaming in the brawl.
Then, a glance to his left, the mirror reflects,
His dark, shadowy image, he quickly rejects.
He walks slowly towards the window,
Feeling entrapped within night's starry gaze
And below the fences in a walled maze.
As thoughts of cowardice and self-doubt grow.
His hands against the bars become fists,
As he now thinks of cutting his wrists.

Early in the morning, Kram awakes,
The bright morning light shone,
He boils the kettle for tea he makes,
As his suicidal thoughts have gone.
Putting the radio on to BBC 4,
Listening to "Prayer of the Day" before,
Welcoming the day, with poetry, say
Reciting aloud or writing away.
As Kram's emotions sway the balance,
Between sanity and insanity
Fighting against man's inhumanity
As he's comforted by his writing talents.
With his pen upon a lined pad,
Words sprawl on his creative clad.

The Prisoner's Sonnet

Wasted time passes for us caged cattle,
From court's monstrous anger of its dark gun
Bellowing judge and galleries prattle
Mocking crowds outside with their hatred spun.
The voices of our souls, like a ghostly choir
Maddening screams cut like thunderous bells,
As screws file us into a stone hate pyre
Before banging us up, in caustic cells.
Life's memories haunt and do age us all,
And with rough, hard, coarse hands and hateful eyes
Ambitions and dreams glimmer their goodbyes,
Armies of pale-skinned prisoners fall.
No flowers of beauty in anyone's mind,
In each and all men's minds, draws down the blind.

5-22

Suddenly, midmorning, his door bolts open,
As a guard directs a prisoner inside
He's grey and old, and lined face broken,
As he nods to Kram, with a smile wide.
'I'm Pete; I'm on a licence recall.'
'I'm Kram, doing life with tariff small.'
Kram lies on his bed and breathes slow,
As he tiredly lies with depression on show.
They engage in light-hearted conversation,
As Kram expresses desire to sleep
Pete unpacks, and Kram goes deep,
Before sitting and assessing his situation.
Kram spends the day, in thoughts away,
As Pete discovers, why he is that way.

5-23

After evening association, Kram does stir,
As Pete offers to make him coffee
'What TV programme do you prefer?'
Pete asks whilst chewing toffee.
'I don't really care,' comes Kram's reply,
And gives a deep, outstretched sigh.
'I know what happened to your mate.'
'He wasn't my mate; let's get that straight!
He was a nonce of the first class,
And he wasted me a year in stolen dreams.'
'What d'you mean, Kram, stolen dreams?
You can tell me I ain't no grass!'
'I wanted to network and be a success,
I'm a bad criminal but want to progress.'

'I know straight where you're coming from,
Networking is a clever move to make.'
As Pete chews on toffee, like gum.
'And working on your own is a mistake.
A good team, men with soul,
And careful planning to obtain the goal.'
'My networking skills, Pete, aren't great,
I should've started earlier in life, not late.'
'It's never too late, to chase your dreams,
Forget society's values and norms,
Just hold tight to soul's mast, thro' storms,
It's never late to pull off clever schemes!'
'Right, Pete, why should I obey man's laws,
And to completely abandon my own cause?'

5-25

'Believe it or not, Kram, I have a solution,
It's been a solution staring you in the face.
My idea to you is a revolution,
It'll knock your head into outer space.'
'What, Pete, tell us your idea,
I hope you're not talking diarrhoea.'
Pete laughs and cries aloud,
As he straightens his posture, proud.
'Have you heard of a therapeutic community?'
Kram looks bewildered, and shakes head no,
But looks interested with mind aglow,
'It's therapy in prison, the perfect opportunity.
You'll make contacts like a star,
And know exactly, what people's charges are.'

'It's hard making contacts in main prison,
All sex cases say they're armed robbers,
Or professional criminals who've risen,
Through ranks of organised crime, in honours.
No one can lie in a therapeutic community,
As during group discussions, staff will guarantee.
I spent five years at HMP Grendon,
The flagship of TCs, where liars are set upon.
But HMP Dovegate's TC will be a breeze,
It's a private jail, and therapy's relaxed,
And cells have showers in, so don't get axed.
Keep to rules, and you'll socialise with ease.
I'll teach you all you need to know,
And what to say and what to show.'

From that moment, they're thick as thieves,
And walk everywhere deep in talk.
Ambitions and ideas to Kram, Pete feeds
As Kram keeps intense focus, like a hawk.
But Kram teaches Pete poetry in return,
And after a year, they both did learn.
Then, at the door, a guard speaks through,
'Skyal, Dovegate's TC is waiting for you.
Tomorrow morning, you are to depart.'
As Kram feels ecstatic and sad,
As he views Pete, like a dad.
'So, start packing now, for your early start.'
Kram packs, and all night, they speak
And Kram gifts Pete with a poem so bleak.

The Black Fly

In my cold, barren cell
A black fly tries to exit,
Within my own private hell
As I lie still, inspecting it.
It was like a hardened con,
Doing time, doing a sentence
As the morning light shone
It then laid still, in penance.
Suddenly, the fly takes off,
As a screw grunted out the air
I coughed a loud cough,
As the fly swirls in despair.
Click. Bang. The door unbolted,
When the fly escaped, I felt exalted.

5-29

In morning, the guard unbolted the door,
'Trolley's here; Skyal, you ready?'
'Yes, Gov, there on the floor,
My kit bag.' As Kram points unsteady.
Kram and Pete look at each other,
'I've got your details, Pete, and your brother.'
'And send us more poetry, mate, it's brill,
As like you, I've oodles of time to kill!'
They shake hands, and Kram departs,
As a myriad of voices bark their farewells
From behind doors, in their locked cells.
Kram cheers, as thro' the wing he darts.
Then, heavily treading down metal stairs,
As the nearing unknown, to Kram's mind scares.

5-30

Going to reception is always unpleasant,
Searching his bag, and the strip search
As the guards stand around, omnipresent
And the bullying vexed guard's lurch.
Then he waits, in a holding cell with others,
Whilst the sodium stark light smothers.
And the lack of water, turns mouths to sand,
As loneliness and uncertainty lie in hand.
Then, one by one, into the prison van
Each locked within a clean white cubicle
Etched with nicknames and lyrics musical,
And a tinted plastic window to scan.
To scan the world like a silent movie,
To scan the world in tinted beauty.

5-31

The prison van moves, through gate it goes,
As the free world, to prisoners, fascinates,
And the music from radio to fantasy throws
And to each prisoner, seeing freedom lacerates.
Kram sees a couple walking down the street,
And thoughts of Gloria to him repeat.
On reliving fantasies in his head,
Of love and comfort to soul it fed.
Kram laughs and talks to himself aloud,
But through his door window, a guard stares
And Kram, on noticing, his anger flares
Then looks away, stoically proud.
His fantasies turn from love to violence,
And sits the entire journey in silence.

CANTO 6

6-1

On reaching Dovegate prison
He goes through the rigmaroles of reception,
As Kram's driven by ambition
His kit bag goes through another inspection.
A thin, lanky guard with flair,
Asks him to sit upon the BOSS chair.
Explaining it searches for metals and phones,
As Kram's tiredness and irritation cyclones.
Before long, Kram, with a trolley are escorted,
To the therapy assessment wing
Where he plans to flourish and sing
And on passing, to therapy, he'll be awarded.
On entering the wing, a sea of faces he studies,
Wondering to which man, he'll be buddies.

6-2

Early next day, Kram sits in a room,
Packed around with prisoners in a meeting,
As anger and bitch barking consume
By prisoners on a sex case, verbally beating.
A guard speaks of a mystery, bizarre,
Of his stolen half-smoked Padron cigar.
The room falls silent as a prisoner speaks up,
Admitting stealing it with sad eyes like a pup.
But this look did not help,
As the guard's fury he feels
In turmoil and horror he reels
And to the guard, he does yelp.
But he's told he's on a commitment vote,
As the vice chairman writes, down that note.

6-3

Kram discovers he's a first-time rapist,
Got life and spent twenty-five years inside.
The guard still in the proverbial red mist
Points out his victim nearly died.
It was at night, in the late seventies,
Outside her house, drunk, fumbling keys.
And with a brick, he did strike,
As to her blonde hair, he did like.
No one in defence speaks up for him,
Kram can sense, he is mentally slow,
As sentences were short, no verbal flow,
You can see to prison; he will stay within.
Kram almost feels pity, as inside, he'll die,
It would've been better, to hang him high.

6-4

Before long, the meeting is over
And people quietly shuffle out,
Kram finds it interesting, but moreover,
To networking, he's eager to scout.
He finds someone for importing class A,
By welding drugs, in a shipment from Calais.
Then, another with possession of a gun,
Who shot a streetlight, when drunk for fun.
Days fly past as he walks the yard,
Then a psychologist calls him, too
Telling him he has psychometrics to do,
As she stands smiling but on guard.
Kram asks others for their advice,
They reply, 'Don't be honest at any price.'

6-5

Throughout the test, his focus is steely
Ticking answers as if he is an angel,
Time passes, as he manipulates freely
As his reading and concentration becomes painful.
Finally, at last, the questions end
And in a stretch, his limbs distend.
And to his cell, he retires,
As stress to his mind, rewires.
But the testing isn't over, he is told,
And so, he must relax and rest,
For an IQ and psychopathy test,
And then to a rainbow, where he'll find gold.
He smiles at the prospect of getting a gun,
As his web of contacts has begun.

6-6

The next morning, in a small group
Kram speaks about his childhood,
To colourful characters in crime's soup
As to Kram, they related and understood.
He grits his teeth as he speaks
As thoughts of his parents leaks.
But no one casts judgment upon,
As they use their stories to add on.
On finishing, he feels he has achieved
After speaking his heart out to all
Without screaming or climbing the wall
But feels strangely calm and relieved.
Then, in the main room, they give feedback,
As other groups also let issues unpack.

6-7

Kram can't see the old man's eyes, just a
Faint glimmer, in a nest of wrinkles
As he writes feverishly in a
Complaints book, in messy words like symbols.
Then, a shout from the two's landing,
As a man, after a review board, is ranting.
His language is vexed and colourful,
As he storms around like a bull.
He got turned down, due to his temper,
Always shouting, arguing, and threatening
Always on edge with face reddening
Whose anger glows on a perpetual ember.
He kicks a bin, which goes flying,
As the old man, the cleaner, starts sighing.

Then, a man, a little on the short side
Broad shoulders, with a boxer's nose
To Kram writing at table, he sits beside,
And questions Kram on his writing prose.
'It keeps me sane, like sitting by a tree,
On a summer's day, also I do poetry.'
'I'm Billy,' as he smiles with gold teeth.
'I'm Kram,' as he cheers beneath.
Then, to each other's crimes, they speak,
Admitting to many robberies, they gloat
Reflecting they're both in the same boat,
As Billy talks of the gym, to change his physique.
They both vex at doing life with tariff small,
Then, to a cell, to watch England play Senegal.

6-9

Then, later in the cell, a man does enter,
And talks in a melodious, quavering voice,
A well-known, serial sex offender
On being accepted to therapy, he does rejoice.
Both Billy and Kram hide their true feelings,
As they both feel he's so unappealing.
But both congratulate him with a smile,
When in reality, they'd rather run a mile.
Finally, the sex case leaves Billy's cell,
As he senses, it is not right
To enter without an invite
And in frustration, Billy does yell.
'Why do we have to do therapy with nonces?
As many have asked to silent responses.'

6-10

Kram lays motionless on his bed
During bang-up, as the sun slaps his face,
As he has no curtains to spread
So, he gets up in vigour and does pace.
He studies outside the concrete fire,
As the sun shatters on the razor wire.
He sees a small bird in distance, fly,
Almost imperceptibly across the sky.
The sun dazzles through the plastic screen,
Stripping the hot cell of air
He sits down on a plastic chair,
Overpowered by the thick, dazzling scene.
His jaws tighten as time stands still,
As drops of sweat, gather in eyebrows sill.

6-11

Kram's thoughts drift to his childhood
As in a group, he spoke the other day,
Recalling the violence at school, he withstood
In mind, like watching movies in Blu-ray.
He knows sometimes; memories play tricks,
As with some memories, he hides with bricks.
Sometimes, he builds a huge wall against hell,
Sometimes, in sadness to his knees, he fell.
He gets his pad and pen to doodle,
And in his mind grows a wild flame
As he starts writing in rhyme again
As creative forces on words, jostle.
Then sparks fly with pen on paper,
And to his childhood, the pain did taper.

The Summer of '79

To the nearing of a seventies summer,
The hay time had now come.
How busy I was in fantasy's thunder,
How webbed my mind, the spider spun.

I walked to school in growing fear,
No happiness like the other kids.
From behind me, tormenting bullies appear,
Gaining bruises, black eyes, and fractured ribs.

Lunchtime at school was hard and long,
As others had meals, I had none.
I spent that time on playground's song,
Where thoughts of crime had begun.

On returning home, I had no fight,
As my parents' presence burnt like mace.
Cold, dark eyes were full of spite,
Like black holes in distant space.

Endless years of pain I endured,
My inner sanctum, a blackened soul.
Those memories stayed, as I matured,
Which fuelled my anger, as I robbed and stole.

6-13

Suddenly, the doors are being unlocked,
As association time has reared its head
It's when devious prisoners lie and concoct
Whilst others in dead weight, lie in bed.
Then Billy, to Kram's cell enters,
Confessing paranoia at CCTV monitors.
As he's bringing drugs in from a visit,
Kram feels nervous being made complicit.
'I'd rather not get involved, mate!'
'I know, Kram. I'm just venting,
As in withdrawal, I'm ascending,
For a week, I haven't felt great.'
Suddenly, the shout for visits is called out,
Kram wishes Billy luck, as their tensions sprout.

6-14

Billy enters into the visits' suite,
And sits facing his visitor friend,
As Billy hides under table, nervous feet
To crisps and Coke, his friend does spend.
The room swells up with chatter,
As Billy talks and devours his platter.
Surrounded by laughter and conversation,
As Billy and friend assess the situation.
Then, into crisps, his friend puts a package,
As guards to children do look
As Billy surveys like a seasoned crook
Then, hand to package, Billy takes advantage.
Billy then quickly plugs it tight,
As nerves and anxiety take flight.

6-15

Billy sees the sparkles of her teeth,
And the little folds of her eyes
Of a guard, as Billy's fear surges beneath
Then suddenly, guards through door surprise.
They immediately take Billy by force,
And quote the rules, they must enforce.
They manhandle Billy in a clamour,
As they admit seeing him on camera.
'I've been fucking grassed up,' he shouts.
'Everything went well as normal.'
As guards laugh and become informal
And in Billy's mind, he has no doubts.
And to the block, he does go,
Grabbed with force, they walk slow.

6-16

Kram hears the news and feels upset,
As he hasn't gotten his details
As Billy is a character, he'll never forget
And hopes to meet again, on life's scales.
As he feels that life balances out,
As there's always an oasis in desert's drought.
He knows one day, he'd have his way,
As life deals him, troubles array.
Kram manages to scrounge a green curtain,
To shade in his hot cell
And clean away the sweaty smell,
By mopping floor, with shampoo insertion.
The cell's finally cool, and to his radio, he plays,
As he imagines himself outside a Parisian café.

Sitting outside a peaceful, quaint café
Somewhere in Paris, along tree-lined streets
As birds sing in springtime May
As he recites to himself, poems by Keats.
He leans back in his creaky chair,
Wondering on the café's history, in sun's glare.
Was this place visited by Nazis?
Or poets and artists in calmer seas.
He imagines women ooze with intelligence,
As he listens to their delightful chatter
Drinking coffee as men do flatter,
In fine mannerisms in delicate elegance.
But back to his stark reality, of prison,
And to his mind, a poem had risen.

There Are No Seasons In Prison

There are no seasons in prison,
No plum tree blossoms,
Or warm breezes with bird calls.

There are no seasons in prison,
No rivers to mirror the sun's rays,
With rippling, glistening sparks of light.

There are no seasons in prison,
Because the background is bare,
With a complete absence of compassion.

There are no seasons in prison,
The sun is black to me,
As the air is death.

There are no seasons in prison,
As I hear my own heartbeat,
And hear my heavy, deep breath.

6-19

Kram sits silently in a community meeting,
When suddenly a psychologist speaks,
As slight depression, on his mind, was seeping,
On hearing his name, adrenalin leaps.
'You're down for your psychopathy test today,
Is eleven-thirty this morning okay?'
Kram nods with his usual fake smile,
And through his hair, his fingers style.
The meeting flies by, in the usual fashion
As Kram watches the room like a TV show
With an undercurrent of agendas flowing below
Within lies, bullshit, and fake compassion.
When the meeting ends, people walk out,
As Kram's nervousness of the test, sprout.

6-20

He reminds himself to answer like an angel,
As he remembers Pete's advise
As these tests are policed, and must be careful,
And he must hide his true self in lies.
The time comes, and into the room, he walks,
Whilst acting polite and courteous, he talks.
Within the room's silence, Kram prepares,
And towards the video camera, he stares.
'We film with everyone, don't be alarmed.'
As Kram fakes a smile, and laughs,
As in stress, and anxiety sweat baths,
But he soon relaxes, as Pete's advice has armed.
And begins breathing deep, and slow, to relax,
As the questions then fall, like an axe.

6-21

'How many sexual partners have you had?'
Kram knew to keep the number low. 'Four.'
Since psychopaths sleep around like mad
And then boast to their friends the score.
'Have you been convicted for all your crimes?'
'No,' as he fights the urge to say 'yes' in rhymes.
Kram knew that that was a test for manipulation,
As Kram grows confident in his deception.
'Do you feel better than others?'
Kram immediately laughs and says, 'No.'
'Have you ever been in debt, though?'
'I never borrow, as to relationships it smothers!'
'Smothers?' 'Owing money ruins a relationship,
Never a borrower or lender be, that's my tip!'

'Can you define the word love?'
Kram knows psychopaths equate –
Love only with lust's glove,
And nothing deep from soul's estate.
Kram gives a prepared reply,
'Someone you feel a part of.' He makes a sigh.
'Are you impulsive?'
Kram knows psychopaths are impulsive!
'No – actually, I think before I act.'
'Are you prone to boredom?'
Kram knows psychopaths suffer such decorum,
'No – as I always find something to distract.'
'How old were you when first convicted?'
Alas, the truth to this, he has to admit it.

6-23

The questions continue, to Kram's delight,
As he is now enjoying himself
For every prisoner, he could write
A book of tricks and tips, for mind's shelf.
For a lot of prisoners to psychology, they fall,
At end of sentences, in hospitals, they crawl.
Drugged and abused in a damaging diagnosis,
Gaining weight with vacant eyes, lacking focus.
But Kram outsmarted psychologists and all
As the test came to an unfortunate end
A cryptic note to Pete he'll send,
As he outsmarts all, in TC's ball.
'Kram, when would you like to complete,
Your IQ test?' Kram pauses. 'At two, after I eat.'

6-24

Kram bounces happily out of the room,
And speaks to Simon, listening to Metallica.
And to sandwiches they all consume,
As Kram studies Simon's photo of Africa.
'It's where I holidayed and started to date,
A black woman from Uganda called Raitt.'
'She looks a bit like Rihanna.'
'Yeah, Kram, and she grew marijuana.'
Minutes fly as time ticks on
As Kram mentally prepares for the test
'Any tips, Simon, would you suggest?'
'Just keep calm and focus upon.
There are no numbers or words on display,
Just numerous patterns in lined array.'

6-25

Kram sits in a small room, waiting,
For the puzzling IQ test.
In nervousness, he's fighting,
In deep breaths from chest.
After a stretch, he is ready,
As his pen in hand is steady.
'Okay, Kram, you can start,'
As he turns it over, he feels his heart.
But immediately understands to his surprise
And quickly completes the pattern,
With each question, carefully in turn
And through the test, Kram flies.
He finishes before time, and so indicates,
And to a high score, he anticipates.

6-26

Days pass, and the psychologist approaches,
And congratulates him on a high IQ,
As to his past education, she encroaches,
Advising him on a degree, he should do.
'Speak to education when you get through,
And start Open University, you must pursue.'
Kram feels excited at that possibility,
And in his mind, a grand symphony.
To leave prison with a degree
As thoughts of going straight interlace
As he drifts towards normality's embrace,
At peace, living life totally free.
But living on licence is like being chained,
Like walking on eggshells, a life constrained.

6-27

Kram's past is more stress than leisure,
As now he intends to use his head more,
To serious contacts, he must treasure,
As he knew he must prepare for war.
He knows even with a bachelor's degree,
He'll never get a job; that's a guarantee.
Especially with a lifetime inside,
And legally, to his past, he can't hide.
The cards were clearly stacked,
And not in Kram's favour, but against
Knowing this, brings him angst,
As his pathway is cruelly cracked.
He knows society doesn't want his reform,
As failure creates jobs, in prison's storm.

That night in his cell
Kram pens a letter to Pete,
To tell him all is well,
And that life in TC is sweet.
Kram's criminal ambitions go supersonic,
Thanks to the TC's structure, which is ironic.
That a place designed to reform,
Is helping him to rise and transform.
From a part-time, failed armed robber
To working in an organised gang,
Now, with a future, he'll rise with a bang,
And then to love without bother.
But Kram is careful what he writes
And also sends Pete a poem, as poetry ignites.

The Lonely Burglar

Walking in night's urban forest
I'm joined by something else,
Besides my quickening heartbeat
With screwdriver itching to go.

Above the starless night sky
I feel it nearing me,
Tugging at my lonely heart
Recoiling through my empty soul.

A cold breeze touches my face,
As I shudder within myself
Then two small eyes greet me,
A fox's eyes green and gold.

Our life's journeys have crossed,
We both with feral pride
Between back gardens, we go
And into houses, we grow.

But then suddenly, flashes of light,
Pulsating in blue with fright
The fox and I did split,
And under a car, I hid.

6-30

In Kram's mind, his thoughts blitz
As memories of Gloria touch his heart
He lies in fantasy, as passion omits,
Plunging him within lyrical art.
Where rhyme in poetry does test,
As stress and calmness do rest.
But he loses himself far in mind's mist,
As memories of Gloria kissed.
Then, an image through soul does rift
Of Gloria crying alone
Alone in pain, he'd sown,
Sown by failing her, to law's clenched fist.
Kram switches the TV off and paces,
Then writes a poem as his mind races.

The Mist

I sat on the top deck,
Of the morning school bus
In my clean-cut uniform.

I wiped the condensation free,
And stared across the meadows,
A thick mist hovers over it.

Its eeriness comforted me,
Like a soft pillow in bed
Ready for the next dream.

That vision gives me hope,
Such hope one day, I would
One day, I would be free.

But no one understood me,
School only taught order
And I wanted to be free.

And life at home was cold,
Cold in love and emotion
And I wanted to be free.

Society buried me inside,
It buried me so deep within
And I wanted to be free.

But now my mind's a mist,
The great mist of creativity
With unbridled thoughts running free,
Writing free.

6-32

Kram sits next day in a small group,
As Simon talks in detail about a robbery
Over fifteen years inside prison's loop
Within lifer wings and camaraderie.
Simon then talks of his future,
As he's different now, and mature.
He wishes he could get a girlfriend,
And has no further interest to reoffend.
Kram knows if he wants to leave, he must lie,
And must pretend and act like a saint,
To a saintly picture of himself, he must paint
If he doesn't want to stagnate and die.
The group comes swiftly to a close,
As Kram thinks of a poem in prose.

The Garage Robbery

Slight anxiety fell, like
A rash upon my skin.
The garage was bathed in
Crisp brightness, as I stood,
Outside in rainy darkness.
The slight smell of petrol
Tickled my nose, as I
Pulled on a balaclava in
Deadly pose. The cashier
Looked at his nails, deep,
In thought, as I entered,
In for a bit of sport.
I brandished the cold,
Metal gun of blackened
Rage, as I burst out from
My inner cage. 'Cash –
No tricks,' I bellowed in
Ominous intent, as my
Anger and desperation began
Its ascent. The urgency of
My voice filled the air,
With electricity, as I
Paralysed his heart with
Fear and lunacy. His
Stomach turned and curled,
Like some black hole
In space, as I walked across
The floor in gallant grace.
As he opened the till and
Gave me the cash, I felt
Like burning this place

Down to ash. Then I noticed
His eyes looking through me,
With venom, as I
Pocketed the cash into my,
Stonewashed denim. I
Noticed his muscle flex
On his jaw, and thought,
I'd rather be in prison,
Than poor. Suddenly,
I heard the sound of an
Alarm, like God had pulled
Me by the arm. But in anger, I
Shot him, shot him dead, and angrily,
I escaped through the streets,
I fled.

6-34

At lunchtime, Simon seeks consolation
As Kram played some Pink Floyd.
Simon is vexed and exhibits frustration,
As him, and others look annoyed.
Apparently, a sex case spoke of his crimes,
And laughed and joked in mocking rhymes.
Simon hates him with a passion,
And Kram notices Simon's face turn ashen.
Kram only pretends to feel the same,
As he wants to blend in and gain
Contacts for drugs, and contacts to maintain,
So, he must act and play the game.
Kram goes to the sex case, in verbal descent,
In words, array, demanding him to repent.

Suddenly, the commotion overflows
Others get involved, with shouts exchanging,
And Kram's temper with punches impose,
As the crazed sex case, in fear is shouting.
Simon holds Kram back, as guards now come
Kram acts innocent, as he and others succumb.
But it is all over, as CCTV had filmed the scene,
As guards explain, that's why they got between.
Kram, with force, is pushed into his cell,
As an officer violently slams his door shut
Kram can't understand what got in his nut,
And knows to this TC, he must bid farewell.
He paces, waiting for the extraction team,
A squad of guards, suited for action extreme.

6-36

Kram's anger in shouts goes supersonic,
As his frustration at himself is burning.
He thinks the incident is ironic,
As his networking plan was working.
Then a mass of heavy boot stomps come,
And through his door, his name they drum.
Followed by a barrage of direct orders,
Which fall like boulders from mind's borders.
Quickly, after ignoring their many warnings,
They storm with force, into his cell,
Grabbing in a stress hold from hell
And take Kram off, without his belongings.
Walking bent over in dire pain,
Barely a breath he could obtain.

CANTO 7

7-1

Kram is still bewildered at his behaviour,
Since he was only pretending to be angry
And screams to himself at his failure,
And cries aloud, 'Oh God, hang me!'
Clasping his hands tight to his chest,
His quickening heart beats in protest.
'Fuck sake, I'm so fucking stupid,
And from success, I'm now excluded.'
He closes his eyes and sighs,
As he desperately beckons sleep
As images of TC creep
Stripped of a future, he then cries.
Soon, he sinks deep, into dream's lake,
Which repeatedly plays his TC mistake.

7-2

Alone without any worldly goods
Trying to be positive with like-minded
The block's full of hardened hoods
Prisoners who fight all, anger blinded.
Kram sits up and rubs sleep away,
No more anger or frustration on display.
The guards to his door, unbolted,
As Kram's heart to hostility hosted.
'Governor's office!' the guard growls
He gets up and exits his cell,
As depressing thoughts, of TC fell,
And into the governor's office, Kram scowls.
Kram sits down on a chair, with back straight,
The governor glares, fists clenched with hate.

7-3

'The TC's there for people to change,
But you attacked a man for speaking his mind.
I saw the footage, you went insane,
Twenty-eight days, you'll stay here confined.'
Kram didn't reply to what he believes,
So, he's motioned up, and with that, he leaves.
He walks back to his cell quick
As he didn't want any conflict.
Sensing a trap, they want him to enter,
But he is smart and says nothing,
But then a guard comes strutting
Hitting Kram hard, in order to render.
To render in fear, in hostility's arms,
As Kram, in distress, recites the psalms.

7-4

Days go past, until now, a shower
As he relaxes himself with warm water
It soothes his body as his thoughts tower,
As he reminisces of good times in laughter.
Then two men walk in, giving him daggers,
Telling him, 'Shut up!' Calling him, 'Crackers'.
Suddenly, he notices one of them is Billy,
As he reintroduces himself until he,
Starts shouting at Kram, calling him a grass.
'You're the only one who knew,
That I was smuggling through.'
Kram's in shock, as Billy's shouts harass.
'You're fucking wrong, I'd never do that!'
As they, with fists, knock Kram flat.

7-5

But Kram's angered and fights back bold,
As he smashes his fists into each one
Targeting them with punches of gold,
Both men lay still. Unconscious. Done.
Kram dries himself off, then gets dressed,
Feeling stunned and shocked, in mind's unrest.
Kram walks to his cell, grinding teeth,
As paranoid thoughts pull strings underneath.
He knows this is the beginning,
As he knows, his name is now mud
And within his mouth, he tastes blood,
As his mind, is now spinning.
Suddenly, a guard enters, 'You're on report,'
And Kram, with violence, does retort.

Voices shout, as the alarms go off,
As a rain of punches to Kram falls
Knocked down, to a blood spurt cough,
Against the blood-splattered walls.
He goes unconscious in torrential pain,
Then stripped, and put in body belts restrain.
Hours pass, and he awakes shivering,
As the windows open to night's snickering.
Each minute feels like an hour,
His thoughts on reality blacken,
From reliving guards' reaction,
And being called 'grass' in the shower.
But then he thinks of Gloria and making love,
In the garden of Kent, in ecstasy's glove.

7-7

On awakening, the governor stands by door
Leaning against a wall with a smile,
'I'm putting you, Skyal, on a 10-74.'
As the guard's grin looks hostile.
'What does that mean?' Kram asks,
As blood across his face, masks.
'You'll be shipped from prison to prison,
Block to block, without any notice given.'
They all laugh at Kram on the floor,
As he aches from head to toe
He closes his eyes and murmurs, 'No.'
Then they all left, slamming the door.
When will this torment end? he thinks,
Could killing that man be a jinx.

Hours later, free from the body belt
He eats a sandwich, swallowing slowly,
With each breath, a soaring pain felt
Picturing their faces, the uniformed unholy.
Days in desperation, wriggling in pain,
He attempts suicide by biting a vein.
Then again, in visions, he pictures Gloria,
And laughs and talks to her in euphoria.
Then, suddenly, a flap opens in the door,
And Kram sees the end of a hose pipe,
Suddenly, water hits him like a spike,
And he's thrown from his bed, onto the floor.
He hears a chorus, of laughter and cheers,
Not just from the guards, but also his peers.

7-9

Clothed in undersized prison clobber,
He's escorted into a van, at night,
Shouted and pulled by his collar,
He relaxes, dreaming of love's unite.
That one day, he and Gloria will hold hands,
As he fantasises of her on windswept sands.
Sitting in a cubicle, locked alone,
As to his reality, his thoughts cyclone.
And to Gloria's image, he holds tight,
Holding him away from reality's strife
Hoping one day, she'll be his wife,
And with that thought, his soul takes flight.
He rests his head, to draw on sleep,
As the engines sound, sends him deep.

7-10

He wakes to rain wrapping furiously,
Upon the van along the lone highway
Driving to where? he thinks curiously,
As Kram sits happily as memories sway.
He thinks of the old man whom he killed,
And now of that death to Kram, it thrilled.
His crimes he committed, the police still sought,
And of which he knows, he'll never be caught.
Thinking of all the crimes he's committed.
Within the justice system, I'm not dead,
And I'm not a victim at this point; I'm ahead,
He smiles to himself, feeling very wicked.
Nothing can balance out justice, he feels,
Imagining the grim reaper to the old man, kneels.

7-11

Soon, he recognises London's streets,
And its many shops and car lights
Then noticing near, the awful police
As he tries focusing on other sites.
He stares at people walking alive and free,
Like watching animals in a chaotic sea.
In stark contrast to prison's routine,
Only witnessing life through a TV screen.
He remembers characters from a soap,
Identifying with each, like a friend
Feeling their lives are real, not pretend,
As they laugh and cry and give out hope.
But soon, the van heads through a gate,
As Kram braces himself, for guards' hate.

7-12

The stark prison reception light
Glares at Kram's eyes like the sun
From hours in darkness, sitting tight,
Now, in prison's pressure, under the gun.
During a strip search, his mind turns off,
As they shout to him to squat and cough.
They deck him out in wrinkled prison grays,
As thoughts of London, to mind replays.
He remembers a woman without an umbrella,
As rainstorms down from God's cry
She stands elegantly with head held high,
He knows to her he'll remember forever.
Then suddenly, in the block, guards attack,
And in his mind, his fantasies fight back.

7-13

The birds sing on springtime song,
As a gentle breeze to Kram saves
In a land where love and beauty belong
In flowering fields like motionless waves.
Kram stretches carefree in the shade,
Caressing through, with fingers, each blade.
As the grass feels cool to every touch,
And with his fist, he does clutch.
Kram laughs to himself in tranquillity,
As Gloria approaches to his right,
Then, holding him, warm and tight,
The world's beauty is its simplicity.
He muses to himself in distant thoughts,
Then reality hits of prisons and courts.

7-14

In agony, Kram crawls along the floor
Noticing dried blood and dirt intermix
Feeling he's been in some kind of war,
His mind readjusts, as reality grips.
With flashbacks of fists and black boots,
By the numerous uniformed prison brutes.
A taste of blood, with tongue underneath,
He feels out in shock, broken teeth.
He manages to climb up on the bed,
And curls up into a ball and cry,
Reciting poetry to say goodbye,
As he imagines his soul from body shed.
His dinner is plain, with an apple for desert,
As he crawls over to eat, he sees on it, dirt.

7-15

This treatment of Kram goes on for years,
Sometimes better and sometimes worse
He loses his feelings, and cries without tears,
As he feeds on hatred, as thoughts disperse.
Then, in his cell, he screams, and talks aloud,
As thoughts of revenge, in murder shroud.
A shroud on his mind in blood and poetry,
As he lives with the dead, in block's cemetery,
He thinks a lot of that dead old man,
Knowing that man's pain only lasted seconds,
Whilst his pain, cast by society's weapons,
Is far more painful than hell can span.
He needs revenge on guards and all,
And needs to kill in destiny's call.

Suddenly, one night, he hears a voice,
And banging on the wall from next door.
'Oi, mate, how ya doin'? I'm Royce.'
'I'm Kram; I'd hear you better by the door.'
'I heard, Kram, that guard giving you stick,
Don't let him get to you; he's a prick.'
'They all are, don't worry, I'm used to it,
I'm known for giving them hell and shit.'
'The best way, Kram, is a dirty protest,
They won't come near you in that cell.
It'll drive them all crazy to hell,
I've done it myself, when oppressed.'
'I'll give it some deep thought, Royce,
Thanks, mate, at least now I have a choice.'

7-17

Next night Kram's shipped out,
In the van, laughing out loud
As his imagination and ideas sprout
Amusing stories storm pain's cloud.
Then, to his surprise, he hears Royce,
'Oi, Kram, remember you have a choice!'
Kram shouts back to his only friend,
'I think I will; to them, I'll offend.'
They talk throughout the entire journey,
As Kram says, he supports the death penalty
'As prison life is such a soulless immensity,
A quick exit is best, strapped to a gurney.'
Kram starts reciting psalms from the bible,
As Kram's mind in solitude is never idle.

7-18

In his new prison, guards to violence ply,
As Kram feels amused and smiles
'You give us trouble; we'll hang you high,
And write it down as suicide in our files.'
'I only fight back in self-defence.'
A guard then hits him, on taking offence.
Kram holds his temper as he plans in mind,
As he knows what to do, revenge, he's rhymed.
They lock him up after kicking him in
As Kram rolls upon the floor, laughing
And wishes for freedom in hanging,
As he's planning, a dirty protest within.
He waits all night, for that time to come,
Instead of the toilet, the floor has become.

7-19

When next day came, he finally pooes,
And across the wall he spreads it
The smell to the wing immediately imbues,
As he layers most of the wall in shit.
After finishing, he washes in sink,
Then sits by his cell door, within the stink.
His thoughts drift back and forth,
As Kram's determined to protest, thenceforth.
Then, soon a guard moans in disgust
As Kram laughs on hearing him swear
As his laughter echoes his boxed square
As a poem through his thoughts had bust.
So, with a finger though shit he writes,
A Haiku poem, to his mind fights.

The Dirty Protest

Soundly, quietly
Shit-covered walls stink up,
To gentle breath.

Midday comes, they unlock his door,
His sandwiches are thrown in quick,
And Kram in anger curses the law
Before being locked up, by guards feeling sick.
Kram's tense, waiting for his usual kick in,
But nothing comes; not even an ugly grin.
He eats the sandwiches of cheese and pickle,
As images and rhyme, to mind does ripple.
Kram smiles at having the upper hand,
'You bastards won't beat me,
And I'll kill you all, when free!'
Growing with ill feeling, within prison's land.
He starts drifting in and out by the door,
As sleep, through resentment, washes ashore.

7-22

On Yorkshire's moor, green and hilly
A thick fog hovered fat
And running towards him, his foe, Billy
Looking like a grey-coated cat.
Billy smiles whilst rollerskating,
Around Kram weaving his way, snaking.
Then suddenly in his back a knife,
A scorching pain, uncorking his life.
Red liquid spurts from him,
As he cries, 'Oh dear God, why?
My life's lost, my soul's dry!
And my blood's cold.' His thoughts spin.
He suddenly smells a beautiful scent,
As he leaves Earth, in love's ascent.

7-23

Kram wakes in a deep gasp for breath,
As his eyes adjusts to the gloom
From his vivid dream of empty death
To window's light, his eyes zoom.
He imagines the universe's growing boundaries,
As it expands endlessly, through the centuries.
And he visualises multiverses in space,
As his mind stretches beyond God's grace.
Is there really a God? Or an impish devil?
Or are there dreams beyond dreams?
Is everything an illusion; is life what it seems?
And Is existence on a spiritual multilevel?
Kram stretches himself up, and begins to pace,
Listening to his breaths, in his echoing space.

Kram imagines the Chinese poet Po,
Who died attempting to kiss the moon,
Well over a thousand years ago,
In moon's reflection in a dark lagoon.
Kram notes he died in poetic grace,
Not like hanging himself, in cell's embrace.
He can't give the guards the satisfaction,
As all guards would just smile in reaction.
Kram continues with his dirty protest,
And spreads more shit across the walls,
In an artistic manner, the shit he sprawls,
Feeling like a nonentity, as life rode west.
Then like a light, to his shadowy thoughts,
With a finger, he writes and talks.

7-25

In Despair

In despair I cut my arm
In wild lines
Like Chinese writing
To distract.

In despair I drink myself sick
On clean pavements
Like Pollack's canvas
Runny and thick.

In despair I fight
In a wild manner
No organised style
I hurt quick.

In despair I take drugs
In a haze of smoke
Watching the world fade
In a blur.

In despair I sleep
Dreaming deep
Completely unaware
Of my despair.

7-26

Suddenly through his door water flames,
From a hosepipe through a circular slot
This is now one of guard's new games,
As Kram uses his mattress to deflect the shot.
'Keep it up, Kram,' shouts a familiar voice,
As Kram then realises, that voice is Royce.
Then, a barrage of shouts from next door,
As Royce to his door, curses the law.
Finally, the water stops, and the hosepipe leaves,
And the slot in squeaks they finally close
As Kram's thoughts juxtapose,
Of anger, relief, while paranoia weaves.
Kram stands still, dripping wet,
So, he strips naked without regret.

7-27

Kram runs to his door in laughter,
'Royce! Nice to meet a fellow on a 10-74,
Christ, aren't our lives a fucking disaster.'
As Kram tells of his dream on the moor.
Royce declares he wants to kill Billy,
As Kram starts to shiver, feeling chilly.
Kram hugs himself and walks on wet,
Thinking of how he could escape prison's net.
God or the devil, I don't care which,
Give me strength, Lord, and direction.
As Kram lives in memory's collection
Mostly of Gloria, to which he feels rich.
Rich in love, desire, and completeness,
Light years away, from his cell's bleakness.

7-28

Months pass as Kram's mind slowly fixes,
That he will not break nor bend.
The dirty protest to Kram's life, eclipses,
With Royce, his dear and only friend.
Up and down the country they went,
Up and down in prison's torment.
Then, through the hatch, a woman speaks
As Kram talks aloud, which he's done for weeks.
'Hello, Kram, why are you doing this?
What are you protesting, why d'you do this?'
Kram approaches the flap, 'Hello, Miss,
I want to escape this violent abyss!
Of guards' physical and verbal abuse,
And threats to me, on using a noose.'

11

7-29

'I'll give you some paper and a pen,
I want you to write this all down.'
'Thanks, Miss,' Kram replies. 'Amen.'
As the woman stands with a frown.
Sheets of paper and pen slide under,
As Kram stares at them in wonder.
On one sheet, he writes his grievances,
Of himself and Royce. The other, some verses.
Rhymes and images, to his mind stretches,
As Kram in passion does write
Throwing his dark mind into light,
As light cuts through torment's edges.
He pauses and thinks, with a look so intense,
Thinking of his life, trying to make sense.

7-30

This Torment

This torment
This torment my life, this torment my pride,
Where no love lives, and where all love died.

This torment
Death was born in this cell beside.
This hell I surf, this hell I ride.

This torment
Where my thoughts escape, where thoughts shape,
As flesh flakes off, in graves gape.

142

This torment
Thrown into limbo from sunshine,
Like a golden coin in shit of swine.

This torment
Where music in screams do laugh,
And in murders game, in blood I'll bath.

This torment
This torment of mine, as thoughts gape,
As sanity and memories, I leave to escape.

7-31

A Smashed Cell

Cell smashed and a cracked sink,

Water flowing and dripping,
Though jagged cracks
Onto the wet floor.

Sodium light flickers upon
Reflecting my blurred face
Without features.

Reality flickers

A memory of a life dreamt,
Whether real or not
Whether I was present or not.

I continued kneeling within.

A Solitary Mind

A memory of

Gloria so

Gentle

Lost

Where I
Can't go

Distant images
A tear
A breath
A smile

A look

7-33

The woman returns hours later,
And Kram sends her under the door,
Slips of paper and pen for her
Clean, from his shit-covered décor.
He tells her of the guard's attack,
And his safety in shitting up to the max.
'It protects me from getting hit,
As the bastards fear touching shit!
So now, when getting shipped to a prison,
I roll around the shit-covered walls,
No more attacks to me befalls,
And above prison, me and Royce have risen.
Go speak to Royce, he's next door,
He's my pal and witness; you must explore.'

7-34

The woman thanks him and walks away,
As Kram's laughter is heard by all
'Royce, I told her and in poetry's display,
All the guards who crossed us, will fall.'
'Well done, Kram, they'll get a kick in,
When convicted and sent down within.'
'Even on the numbers, Royce, they can't hide,
For the beaten, they'll meet and will collide.
Their faces and names are too well known,
Even walking free, they have to disguise,
Because all prisoners scan with distant eyes
Like on all our minds, their faces are sown.'
Kram and Royce shout and laugh aloud,
As Kram straightens his back and paces proud.

Kram at sink washes himself clean,
As he feels the soap dissolve
He hears the guards in teatime routine,
Feeling better with letter's resolve.
The door opens to a plate of curry,
As guards in white, stand in three.
Kram takes it, naked, staying mute,
And quickly grabs some fruit.
Then the door is slammed shut
As he feels more astute
And eats quickly in pursuit,
Of contentment in warmth, in gut.
Then a thought enters, as his lips moisten,
Is it possible they've put in poison?

In anger, he throws it on the floor
The curry and rice and shouts
Whilst banging and kicking his door
Warning Royce of his doubts.
Royce shouts and voices the same,
As they both react furiously, insane.
Banging, shouting, and screaming aloud,
As Kram hears feet, near door crowd.
'The guards are fucking poisoning us.'
Kram shouts to warn everyone,
And within mind, his fury spun,
Then forces himself to chuck his guts.
With fingers, he forces down his throat,
As undigested food, in toilet does float.

146

Kram goes days without a food source,
As anger and rage, cut like a sword
He barely sleeps and incessantly talks,
As Kram cries aloud, 'Oh Lord!'
Then the woman again to his door visits,
As Kram explains his suspicions in minutes.
She says she'll bring him food in sealed packets,
As the woman develops friendly dynamics.
Kram thanks her, as he is so hungry,
And regularly, the woman with food comes,
And Kram smiles to her with raised thumbs,
And in his mind, his thoughts run free.
'Fucking hell, Royce, our lives are crazy!'
'Fuck's sake, Kram, like a film by Scorsese!'

7-38

Kram sits at his table eating,
Shop-bought sandwiches and biscuits,
With paranoid thoughts creeping
As he imagines guards like midgets.
He laughs as they bump around,
And speaking without any sound.
He thinks of that woman as hope,
And stops imagining himself with a rope.
He saves the biscuits for later,
As he imagines a different life
A different life with a wife
As he wishes for a pen and paper.
Hours pass by without a change,
As Kram feels edgy and strange.

The night of hatred grows dense,
As Kram paces barefoot, to and fro,
Not knowing when to make his defence,
On meeting the ship-out-crew's show.
As the night guard's feet grow near,
Kram gets tense, in paranoia's sphere.
Then, through the spy hole, the guard looks,
And on each time, Kram's anger cooks.
From day to day, there's no relief
In his bubble tank, like a goldfish
Spied on by cats, as a potential dish
From night to night, in stress and grief.
With a damp and shit-stained mattress,
He lies on the bed's metal-framed lattice.

7-40

At his table an hour, he rests,
Then suddenly awakes to door unbolting.
And inside the cell, a guard steps,
In white, with handcuffs holding.
'You're being shipped to a hospital,
Don't shit up, be logical.'
Kram looks confused and dazed,
'No more prison?' He looks amazed.
Kram follows the protocol of the search,
Unable to comprehend this move,
Why to hospital did doctors approve?
As a hundred questions to his mind perch.
'Wow – what about Royce? Is he coming, too?'
'Yeah, Skyal – Royce is going with you!'

CANTO 8

Kram sits in a white people carrier,
A polar opposite of a prison van
No cubicle, and on a soft seat, happier
With many glass windows to scan.
The world outside seems fascinating,
As he feels his soul saturating.
But then the police silently drive past,
And knows on the outside, he wouldn't last.
As on life licence, your reins are short,
One wrong step, the police will call,
And back to prison, you will crawl,
But for now, the hospital is his resort.
No one to hold Kram down in an attack,
With kicks and jumps upon his back.

8-2

Through the busy streets, they go
Up clogged roads the choking traffic,
Then, on motorways' arterial flow
A motorbike glides past, riding erratic.
Kram notices cars looking more modern,
No old Ford Sierras in blue, rusty, and rotten.
They turn off from the left lane,
As Kram laughs to himself, looking insane.
If they think I'm crazy, great
No more needing to shit up,
No more feeling tensed up,
I'm safer than ever, in hospital's estate.
'Where's Royce? Has he shitted up as well?'
'He'll come later; he's still in his cell.'

8-3

Finally, they drive through hospital's gate,
A newish-looking building within a city
Amongst a dirty rundown housing estate
Of council houses, stark and gritty.
It reminds Kram of the realities of life,
That he must fight poverty with a knife.
Without money, laws and morals are lost,
Laws and morals, the poor man's cross.
But Kram fears the costly fight,
As being caught again, has a huge price,
As crime's a gamble, with loaded dice,
With huge sentences, from judge's bite.
But the real world is years away,
Locked within the cold and grey.

8-4

Kram is escorted to the acute ward,
After a mild-mannered pat-down search
As patients scan Kram on record
As relief to Kram is like an electrical surge.
A myriad of windows, light the scene,
With a smell of bleach, as cleaners clean.
A tall thin man with tattooed skin,
Walks past Kram, with a toothless grin.
Kram, to everyone, smiles and nods,
As slight unease grows to cold shoulders,
And nurses near with smiles and folders
As they rule and run like ancient Gods.
Like Zeus and all, in clouds and trumpets,
Running lives, with strings to puppets.

8-5

The prison guards uncuff him and leave,
As nurses sit with Kram, smiling in a room,
He feels relaxed with clean air to breathe,
Expressing a need for something to consume.
They go through the basics of hospital life,
And Kram explains, 'Abuse in prison is rife.'
Detailing the beatings he received,
And now, in hospital, he feels reprieved.
They soon give him a salad baguette,
And with other patients, he tries to blend,
Attempting with a smile to make a friend,
Until a man approaches in a growing threat.
In shouts at Kram, he grimaces his face,
Kram backs up, giving him plenty of space.

8-6

Alarms go off, and nurses come running,
As Kram looks at the growing circus
They grab the man in a hold, crushing,
As the man struggles, looking nervous.
The rest of the day is calm and stress-free,
And he receives medication after tea.
He's told the pill is called Risperidone,
And, after swallowing, he walks to his room, alone.
But outside his room, a nurse is on watch,
When Kram's told, he's on one-to-one obs
Slight tiredness to his mind mobs,
And to this day, he carves a notch.
Suddenly, he hears Royce's voice shout,
Kram shouts back, then goes on the scout.

8-7

'If they try anything, Kram, shit up!'
'Royce, I know, but I'm safe here.'
'And when throwing piss, use a cup.'
Kram laughs loudly. 'That's severe!'
Nurses on watch look at him curiously,
'Christ, Royce, where are you, seriously?
I can't see you anywhere, mate?'
As a nurse whispers, 'We need to sedate.'
Kram tries opening other patients' doors,
Aggressively questioning all,
As he still hears Royce's call,
'What's going on?' As Kram's voice soars.
The alarm's pressed, boots come running,
And Kram feels anxious at them coming.

'Don't let the bastards win, Kram.'
As Kram looks about the ward
'Where are you, Royce? Fuck. Damn.'
As nurses bunch up and rush toward.
'There's no Royce!' as those words spiral,
As Kram's mind, is in agitation and denial.
'Kram, you're delusional; let calmness resume.'
And to his heart, these words consume.
Suddenly, they grab Kram in a struggle,
And to his bottom, they inject
As his anger flares direct
In shouts and threats, as Kram's legs buckle.
But before he knew it, his mind falls south,
As drugs take hold, he dribbles from mouth.

8-9

After hours in seclusion, Kram comes round,
Disoriented and lost in echoing gloom,
Getting up dazed from mind's dull crown,
In a cold, dim-lighted, green-painted tomb.
He notices a camera boxed in a corner,
Feeling tense and on show, like a performer.
He thinks hard to reassess from the chaos,
As the cold room's gloom captures the pathos.
Am I really mad, or just confused?
Is this the result of a loveless life,
That cuts the soul with a knife
With a burnt, dry mouth, and anger diffused.
He bangs hard on the door for some water,
Then hears in distance, Royce's laughter.

8-10

'Royce, mate, is that you?' Kram shouts.
Then a nurse comes to his door
With dyed black glossy hair, she pouts,
'Give me fucking water, you whore!'
Royce's laughter gets louder and louder,
Christ, I need water; my saliva's like powder.
'She's going to poison it, Kram!'
'Fucksake, Royce, no! Damn.
Where are you, Royce? I don't…
Royce, are you playing a game?
Is this all a fucking game?
Stop fucking shouting, just don't…
I don't understand,' as Kram to floor sits,
'If she's poisoned the water, I'll see the bits.'

8-11

The nurse walks away in hard shoes,
Clomping in descent across the floor,
'Should I drink, or should I refuse?'
And around the room, his eyes explore.
Soon, the clomps sounds get louder,
As paranoia to mind tower.
Then, at his door, a blue plastic cup,
Resting on the hatch, as he crawls up.
He grabs the cup and studies the water,
Then smells it, as a sense lingers.
Then swirls it slowly with his fingers,
And replaces it on the hatch and applauds her.
'Nice try. I can see there's poison!'
As his tongue to lips attempts to moisten.

8-12

He paces the room in agitation,
As a small headache grows
Then he hears a voice, 'Medication.'
As words to a poem compose.
'Kram, medication, please; it'll help,'
As he sees fingers on the hatch, like kelp.
He closes his eyes and turns away,
As Royce's voice to his thoughts prey.
'They're conspiring to kill you.'
Kram's heart races
Noticing twisted faces,
At door's window, looking through.
'Medication, please; it'll help you relax.'
As he notices on floor, widening cracks.

8-13

'Fuck off, go away, leave me alone,
I fucking know you're trying to kill me.
I can feel it deep within my bone,'
As anger's tidal wave crosses soul's sea.
He listens intently at whispering near,
As he imagines them getting into riot gear.
He tenses up with fists clenched tight,
As blood to muscles flow, with face white.
Kram stares at the widening cracks upon the floor,
Feeling it's a sign, his life will fall,
He jumps on bed as the cracks crawl.
His stomach churns at an eventual war.
They study him through the plastic window,
As Kram feels dazed in a soulless limbo.

8-14

The nurse goes away to the whispering,
'I'm fucking ready, you bastards,'
Kram shouts as the lights start flickering,
As Royce shouts, 'Your last words!'
His mouth grows dryer as sweat pours,
And notices the cracks widen, like doors.
And the walls pulse like heartbeats,
As Royce's voice in his mind repeats.
'They're going to kill you, Kram,
Kram. Kram. You're going to die.
Kram. Kram. They'll take your eye.
They're going to kill you, Kram.'
A large muscular man to his door stares,
As Kram to himself curses and swears.

8-15

Suddenly, it goes quiet outside,
Which made Kram more nervous,
Feeling outpowered, he sighed.
Why? Why? What's the purpose?
Why do they want me dead?
Is this real? Or have I misread?
Is Royce lying, or is my paranoia flying,
Why's existence dying with thoughts crying?
'Help me, God, if you exist!'
As Kram shouts in desperation,
'Help me; I'm your creation!
Why let me die? Please assist!'
Suddenly, in the room, they all come in,
Rushing Kram in force, as the cracks grin.

8-16

They hold him down on the blue mattress,
And inject him in his backside,
Kram's unable to move and lay hapless,
As terror and panic to confusion slide.
He feels surprised at the slight prick,
They then get off, retreating quick.
As his fears of death, he grabs by the handle,
As faraway hopes glow like a lit candle.
They depart the room and lock door shut,
As Kram gets up, slightly dazed,
And to God he praises, unfazed,
As he slowly rethinks, his thoughts rebut.
They didn't kill me; I'm still alive!
As logical thoughts and calmness arrive.

8-17

Then, a man in a suit appears at the door
'Hello, I'm Doctor Kautz,
That drug injection will help to restore,
Normality from terrifying thoughts.
If you take tablets, they'll be no more,
No more forced injections to endure.'
'I agree, Doc, as they didn't try to kill,
Next time, I'll happily take a pill.'
'Here, Kram, would you like this to drink?'
As he passes Kram a Coke bottle through.
'It's poisoned,' Royce warns with voice askew.
But Kram ignores, as logic begins to sink.
Kram unscrews the cap despite Royce,
And gulps it down, as his thoughts rejoice.

8-18

Despite the cool Coke, flowing down south,
He still sees large cracks upon the floor,
Now opening and closing like a mouth
He jumps clean onto his bed like before.
Kram hears Royce's evil, horrid laughter,
Laugh, you cunt, I'll get you here after
Kram feels alone from the human race,
Like a distant asteroid in far-reaching space.
The terror soars from his dark vision
And wishes badly for peace and love,
And fit into society like hand to glove,
But knows here, he's safer than prison.
He convinces himself it's all in his mind,
And stands on cracks with eyes closed blind.

8-19

Kram remembers the dark cracks' descent,
But feels the floor, solid and intact,
And realises now that madness does invent,
As his courage around fear is wrapped.
He opens his eyes in terror and frowns,
On seeing dark depths, in fear, he drowns.
But remains standing as his body trembles,
As cracks gape open, like *Jaws,* it resembles.
Then he jumps on bed, to rest his nerves,
I'm mentally ill! He's of that belief,
It's all in my mind; what a relief!
But feels unease as realisation disturbs.
Will I ever be normal and free from this?
Will I ever see the world as it really is?

8-20

Within hours, sleep beckons
Like sighting an oasis in a desert
Lying on bed as a crack still threatens
He drifts to dreams with little effort.
He studies the delicate, gentle night,
And the fluttering of leaves in moonlight.
The coolness of night's air embraces,
As Kram walks in gentle paces.
An owl hoots aloud, within a tree,
To announce his feathery face
As Kram wants to near and embrace
But resists and watches it fly free.
Suddenly, a loud voice resonates within,
As he awakes to food, and a nurse's grin.

8-21

He grabs the plate from the hatch,
As he suddenly realises the floor's clear
No dark, jawing mouth, trying to catch,
But slight fear that they might appear.
He eats the food with a plastic spoon,
Laughing aloud at the thought he's a loon.
Through his pain, humour raises its head,
Like British spirit through the blitz, it's said
What world am I in?
Like an episode from Dr. Who
A new world in Tardis' view
Will medication win?
He finishes his meal by drinking water,
From a plastic cup, feeling stronger.

He paces room and stretches from pressure,
As Dr Kautz comes smiling to his door
'Hi, Kram, you look like you feel much better!'
'Hi, Doc, I think my sanity's come ashore.'
They both laugh as Kram talks like a veteran,
Like recalling war stories to his grandchildren.
He gives details of the unearthly cracks,
As the vivid images, to reality smacks.
'I want to get better. The meds I'll take,
I didn't realise until now,
That I was as mad as a cow.
The meds I'll take, no more will I snake.'
'You're not out the woods yet, you know,
As it will take time for symptoms to go.'

8-23

'So, when I improve, I'll go back to prison?
'I don't think, Kram, that's your best move
It's stress from prison where madness had risen,
Your future is in hospital, where you'll improve.'
Kram's anger boils on hearing this,
'You mean, Dr Kautz, they did this?
Their bad treatment of me drove me insane,
The police, the guards, the system's to blame!'
'Calm down, Kram, it's more than that,
You were probably also genetically prone,
And together with stress, madness had sown.'
'But without prison, madness wouldn't have sat!'
'I understand, Kram, at how you must feel,
Try calming down now, as you've had an ordeal.'

8-24

Kram looks down, 'You're right, Doc,'
As something new glares from Kram's eyes.
'I think, Kram, this door we'll unlock,
And back to the ward, I'll advise.'
'Thanks, I just want to settle and relax,
But, Doc, I really do fear those cracks.
Will they be back, and that voice?'
'I don't know, Kram, or about Royce.'
The doctor leaves, as Kram then paces,
Killing screws and all, was only fantasy,
But now I must make it a reality
Kram repeats to himself, whilst picturing faces.
Nurses approach, and the door opens,
And Kram walks out, with new notions.

8-25

He walks back, whilst in casual conversation,
Onto the acute ward, and to his door
People's faces stare in fascination
As he walks into his room, and does ignore.
He hears talk and laughter behind him,
But then suddenly he fears madness's fin.
Nearing him slowly like a great white,
To chew his mind, in an uneven fight.
He walks outside to appease his mind,
And feels at ease at what he sees,
People are talking in calmer seas,
So, he returns to room to relax and unwind.
He puts the television on with volume loud,
To disguise the noise, and to voices cloud.

8-26

After an hour, he gets off his bed
And turns the television off,
Words and rhymes bounce in his head,
And gets attention, with a cough.
'Alright. Could I have some paper and a pen,
As I need to write. Poetry's my Zen.'
The nurse smiles. 'I'll ask over to Dwight,
Dwight, could Kram have a pen to write?
And some A4 sheets of lined paper,
Kram wants to write some poetry?'
'It'll help, Dwight, to set my mind free,
Poetry's my calling, my love's labour.'
'Sure,' replies Dwight, 'I won't be a minute.'
As rhyme and imagery fill Kram's spirit.

8-27

By the Prison Wall

As I sit alone by the prison wall
Buried in thoughts and pain,
Prisoners caught in society's trawl,
As they circle around in a chain.

Buried in thoughts and pain,
Because I so loved the sky
As I dreamt of the sweet rain
As I wished, I could fly.

162

Because I so loved the sky
Like a light blue summer's sea
Such beauty made me almost cry,
As I fantasised about being free.

Like a light blue summer's sea
In thoughts I swam within
As I rested my chin on knee
My thoughts made my head spin.

In thoughts, I swam within
As anger and pain collide
No sane mind could ever win,
As freedom beckons in suicide.

As anger and pain collide
As I plan to end my life
As prisoner's walk slowly by
If only I had a knife.

As I plan to end my life
Maybe with a bedsheet noose
I wonder if there's an afterlife,
Maybe a razor blade I could use.

Maybe with a bedsheet noose
Christ! I almost stitched my shroud,
I can't give into prison's abuse,
As I look up at a passing cloud.

Christ! I almost stitched my shroud,
I can't let these bastards win,
'Revenge, fucking revenge,' I cried aloud,
I must survive through thick and thin.

I can't let these bastards win,
As I sit alone by the prison wall
Buried within for my so-called sin,
As I hear my madness call.

8-28

The Exercise Yard

The cold exercise yard,
Brick, concrete and metal
My feelings spin within.

An ogling smug guard
Adding to the unsettle
Like a shark's fin.

Emotions hidden hard,
Within prison's fettle
With a twisted grin.

Thoughts jagged shard
Coloured in gunmetal,
Yearning for more sin.

Like a deadly pard
Dreams I do throttle,
In scarred tattooed skin.

Always keeping guard
My future's ever brittle
Within society's bin.

Through Dust of Lost Time

Through dust of lost time
Dark soul's inevitable climb.

Until I experience bloody awe
Through jungles of shadowed law.

Then what I do, you will see
On a moonlit night's divinity.

They thought I'd reformed,
But merely I'd transformed.

Beyond good and evil, I am
God and society's laws, I ram.

Pacing My Cell

I place one foot forward, then the
Other. Feeling my leg muscles ache
From hours and hours of pacing.

I pause by the barred window and
Glare at the coming and going of screws,
I breathe out a sigh and continue.

Suddenly I shouted out 'cunts', the word,
Was building inside me like a pressure-
Cooker. I felt better, as I continued pacing.

I imagined I was walking through the forest,
Then, the colourful streets of a rainswept
City, before landing on a sun-soaked beach.

It was now night, and my feet
Ached as I now had a slight limp,
Due to a small blister. But I continued.

Suddenly, the observation flap tapped,
Bringing me to reality. I paused and
Listened to the guards' footsteps fade.

I continued on.

8-31

Days pass by into weeks,
As Kram's mental health stabilises
But Royce's voice sometimes speaks,
And of prison guards he fantasises.
He sits within a ward round meeting,
As Dr Kautz and all make greeting.
With niceties and smiles, they go on,
As to his mental health, they speak upon.
'You've come on, in leaps and bounds,
And we've all agreed, and are all on board,
That you should move to another ward.
A long-term ward with quieter surrounds.'
'Yes,' Kram replies without blinking,
'As my grit on the acute ward is thinning.'

8-32

'I know I'm a long way from being free,
Free from all voices and visions
And meds will kill them to a great degree,
As to a normal life, I've great ambitions.'
Kram holds his hands upon his lap,
And studies their faces like a map.
'You'll be moving soon in a few days.'
As Krams eyes smile with a cold glaze.
Kram's body posture stays the same,
As he's motioned by a nurse to leave,
He smiles and wipes his mouth free,
Then gets up slowly, dazed, and tame.
'Thanks,' he says as he walks to the door,
Noticing the room's light green décor.

8-33

'That's bloody great news,' the nurse says
Whilst walking back to the acute ward
As Kram rubs his head, and with hair he plays.
'I'll be pleased on leaving, thank the Lord.'
Best though, keep this to yourself, mate,
Others might get envious in their unwell state.'
'I don't talk to anyone; I'm a bit of a loner,
Just battling by, like in the *Odyssey* by Homer.'
They enter the ward to unfriendly faces,
As Kram feels he's made an important step
But the losses in his life, to mind, has swept,
Like a tidal wave, as to his past, he gazes.
But to his rescue, through window's light, he sees,
Then writes a poem, as words to mind breeze.

Out of My Hospital Window

Out of my hospital window
I see the litter flutter by
To dreams I couldn't utter,
Swimming in the shining sky.

A tree like a tramp below
Poised in old, mangled clothes,
Absent of all human desire
Like a copper in plain clothes.

A dream of a vision then falls,
Like feasts around my head
The bark twists and twirls
By the Earth's spinning bed.

I stretch my hands outside,
As the branches click and hum
With lifeless, deformed arms
I felt myself go numb.

I bared my hands to sky,
As they collected pools of rain
Like a puddle, each one grew
As I grow deadly insane.

But arms like branches endure,
Endure through winter's season,
Plagued by dreams of loss,
Lost for no rhyme nor reason.

I know one day I'll die,
Too a bundle of bones beneath
So, I'll fight for all my rights,
With fists and sharpened teeth.

8-35

Today, Kram prepares and packs,
As he senses jealousy around,
Whilst collecting his poetry, he wraps.
As thoughts on his mind compound.
Will it really be, a quieter, nicer ward?
And will meds be, my literal sword?
To hack to death the terrifying visions?
And to Royce's voice cut all transmissions?
And will I be able to hunt like a hawk?
All those who abused and hurt me,
And to fight again in London's Sea
The societal prison where I once did walk.
These thoughts to Kram's mind chills,
As he fantasises about future kills.

CANTO 9

9-1

He lands ubiquitously on Helvellyn ward,
And to his room, he arranges his stuff
And to the calmness, he thanks the Lord,
As of people's dramas, he's had enough.
He gets his own room key, a real surprise,
And lies on his bed, then closes his eyes.
Then suddenly at his door, his neighbour speaks,
Explaining life's quiet here, as no one sleeps.
'We're banned from rooms throughout the day,
As there are no lie-ins or afternoon naps
And throughout the day, your energy saps
And if you're a night owl, your mind will sway.'
He walks away before Kram can say a word,
But Kram isn't fazed as he's done some bird.

Focusing on the cleanliness of his room
He glides his eyes across the walls,
As anger in his soul, does resume
Of uniformed faces, to mind recalls.
He presses his hand against his forehead,
A sentence with no end date is pure dread,
How long will it take until I'm free,
How many waves do I face, to cross this sea?
He clenches his jaw and grinds his teeth,
In suffering and pain, he does swim,
On picturing guards beating him
But focuses on keeping it all hidden beneath.
All beneath a calm and pleasant façade,
But itching to turn over the grim reaper's card.

9-3

He flinches hard as mind recoils,
And back to reality, he jumps to
Feeling hot, as his blood boils
He focuses on walls, of light blue.
He chokes to an uncomfortable swallow,
Feeling invisible, insignificant, and hollow.
He gets up from his bed and stretches,
With each flashback, his mind etches.
Pressing his fist against parched lips
He lets out a deep sigh,
Can I really to the system defy,
As bad memories lacerate, and whips.
With deep lashes against heart and mind,
To his present life, they keep him confined.

9-4

On being a night owl, Kram barely sleeps
As no one can change their body clocks,
In misery and depression, he barely speaks,
As nurses shout with rattling knocks.
'Get up!' they shout, 'Get up, morning meds!'
They repeatedly shout, 'Get out of beds.'
Each day goes by, regimented and slow,
And counted twice, when lined up for show.
For breakfast, lunch, and teatime
Like zombies on a slow march
No one talks, under nurse's arch,
Feeling dull, withdrawn, and without rhyme.
The nurses seem cold, dead-eyed, no smiles,
And everywhere they go, they're in single files.

9-5

In a few months, he notices weight gain,
And realises everyone's misshapen,
As Kram sees it around stomach's domain
Due to no exercise and meds taken.
And not being allowed in room, during day,
Strangles his thoughts to Kram's dismay.
He's unable to read or write poetry,
Due to the stranglehold of psychiatry.
But at times, he's cheered up, with a one-to-one,
Either with a psychiatrist or psychologists
And by freely chatting, his spirit lifts
But forever careful, at past lies he's spun.
But Kram's only friend is his colourful TV,
And within its world, he feels alive and free.

At night the telly, in warm light glows
As Kram's eyes dance, sparkle, and shine
From drama series to comedy shows
He feels out words and slight rhymes.
He imagines himself on various talk shows,
Giving tips and advice that only he knows.
With anecdotes of the rich and famous,
In enticing charisma and ever efficacious.
But now he pulls out a pen and paper,
As words dance and skip about
From months, where words hadn't sprout
Since hospital life formed a dull crater.
A crater, in the creative section of his mind,
Where poetry and rhyme are designed.

I've Witnessed

I've witnessed many wars and battles,
From ancient times to Iraq
Scores of young men, killed like cattle,
Whilst drinking a rocky Cognac.

I saw the great plague of London,
Before it being consumed by fire
I've witnessed lowly soldiers grow emboldened,
As great leaders roar and inspire.

I've seen the great monster of Transylvania,
But Jack the Ripper tops the lot,
And this world is moving to dystopia,
As Big Brother ties the knot.

I've witnessed Jesus nailed to the cross
As a Roman stabbed him with a spear
And Nazis slaughter Jews in Hugo Boss
To Van Gogh cutting off his ear.

But back I go into this dull world,
As I get out of bed to pee
Wheezing and coughing in the cold
As my flat-screen TV calls back to me.

9-8

Kram sits in the gloomy day area,
Feeling sleepy and shabbily dressed
As a patient cries in hysteria
With his head against the armrest.
Then, within a snap, a nurse to Kram breaks,
Breaking Kram's sleep, as she roughly shakes.
'You don't sleep here, Kram; keep awake!'
In growls, before slithering off like a snake.
Kram rests his head against his right palm,
Positioned away from the office angle,
With closed eyes, nearing tranquil
His face is hidden, as nurses' eyes alarm.
Kram cunningly steals a few moments of rest,
And throughout the days, sleep is his quest.

Another day in the day area
As a nurse shakes Kram awake
As he dreams about Gloria,
Wishing he could erase his mistake.
A dusty beam of sunlight cuts through,
Landing upon the eyes, of an old man's view.
The old man gets up, cursing in fight,
Then raps the floor with fists tight.
And moves to another chair out of light,
As two men either side look unfazed,
With eyes and faces glazed,
Looking worn out, tired and contrite.
Kram diverts his gaze to a blank screen,
Since TV's not allowed in daytime's routine!

9-10

A year goes by, the system has claimed,
Only Kram has grown much fatter,
He feels the 'day area' must be renamed,
To 'the hope and sanity attacker.'
His eyes then close for seconds of rest,
Until a nurse shouts in protest
'No sleeping here; you must stay awake,
Or I'll go round and vigorously shake.'
Kram fantasises about killing that snake,
With a multitude of vicious kicks
As a torrent of anger to mind eclipse
With a final stab in heart, with a stake.
Hours pass by, and Kram closes his eyes,
Then a shout and a glare of a nurse, decries.

9-11

Kram lines up as lunchtime comes
As people speak at low volume
Nurses call, in grimaces showing gums,
As someone is still in the washroom.
Nurses then snap behind his back,
'You're holding everyone up. Come on, Jack!'
After a short while, Jack joins the queue,
Then off they go the motley crew.
They eat quietly, their midday treat,
A factory-made sandwich. Cut and sealed,
And in these moments, they're life's appealed,
Before lining up for their slow retreat.
Kram sits quietly in the 'day area care!'
Focusing on the floor with a stoic stare.

9-12

The second year comes, tortuous and long,
As Kram sits staring at the wall
He doesn't feel alive; he feels wrong,
And all he does is picture faces and recall.
The courtyard doors are opened,
As thirty minutes of air gives hope, and
A wooden seat to sit and talk,
As it is too small to get up and walk.
One of the nurses has a striking beauty,
Even clear features with long hair
He imagines with her, an illicit affair,
But doesn't approach as she's too moody.
Kram's thoughts wander, into fantasy,
Wishing for a royal pardon and amnesty.

9-13

'Kram! Kram!' a man shouts. 'Fantastic.'
Kram turns to see a blur,
'Kram, it's me!' he said, enthusiastic,
And in Kram's stomach, a stir.
'I'm sorry. I don't know you, mate,
I've done past a half decade straight.'
'I spoke to you after your trial,
To your sentence, you seemed in denial.'
'Christ, yeah, Mark, why you here, mate?'
'I suffer badly from depression.
Too many years in fucking prison,
My mind's like a thick fog, a right state!'
'I understand, mate; I was on a 10-74,
I felt like in limbo, close to heaven's door.'

9-14

'Wow, Kram, you've put on weight!
Is this your meds or hospital's lifestyle?'
'I don't know how much I can take,
I'm sleep-deprived, and nurses are vile.'
Sometimes I sleep in the communal toilets,
But people bang on the door to spoil it.
I hear they have a new initiative,
To us, the uneducated and primitive!
They're forcing us to play bingo,
Paint by fucking numbers and so on,
My thoughts just can't grapple upon.
I wish I could hide and lay low.
It's like another kind of fucking torture,
But having no release date, is the real horror.'

9-15

'I'm with you, Kram, on that one,
No release date must be hell,
I'm doing a sixteen with eight done,
Eight lost years, in a fucking cell.'
'And they call this, Mark, rehabilitation,
Who on Earth believes in that notion!'
'It would be better, to our throats, slit,
This is why most prisoners' minds split.'
'And then you're released to the streets,
So, it's either homelessness or crime,
What else can you do after such a time
As prison's cruelty to your soul secretes.
Then, when caught, your sentence is long,
And again, thro' system's, same old song.'

9-16

After teatime, Kram retreats
And plays Lana del Rey on stereo,
Nodding head slightly to the beats
Then a nurse orders, 'Turn the volume low.'
He puts on headphones, as music spells,
And turns up volume to high decibels.
The calmness of his thoughts disarms,
As the hope of freedom charms.
He pulls out a pad and writes,
Biting the end of his plastic pen
With thoughts of imprisoned men
As a poem in prose to mind ignites.
At the thought of rehabilitation's farce,
And heated feelings in imagery has cast.

Rehabilitation?

Click, bang,
The cell doors open,
Noises rise,
Shouts, loud talking.

I go downstairs and grab a toilet,
Roll, on the pool table, and put my,
Name on the gym list, before walking
Upstairs to my cell. I pass a cell
Door, encompassing a fight between
Two men.

Smash, ahhh, ahhh.

A man runs out, looks at me,
And punches me in the face.

Argh! I moan,
'If you grass, I'll smash you too!'

I made it to my cell, and nurse
My wounds. The dirty magnolia
Pod echoed its emptiness right
Through my soul.

Alarm sounds. Another fight on the
Landing. Screws come running.

Suddenly, my door is bolted
Shut. I lie on bed. 'Just six-
And-a-half years to go,' I
Mutter aloud.

Doors unlock for lunch, and gym,
But is cancelled due to short staffing.
I grab my blue plastic plate and
Join the masses.
Noises soon rise again.

Bang, shouts, bang, shouts, bang
Arguing, shouts, arguing, shouts.

'Gov, why no gym?'
'You know why.'
'It's out of order, gov.'
'Move on, lad.'

I collected my sandwich and
Apple on plate and walk back,
To my cell, letting the apple
encircle around my sandwich.

'Aye. Oi. Gov. Got any burn.'
Bang, shout, bang, shout, bang.

I watch the TV, whilst drinking
Hot tea, whilst eating my tuna
Sandwich. I watch a programme,
But didn't take it in.
I never did at this time of day – I
Just like the TV on for company.

Click, bang. My door is unlocked.

As a screw opens my door,
'Education!' 'Yes,' I answered.

*****

The maths class is simple as they
Only teach to level two. So
It didn't benefit me, so I just
Sit and fantasise about my
Release – my chance of unleashing
Anger and revenge back on society.

In robberies, burglaries and arsons.

*****

The walk back to my wing is
Ordered and controlled. We're
Like sheep to dogs in uniform, and
Instead of a shepherd, orders crackle
Over their radios, clipped
On their belts.

Murmurs. Laughter. Murmurs. Laughter.
'Ee' – 'aye' – 'oi' – 'gov' – 'got any burn, mate?'

Then back on the wing to a
Rise of voices. Shouting soon came.

I was still imaging the burning
Police car, crackling, with bangs of
Exploding tyres, bursting in the flames.
As I'm locked up.

I sat with the TV on, waiting
For tea. I made another coffee,
With half a spoon of sugar.

Occasional footsteps walk around
Cells, doing a count through the obs flaps.

Tap. Footsteps. Tap. Footsteps. Tap.

I stand in front of the window,
Resting my forehead upon the plastic
Screen.

Large trolleys of heated food, pushed,
By prisoners behind screws.

*****

I sit in my cell and make
A sandwich with my chips in
Slightly stale bread. My mouth
Became dry after swallowing,
No fizzy pop till Wednesday's canteen.

Suddenly, a tap at my door
The obs flap window is filled with
A wrinkled face of a cleaner.

'Got any burn, mate?'

'Don't smoke,' I replied. *Fuck off*,
I thought, since I've told him
Dozens of times before.

I noticed one of my photos had
Fallen, leaving squashed dried
Toothpaste on the wall.

'Fuck's sake!' I murmured, as I got up
And restick the photo with more
Toothpaste.

Outside my window,
Sunset in distant land, distant
Faraway trees, a distant world
A shadowy world, world's away.

Association came and went.

I spoke to no one, I couldn't be
Bothered. It's the same old shit,
Which I couldn't stomach.

Taps. Footsteps. Taps. Footstep. Tap.

I put the light on in the autumn night.

The light made me look yellow,
As I stare at my reflection in
The scratched plastic mirror above
The sink.

'Another day gone,' I murmur,
Another day – six and a half left.
Filled with suffering, pain, and loneliness.

Years of rehabilitation, alone,
Cold. Dead.

*****

9-18

Kram and Mark are thick as thieves,
Playing bingo and painting shit
And to stale air, each one breathes,
As hopelessness to mind does knit.
A vexed nurse turns to both of them,
Giving daggers at Mark, for spitting phlegm.
'Wake up, both of yous, right now!
And again, to bingo, you both must plough.'
Later on, they line up for shop's bliss,
With bags held tight
And faces of delight,
That nothing in the week could top this.
They move off, sluggish, slow, and quiet,
To a chocolate, crisp and fizzy-pop diet.

9-19

Kram goes through his shop goodies,
Like flipping through old photos
As chocolate to stress does ease
With TV's volume down on low tones.
He savours each bite with slow chewing,
Together, watching TV in comfort viewing.
He tries forgetting the mind-numbing day,
Where rhyme, rhythm, and verse decay.
He eats crisps with his fizzy drink,
As the taste strikes hard
Against tongue's yard
And on finishing, his heart does sink.
As chocolate's taste to memory enraptures,
But on seeing wrappers, depression captures.

Kram's mind flashes back to prison
From the strip search, and the cell spin
It's not a holiday camp, it isn't,
Just an existence in a cold, lonely coffin.
He draws the curtains to see the moon,
As he feels suffocated in hospital's cocoon.
For some, it's a mental health citadel,
But for Kram, it's an empty wishing well.
With the toilet light on, he writes,
In between looking at the Northern Star,
Whilst sucking on a pen, like a cigar
He forces himself, and mentally fights,
Fighting the urge to give up and weep,
So, he writes a poem from thoughts deep.

9-21

Grey Stone-Cold Faces

Grey stone-cold faces
A prison of lonely men
In boxed coffin spaces.

Doing time races
Within towering walls
Where the devil gazes.

A tough judge embraces,
The two-strike laws
To lengthen cases.

And darkness chases
Away all humanity
As sentences effaces.

But poetry retraces,
As emotions recall
Dreams of better places.

And poetry retraces,
A prison of lonely men
Grey stone-cold faces
In boxed coffins' spaces.

9-22

Flickering Silhouettes

Silhouettes move in golden browns,
In late evenings, half-light.

And in my mind, shadows dance
Beckoning me to life.

As days dark blues exits the stage
Slowly morphing into night.

From a world I don't care for
Being an actor, always acting.

And I feel sick of realities light,
As night unravels its arms.

186

And embraces me in shadows,
Where my darkness turns to life.

And the only silhouettes that move,
Are from my soul flickering bright.

And as I burn with fantasy's flames,
I wait for day to kill and maim.

9-23

Farewell Body

Dear Body,

We won't be entwined together,
On fate's path anymore. As this world
Is too… too much to bear. We've
Grown together, scared, swelled with
Fat, and tasted drugs, and alcohol
Together. We've cried!

I took you for granted, and
Mistreated you, sending you,
To imprisonment for life. You
Didn't deserve this pain. It
Was me. I'm full of so much anger.

We did have good times, remember!
Remember all those girls, blue-eyed,
In blonde hair sails. As love
Stormed through both of us!

But I need to go, prison's too much,
Violence is rife, no beauty to
Behold, no beauty to hold.

You warned me of my mistakes,
With that heart attack.

I didn't listen. The drugs are taking hold.

Goodbye!

9-24

Kram sits sluggish within ward round,
As they revise his monthly progress
And having no incidents or issues found
And to his past, he expresses regrets.
He fakes empathy by looking down,
Trying not to smile like a clown.
'You've acted sensible and mature,
Throughout your stay in medium secure.
So maybe now it's time for you to move on
As you've now passed your third year.
As to your illness, you're in normality's sphere,
And with psychology, you talked upon.
Discussing your past, showing regret and insight,
And it's now clear, you've seen the light.'

9-25

'A return to prison isn't on the cards,
So, to a low secure hospital for you.'
A firework of feelings to Kram bombards
As he imagines a rainbow in sky blue.
'No one here is in dispute,
And your move on, is absolute.'
Kram feels dizzy at the news,
As he listens intently, at their views.
'In the next few weeks, you'll get
An interview by a team
From a low secure regime,
And as to your past, you must forget.
You're relatively young and extremely bright,
And to a good future, you'll clearly bite.

9-26

Despite your vast criminal record
I'm sure in society you'll pull through,
Just work hard, and God will reward,
And to a better world, you will view.'
Kram leaves the meeting feeling happy,
And back to the ward, goes he
As thoughts of revenge fall,
He feels his pain call.
Through jungles of shadowed law
I'll manoeuvre around each day,
Careful, as to what I say,
And soon, the world will be in awe.
Into bloody infamy, my name will rise,
In blood-soaked history, I'll storm the skies.

9-27

Kram walks onto the ward,
And approaches Mark, his only friend,
Looking wide-eyed and restored.
'You'll never believe or comprehend.
Within my ward round, I felt shocked,
As soon my freedom, will be unlocked.
They're all recommending low secure,
So, I could be free soon for sure!'
'Oh no, Kram, you're leaving me here?'
Mark laughs. 'Who will I talk to?
Everyone acts like they're sniffing glue!'
'You'll be leaving soon, Mark, probably this year.
Just act normal, pleasant, and sane,
And you'll be riding in freedom's train.'

9-28

Suddenly, Jack attacks Kram
With punches, kicks, and bites
Jack's emotions burst its dam,
As Kram in defence fights.
Alarms blaze, as Mark holds Jack,
And Kram, with hands up, walks back.
They explain how Jack went ballistic,
But nurses grab, in stress holds, sadistic.
And all three are injected and carried away,
As nurses gloat in laughs
As unconsciousness to all, baths
To separate seclusion rooms, for a stay.
Kram's clothes are stripped to naked dress,
As he lies dribbling on a blue plastic mattress.

9-29

The next day arrives slow,
As Dr Kautz to door approaches
Kram's fears are on show,
As he talks to Kram about upping doses.
'Doc, I'm sane; don't do a meds review,
Jack attacked me. What else could I do?
Ask Mark, he'll say the same,
I was happy with my news and did proclaim.
Upping my meds is overkill,
As I didn't want to fight
My happiness was on flight.
Inside, I was calm and tranquil.
Please don't turn me into a zombie,
As being slow, will be the end of me.'

9-30

Dr Kautz nods in agreement,
'I'll speak to Mark when he's awake,
And you seem too calm for confinement,
But your move to low secure was a mistake.'
'Speak to others who were there,
Old John and Steve saw the affair.'
Kram's heart aches at losing his move,
Despite knowing they're witnesses to prove.
But the witnesses' mental states aren't okay,
To recall what happened
And to detail the attack, and
Clearly explain from their mental decay.
Depression and frustration seep within,
As he feels his patience wearing thin.

9-31

But Kram realises there's no victory,
For getting out of the system
The trick is no mystery,
As he remembers Pete's wisdom.
The most important skill is resilience,
And rely on mind's creative brilliance.
You must keep dreams and passions alive,
Until the death knell does arrive.
Keeping calm and silent is best,
No matter what's thrown at you,
Keep that dream in fiery view,
And let the idiots cry and protest.
Your day will come, it will come,
Repeat this to yourself, in times to come.

9-32

The tension rises as hours pass,
As his lunch is given to him
He eats slowly, like cow to grass,
As positive thoughts fight to swim.
Suddenly, his door opens out,
And sees nurses around him sprout.
'It was wrong to stop my move,
Did Dr Kautz to my story prove?'
'You're fit and sound to go back,
Just move, as we don't have all day,
As to your future, it's looking grey,
So, no more fighting, or you'll be back.'
'Can I see Dr Kautz?' 'Just move.'
'Please, I need to…' 'Just move.'

9-33

Kram sits in the day area,
As he notices Mark walk in
He seems to be in dysphoria,
With slight shakes, and reddened skin.
Kram approaches and sees glazed eyes,
And immediately notices Mark's demise.
Why, Kram thinks, *he only held him back,*
Or Jack would've continued the attack.
Kram pats his shoulders and walks away,
As Mark doesn't recognise him
He is a shell hidden within
No character or banter on display.
Kram sits in a chair as his eyes well,
As anger and sadness in tears dispel.

9-34

Kram retires to his room after five,
And lies on bed, deep in thought,
I must keep quiet and survive.
Feeling tired and overwrought.
But he feels he's learnt two valuable lessons,
As his thoughts storm, upon the heavens.
He knows how fast and slow things occur,
As depression and anger within him stir.
Whether I lose or prevail
I must focus on tomorrow,
Where society will feel my sorrow
Of that goal, I cannot fail.
Wearily, he sits up, and grabs his notebook,
To write a poem with words that hook.

Camden Town

Clouds of rain hover over Camden Town
Haunting shadows below me grew,
Reflecting my heart upside down.

Dressed within in a morning gown,
With gusts of wind through window blew
But in minds bayou, thoughts drown.

A murky bayou of black and brown
Brown logs of sadness I did view,
As I forced a smile like a tired clown.

Suddenly, sun's dazzling rays shot down,
Inspiring, happy thoughts grew,
Logs of sadness began sinking down.

And memories start dancing around,
As a calm and happier time ran through,
Dancing happily, breaking my frown.

Hope sprung as heart slow down,
As my passion for poetry grew through
And above my head a rainbow's frown
No more being sad, not in this town.

9-36

And the days roll into weeks,
As Kram goes with the motion
Within his mind to himself he speaks
Of revenge in which he has devotion.
To the memories of Mark, he does grieve,
But is cheered up at having leave.
Escorted on an hour's excursion,
As outside life is a great diversion.
Weeks roll slowly into months,
And Kram feels strong,
He ignores what's wrong,
And only within his mind, he confronts.
He thinks of what could have been,
A low secure hospital with a better routine.

9-37

Kram sits within ward round,
As everyone seems very laid back
As smiles and niceties surround,
Kram relaxes not sensing an attack.
'It's been nearly a year since the fight,
And your behaviour has been a delight.
You're never late for activities,
And you've taken responsibilities.
You take your meds unprompted,
You don't argue with staff,
And your jokes make us laugh,
And to a new and better you, you've adopted.
Your interview for low secure is tomorrow,
With a Mr Andrews and Mr Gennaro.'

Kram leaves the meeting on a high
But this time, he keeps lips tight,
So, no jealous attacks will fly,
And needing to defend himself in a fight.
To sly extremes, I must be committed,
So far, the system, I have outwitted!
Kram feels his time is coming,
As he hears himself humming.
He sits in a chair in the day area,
As Mark dribbles from mouth, in stale breath
Kram wishes he would have a quick death,
Than suffer within, in silent hysteria.
Go to hell, world, go to hell!
And take your fucking meds as well!

In the interview room, Kram does talk
Presenting himself as normal and well
At times, he imagines an eagle's squawk
From their mouths, like demons from hell.
Within minutes, it is all over,
As they are literal and sober.
'That was painless,' Kram replies,
And Mr Gennaro smiles and sighs.
Kram rejoins a group, paint by numbers,
As his mind soon goes dull
As paint by numbers lull
But then he fantasises of distant wonders.
Wonders of poetry, murder, and sin,
And no nurses scanning or staring at him.

A week passes and he feels a smile spread,
While he refreshes in shower's rain
Then dresses, as dreams of freedom embed,
And escaping the dull and mundane.
When will I leave for the hospital in Essex?
A life with more sleep, and poetics.
Then, to his room, Dr Kautz appears,
With an animated expression, he nears.
'You're leaving, Kram, tomorrow morning
If you could start packing today,
And so, there'll be no delay.'
Kram smiles wide, with face distorting.
'Thanks, Doc, my day has finally come.'
As relief in tears, he does succumb.

9-41

Kram moves throughout the day secretively,
As he doesn't want people to know
He packs and discards decoratively,
Carefully wrapping poems with a bow.
With a lidded look of satisfaction,
He finishes with little distraction.
Then, tightly lacing fingers behind his head,
He lets negative thoughts unthread.
By imagining the worst is over
With slow, and steady deep breaths
He envisages many police officers' deaths,
As he then lies on bed, in full composure.
He sings "Wonderwall" in a loud voice,
And wishes farewell to his delusion Royce.

9-42

The morning comes like Christmas Day,
As he fills a trolley with bags
Then, off the ward without delay
As the trolley to Kram's jumper snags.
Then, through a maze of corridors leading,
At a brisk walk, they go speeding.
And through reception, a driver approaches,
As feelings of freedom, and life encroaches.
They load Kram's bags into the car,
As Kram's dream of revenge nears,
As the car represents freedom's spheres
And to a blood-red horizon, he sees afar.
After farewells to the medium-secure team,
He dreams of living a more relaxed regime.

9-43

They slowly drive away from hospital,
The medium-secure mire
Down the road it looks so little
As he imagines the hospital on fire.
The smoky exhaust to air defies,
Its breaths of black, to nature's demise.
The road to highway, he does heed,
As the accelerator down touches speed.
He sees his tortured past like a dream,
And with speed to the future, he goes,
As his nightmares behind him finally close
As words and rhymes and rhythm stream.
Kram falls asleep to engine's cosy roar,
Towards the new hospital, he does snore.

CANTO 10

St. Andrews Hospital comes too,
Like a white manor house at front
Kram's nerves dig in, at such a view,
To new patients and staff to confront.
So, here's to my new home,
My universe, like ancient Rome.
In the middle of Essex's glare,
With hope of a full sleep and good care.
He goes through the rigmaroles of reception,
Whilst chatting with grins, and laughs,
To a good relationship, he cunningly grafts,
As staff search bags for signs of deception.
Then, to his new ward, Kram quietly goes,
With his bag, as curiosity grows.

10-2

His room is large, almost twice the size
Of old. With an en-suite shower
Kram was shocked at that surprise,
As sharing a shower did overpower.
At seeing other patients' pubic hair,
And semen from a masturbatory affair.
And sometimes shit stains, across the walls,
As some think that's funny as madness crawls.
Within minutes, staff leave him alone,
As he feels, he's wearing rose-tinted glasses,
And feels towards freedom, he's making advances,
As happiness and peace to his soul has sewn.
He breathes deep into his expanding chest,
And to his bed, he lies in rest.

10-3

Kram wakes up and has a shower,
Then watches some TV,
Like lying under nature's bower,
Feeling relaxed, feeling free.
He stretches wide to awake his body,
And leaves his room to make some coffee.
The ward is quiet, calm, and quaint,
No bullying nurses in verbal restraint.
Kram feels his mind has more focus,
Without nurses trying to uproot
With scanning eyes in pursuit
Of sleeping men with psychosis.
And no one is suffering a lack of sleep,
As anyone, at any time, can fall deep.

Sipping coffee in his room
Watching a black-and-white movie
As shower gel to his room did perfume,
Whilst he eats a chocolate toffee.
With total release of bodily tension,
The hospital feels like another dimension.
To the ward's newspaper he does scan,
Whilst lying on his bed, like a divan.
Suddenly, a headline he reads in shock,
Of a serial killer who got caught
And to a death sentence, he bought
For killing seven women in Bangkok.
Seven minor murders? What a pussy!
Wait for the world to read about me!

10-5

Kram's daily routine starts at ten,
With a short morning meeting
Then lies and rests with TV, again,
Before hospital's café, for some eating.
Then more rest, and maybe a nap,
Or some self-reflection, to unwrap.
And when his head is calm and clear,
He plots and plans his murderous career.
Then, unfortunately, at five, he has his tea,
Where he has to queue up with others
As being close together smothers
But after meds, he's totally free.
At times, in his room, he plays some blues,
With murderous fantasies of killing screws.

With an intensity of concentration
He imagines the newspaper headlines,
From the justice system's education
He writes poetry with haunting lines.
In a way, he's thankful to his enemies,
For giving him purpose thro' bad memories.
A purpose where age doesn't matter,
A purpose in death with blood splatter.
The prison guards, et al., will pay,
As I'll follow them from their prisons
Then judges, police, and politicians,
I'll hold in terror, then slay.
On lined paper with pen, he strikes,
As a myriad of imagery and rhyme spikes.

I'm a Prisoner in This Land

I'm a prisoner in this land,
Society had turned away,
So, I turned my back and planned,
To the upturned sea all day.

I watched the time pass,
In this ship's, cold concrete hull
Kept locked in due to a grass,
Can't wait to smash in his skull.

Each prisoner wants that bit more,
Whatever their truth, maybe
Soon freedom does come ashore,
From a deep, cold murky sea.

But prisoners don't look too far,
As they'd probably fall and weep
Since true freedom is much too far
As habits are sown too deep.

The Screams of Corpses

Prison nights – prison rites
Echoes of footsteps along the wing
As I'm spied on routinely by a screw
Like a damned animal in a zoo.

The eerie, cloudy night sky
No stars or moon to be seen,
Winter's bite has nearly gone now,
With endless more to plough.

I get in bed and close my eyes,
Feeling surreally like I'm dead,
I can barely hear myself breathe,
As I begin to feel myself seethe.

I then stare blankly at the ceiling,
Hearing screams every now and then,
Snapping hauntingly like a whip
As I dug teeth into my bleeding lip.

Suddenly, the noise left me,
A loud scream like a dying animal
As I lay still against the night
Like a corpse dead with fright.

People are lucky to have love,
Especially on such a bleak night
Dreams I try to hold on tight,
But coldly, reality does bite.

Be grateful you're in bed,
Making passionate, sweet love
Away from this passionless place
Where at night, nightmares chase
Together with the screams of corpses.

10-9

What Hell is This!

'What hell is this!' said the prisoner,
As he glares through the window
At the cold, barren, empty sky
As a blackbird swoops calmly by.

Then he hears a few officers shouting,
Echoing through the empty, cold wing
Uniforms of black and white on burnt marble,
Clanging and tapping with keys on metal.

Footsteps soon run by his cell door,
As voices surge back at the emptiness
Shadows of feet scatter under the door,
Eager to escape the devil's own claw.

He stares at his own haunted reflection,
On a square piece of plastic mirror
Cold grey eyes are vexed with rage,
Eager to escape the small concrete cage.

Dreams of love, as smouldering metal
Smashed on prison's anvil,
Hammered by painful lost years,
Moulding endlessly with paranoid fears.

Then, suddenly, keys jangle loudly near
Clanging and twisting at his metal door
Then, exploding open with noise and light
A myriad of voices of prisoners' plight.

'This world,' said the prisoner,
'As you lie in false comfort,
You citizens will never know,
Your futures are cold as snow.'

'Safe and warm poor citizens,
Oblivious to a madman's tears
Growing hysterical in prison sadness
Hell's coming from prison's madness.'

From Devil's Grace

I didn't want to be,
I thought I'd never be free,
Forever in that heartless place
Deep within Devil's grace.

Injustice was all around me,
Like a curse around my soul
Like Jacob Marley's weighty chain
Weighed down with so much pain.

The justice system's umbrella of darkness,
Covered me in murderous fantasies,
In which you all will fear me,
In which my vengeance will burn free.

But now I'm out within this train,
Amongst empty, unfriendly faces
Cutting through this loveless land,
Cutting through fog's-clenched hand.

I felt inside my soul like a clockface,
With slow-moving skeletal hands
As I stagnated, watching time pass by
And now I live, by watching you die.

10-11

Sitting within the bustling ward round
After six months of relaxation
A doctor, nurses, and carers surround,
Saying they've done an evaluation.
'We've all agreed on you having leave,
Three hours, if you can believe.
And also, we'd like you to do therapy,
To help, and give you more clarity.'
Kram agrees, smiling, feeling ecstatic,
Focusing on visiting Burger King
As he imagines his tastebud's cling
From years of hospital food like plastic.
He returns to his room in thoughts afar,
To continue reading Sylvia Plath's *Bell Jar*.

10-12

Kram's mind is filled with awe,
At the character's deep understanding
With its detailed descriptions, raw
With Sylvia Plath's suicide implanting.
He wishes he could've saved her,
And to hug and comfort her.
And to turn her thoughts to life,
And fight her darkness with a knife.
To cut hard and fight back,
Death is no sweet dream,
It's nothingness in the extreme
Life's a puzzle you must crack.
The book resonates, as he finishes in tears,
And feels his destiny, from locked frontiers.

10-13

Leave comes, with breaths of freedom's flame,
As Kram exits the car with his male escort
A short man with a slight frame
As to everything Kram does, he'll report.
Kram hits Basildon's streets in eager tread,
And through crowds, little is said.
Then Kram shouts, 'Let's go to Burger King first.'
As his hunger in his imagination immersed.
Then, finally, on first bite, tastebuds took flight,
Together with salted fries
And with fizzy pop, Kram sighs
Savouring this moment, as thoughts ignite.
He finishes, and relaxes in his plastic seat,
Realising he needs DVDs, to feel complete.

10-14

Kram buys *The Fog*, then *Jaws*
And the *Godfather* trilogy
Also, a novel for mind to pause,
From cinematic history.
Together with chocolate sweets,
With toffee popcorn and savoury treats.
In a talkative and polite manner,
Kram heads back to psychiatric glamour.
The romantic glamour of a mental asylum
With tormented lost souls
Burning like hot coals
Split minds kept under the thumb.
But Kram knows the reality, he truly does
Just empty lives, whom nobody loves.

10-15

Kram, with a joyous expression
Thumbs through his new possessions
As the films spark a mental regression
Of happier and ecstatic recollections.
Jaws reminds him of Kent's summer sea,
Where he was with Gloria, running free.
The Godfather reminds him of Italian food,
Eating spaghetti, before making love nude.
Popcorn reminds him of cinema's frolics,
Seated in the back row,
Kissing and stroking slow
Before the law and all its bollocks.
He replays the film *Jaws* on his TV,
Mesmerised by the sun's flickering sea.

10-16

Years go by without much fuss,
Reading and studying poetry
Talking deep of his past, they discuss
With Haylee, in his one-to-one therapy.
He had to lie almost throughout,
As he feared she'd be, of no doubt.
That his risk to the public was very high,
And to his freedom, she'd definitely deny.
He spends his days planning and plotting,
In his mind with each crime
How, where, and what time
And the types of weapons for each killing.
As he has no guns for an easy kill,
He must be inventive for blood to spill.

10-17

A mental health panel comes on year four,
To decide if they should end his section,
And all experts they did explore,
His time in therapy and introspection.
The panel goes swimmingly well,
And from his section, they did expel.
Which triggers finally his parole board,
And to his freedom, they might reward.
For the parole board, he must prepare
As it's much, much harder to trudge
With a psychologist and a judge
And the dangers of failure, he is aware.
A return to prison's harsh regime,
Back to his nightmare's inner scream.

10-18

He was put in touch with a solicitor,
A Mr Sach of Italian descent
Who specialises in parole board's perimeter,
And to his files, Kram gives consent.
Kram prepares hard each day,
As he wants to reassure and convey.
His wonderful change in nature,
And his wish to work and labour.
To make up for his awful past
And his desire to live in peace,
And never again fall foul of police
This is the image he must cast.
In order to gain freedom, to kill and kill,
To this bloody dream, he must fulfil.

10-19

Months go past as time slows,
Kram studies and prepares hard,
As creeping stress and anxiety grows,
As to his solicitor, he does regard.
His dreams and fantasies radiate,
On picturing the proverbial gate.
But he also plans to escape,
If the parole board doesn't take shape.
As to the results he gets in a letter,
But also has unescorted daily leave,
And if bad news, he does receive,
He won't return to hospital, never.
Suddenly, a feeling of breathlessness takes,
As he knows, he can't make mistakes.

10-20

The day of the parole board arrives
As he eagerly, to the building, walks
As his thoughts of murder drives
But nervousness to his soul stalks.
His solicitor offers encouragement,
As his soul needs that nourishment.
In his mind, he mentally prepares,
But stress on his shoulders bears.
He enters the room gently smiling,
As Kram sits next to people, in the middle
And hands on lap, nervously fiddle,
Opposite three men, presiding.
After pleasantries, the meeting starts,
As nervousness to Kram strangely departs.

10-21

The man in the middle talks first
And asks Kram if he'd like,
If he'd like to be questioned first
As going last, he'll probably dislike.
Kram agrees and sits up straight,
As he starts to feel destiny's weight.
The questions are each taken in turn,
As Kram answers, more questions return.
'I wasn't a good criminal!
And therefore, I don't want to return,
And through honesty, I want to earn
And be a decent individual.'
Kram goes on, giving good answers,
And through tricky questions, he dances.

10-22

Kram's ordeal is soon over,
And then his therapist is next,
'To Kram's upbringing, he has closure,
Which was why, through life, he was vexed.
Kram has shown great remorse,
And to his freedom, I endorse.
He has great urge to go straight,
And realises it isn't too late.'
'Has Kram shown, since you've known him,
Signs of antisocial behaviour?'
'No, as he's with Jesus, his loving saviour,
And regarding ward's troubles, he doesn't swim.'
Haylee's description of Kram does delight,
As Kram feels his murderous goals ignite.

10-23

Haylee's evidence comes to an end,
And his psychiatrist Dr Dove is next,
Kram realises she has to recommend,
As Kram's jaw muscles flex.
'Have you seen signs of criminal behaviour?'
'No, as Haylee said, Jesus is his saviour.
I've been a psychiatrist for fifteen years,
And never seen so much remorse in tears.
He's a sensible, reliable man,
And takes his life very seriously,
Undertaking courses and responsibility
And with his life, he has a plan.
He wants to finish his O.U. degree,
And live a good life, I guarantee.'

10-24

'Also, his risk of reoffending is low,
And I recommend his release,
And as Haylee did show,
His childhood anger's gone. He's at peace.'
The board looks truly satisfied,
As fears of Kram reoffending slide.
Which Kram senses, and feels more positive,
She continues, 'His childhood was causative.
To which fuelled his life of crime
And to which, he's finally come to terms.'
But to Kram, a headache slowly burns
As slight doubt begins to climb.
As this is his first parole board,
And they're known, on first, not to reward.

10-25

The parole board meeting soon finishes
And he's told he'll receive a letter,
Of their decision and wishes
Either to deny or enter the world better.
He walks back through the wards doors,
As Kram to the nurses talk, ignores.
Kram carefully masks his feelings,
Throughout the parole board proceedings.
But knows now he has to prepare,
His escape just in case
And to prepare for the chase
And the huge stress and despair.
As he knows being sent back to prison,
Is much too much a terrifying position.

10-26

Kram, on leave in bookstore rectangular
Skimming books of true crime through
Of glamourous gangster's spectacular
Then, into a café for a hot brew.
On his escape, he needs to buy clothes,
As his appearance is detailed in prose.
By staff on ward's leave procedure,
And a recent photo for the reader.
I need to buy a hat too,
As he drinks his hot drink
Then to catch the London link
The train to escape, as police pursue.
Kram's escape is a living machine,
As the drink inspires via its caffeine.

10-27

With another coffee and a confection
He sees a patient called Paul,
On the same prison transfer section
But on a sentence small.
Paul has a book – *Harry Potter*,
Reading it deep as he's got a
Slight smile with thick glasses
With tied-back hair in thick molasses.
Kram gets quietly up, and leaves,
As to avoid boring small talk
And so, he does quietly walk,
And wipes his mouth upon his sleeve.
Kram feels confident when the chase is on,
As he'll be far away in London's song.

10-28

And to crime, he must soon adapt,
First, robbing a bank with a note
Then a burglary, in night's cloak wrapped,
As he needs stolen ID to stay afloat.
And instead of pulling a major crime,
He'll focus more on a smaller climb.
As that's where he went wrong before,
The jewellery shop job, he does deplore.
So, back in hospital, after the search,
He goes to his room alone,
Where he feels snuggly at home
Then puts a DVD on, for ideas to perch.
Ideas from detective shows to advise,
To escape leaving DNA, the policemen's prize.

10-29

But back and forth his mind does go,
From TV to present-day life
And of his escape in fantasies throw,
Are marked with thoughts of prison strife.
As prison hangs, like death surrounds,
In eerie dark shadows, to soul, it hounds.
But Kram doesn't have any options,
As prison's torture injected toxins.
He must focus now on being ruthless,
Without any lingering doubt
He must focus on crime, and be devout,
And to betray all humanity like Judas.
With a kiss to his true desire,
A desire for revenge, from prison's fire.

10-30

Two weeks pass through mind's storm,
As Kram lets down his sail
As he rows against, as waves deform,
Until suddenly, he's given his mail.
Kram walks casually into his room,
And rips open the letter, as words consume.
With each word, one by one,
Until he sees the word 'approved,' done.
I've got my parole, the final red tape.
No escape is needed,
Christ Lord, I've succeeded,
My murderous plans are taking shape.
Soon my bloody poems, will rhyme my reign,
Across London's city, I'll kill, burn, and maim.

10-31

Everyone in the morning meeting claps,
With a nurse calling him 'freeman'
As to life from darkness, Kram snaps,
To a great future, his fantasies scan.
'Good luck outside,' says old Ed,
As violent thoughts storm Kram's head.
'Don't come back,' says James,
As Kram pictures houses in flames.
'You're lucky, you can get pissed,'
Says Andy, 'I bet your mind is in overflow!'
Kram nods, daring not to put on show,
As his murderous goals and poetry kissed.
But smiles back in dull banality,
As he mentally prepares for his new reality.

10-32

On his last ward round
His probation officer attends,
As Kram sits, crowned
As his happiness transcends.
'Hello, I'm your probation officer, Iveta,'
As Kram bellows attempting an operetta.
'Kram,' says Haylee, 'be serious!'
'Sorry, I'm feeling slightly delirious,
Hello, Iveta, it's great; I'll finally be free!
I notice your slight accent, Russian?
It's got that tone of construction.'
Kram smiles, gently swirling his room key.
'I'm from Lithuania, the city of Vilnius,'
She replies kindly and punctilious.

10-33

The meeting simply dotted the i's,
And crossed the t's,
No sucker punches or hidden surprise,
And it all flows with ease.
Kram, in his room, watches TV,
Then puts on a film of the highest degree.
The film for all romantics, *Dr Zhivago*,
As Kram imagines himself as the hero.
Battling forces to be with his love
Against oppression in violent throws
Of callous police hiding in plain clothes
As his poetry puts him high above.
Above all, the ordinary simple folk,
As the film's message and imagery invoke.

10-34

On the day of his departure
Kram nods, as his doctor speaks,
'Don't forget you're much smarter,
And practise your relaxation techniques.'
With a flutter in his belly,
He places down his telly.
Shaking hands and saying goodbye,
And to his meds, he has a month's supply.
Clasping palms together in prayer's gesture
Give me strength and luck,
Don't let me fall like a schmuck!
As now's my time to leave and venture.
With strong eye contact with each and all,
He salutes the doctor and kisses the wall.

In complete disbelief Kram sighs,
As Kram and nurses load his bags
Into the trolley, his possession dives,
Then, heading off. The trolley he drags.
'Bye, everyone,' Kram shouts to all.
'Good luck, Kram,' their cries sprawl.
He finally breathes deep at hospital's exit,
To a good, honest man, Kram sells it.
Then, into the car, the driver loads,
As Kram sits casually in the back seat,
Then, belting up to complete
As a sudden rush of fear explodes.
Years of planning, his mind has spun,
Knowing one mistake, his freedom's done.

CANTO 11

Kram arrives at his London home,
For released ex-hospital patients
His eyes, to his home, he does comb,
Then spots the CCTV surveillance.
He gets out, and greets staff,
Standing by door, in exaggerated laugh.
And points upset, at the outside camera,
To a jolly-faced woman named Klara.
'I don't like that camera there,
As I feel, slight unease,
And to my bones, I freeze
I suffer paranoia, are you aware?'
'It doesn't work, Kram, it's a dummy.
Please feel free to examine it, honey.'

11-2

Kram examines the camera closer,
Then laughs aloud.
As Kram acts, the charming poser
Free from camera's shroud.
Then he sees opposite a public house,
Bustling full, called The Cat and Mouse.
Which Kram feels its name, is slightly ironic,
As he thinks of having a gin and tonic.
But first, he must examine, every street,
Marking in a notebook, each camera's stare
As he lies in wait, in murderous prayer,
As thoughts of guards, in his mind repeat.
Which remind him to focus on his strategy,
To attack society in blood-drenched totality.

11-3

He talks further with Klara,
As she helps unload the car
Then, further help from a Sara,
As they keep his room door ajar.
After unloading his room, he fills,
And in med's cabinet, he places his pills.
He hides the meds key, keeping it safe,
But feels tired as his inner thighs chafe.
He knows he's not used to exercise,
And really must plan to get fit,
To running and weights, he must commit,
Because being unfit does jeopardise.
As physical ability in crime is needed,
I must first get fit; this goal has seeded.

11-4

He jogs along the local paths,
Within morning's, cold fresh light
Then back home, and with staff, he laughs,
Then, to his notebook, a plan takes flight.
I must totally change my diet,
And to completely focus and commit
Then, every three days, I'll hit the gym,
I must get fit, strong, and trim.
He studies on YouTube, fighting techniques,
On his flat-screen TV
Whilst drinking green tea
As punching angles and kicks to mind seeps.
He fantasies about doing an arson blitz,
Instead of murder, until fitness permits.

11-5

Kram hears his downstairs neighbour,
Walking slowly and softly upstairs
In deep breaths, he does labour
As he greets Kram, with paranoid stares.
'Hi, I'm Henry,' he says with thin cheeks,
'I'm Kram,' as Kram compares physiques.
Henry is thin with a bloated belly,
As Kram charms like Machiavelli.
'Alright, chap, what's life like here, mate,
Any nutters or fruit cakes?'
Henry then slightly shakes,
Then laughs. 'It's been quiet here of late.'
Then, to the upstairs toilet, he goes,
As Sara greets Kram, wearing colourful clothes.

11-6

'Kram, I'll explain how this place is run,
We're staffed twenty-four-seven.
Two staff during day, and night, only one,
And the manager's called Stephen.
But night staff, after nine, only sleep,
As, if there's trouble, we are here to keep.
Keep the peace and your presence of mind,
Also, to help in all matters entwined.
This is a new world you've come out to
Everything is mostly online,
But we'll help; you'll be fine,
Ask if you need anything; we're here for you.'
Kram's relieved that night staff only slept,
As he plans to kill, as night's blanket crept.

11-7

After years inside in maddening brilliance
Kram feels hugely omniscient,
In bloody poetry, he found resilience
Reading them aloud in his room was sufficient.
Twelve long years without a break,
Twelve long years was society's mistake.
As he's determined a kill for each year,
The very minimum before ending his career.
The career of the 'Mad Poet of London',
As he's now certain of that name
And certain of that fame
From prison's years, swallowed and sunken.
I was sunk deep, and drunk with rage,
My times come to kill on London's stage.

11-8

Kram works hard on his first poem,
His first official calling card
Whilst listening to TV on low hum
In words from memory's shard.
In murder and poetry, I will terrorise,
In murder and poetry, I do fantasise.
In my poems, I must rise
As I know, the press will criticise.
And the police will try to outwit,
As they know, I can't give up or quit
As the system made my mind split,
And I must focus hard on getting fit.
Tomorrow, I must use the Tube train,
I must get familiar with London's terrain.

11-9

For most days, he puts on a front
Of a cheerful, kind, and pleasant chap
But in his mind, he's planning a hunt,
And carefully studies London's map.
Then, at day's end, outside a police station,
He follows suited men in preparation.
As he knows, they're likely to be CID,
Of that, there is a high degree.
Most get into a car and drive away,
But one man to the Tube station enters,
Just like in his fantasies, Kram ventures,
Following him like glue in crowd's array.
He changes lines, up to Walthamstow,
As Kram follows him, close in tow.

11-10

Kram walks behind him slow,
Casually looking calm and relaxed
Then, across the road's busy flow
Nearly ninety minutes have lapsed.
The suited man, into his house, enters,
As Kram in pad, the address he enters.
He repeats this with other police stations,
Criss-crossing London at various locations.
Kram uses this technique with London's prisons,
Wandsworth, Pentonville, and the Scrubs
As warmth and joy to Kram floods,
Writing down addresses and CCTV positions.
Five months fly by, of detailed planning,
Entwined with exercise, and constant scanning.

11-11

To all, Kram adopts a languid pose,
Whilst nervously dancing, he wiggles,
Engaging in banter and jokes, he throws,
As staff and residents are in giggles.
Time goes by, as Kram feigns sleepiness,
And to his room, he goes in uneasiness.
He looks through his clever disguise,
A false beard and wig in perfect size.
Whilst wearing two sets of clothes
He puts on his dark green jacket,
Then lies in wait for night's blanket,
As time ticks by, his tension grows.
The time has come, and Kram creeps out,
Towards a stolen car, he walks in doubt.

11-12

'Dan, your mum phoned today,
Reminding you about...'
'I know, I know, it's all okay,
Why does she doubt?
Dad's birthday is only once a year,
There's more to me than a fucking career!'
'I know, love; she just wanted to remind,
Don't snap at me, I was being kind.'
'Sorry for snapping, Diana, sweetie,
As I had a hard day at work
The chief inspector was a jerk,
Let's go to bed and make a treaty.'
Diana laughs, as he tickles her all over,
They both undress, to naked exposure.

11-13

Hours later, they're both asleep,
But suddenly wake to a car alarm,
They both get up, as tensions creep,
And Dan picks up, a cricket bat to arm.
'Diana, I'll investigate, stay put and hide,
It's probably teenagers daring a joyride.'
She gets out of bed, vexed and alert,
And dresses in a blue shirt.
And to the window of flashing lights
From their black Mazda car
Her vision blurs, due to an eyelash scar,
As her soul in terror bites.
Dan exits the house, and in shouts he bites,
As Diana's adrenalin, to heart ignites.

11-14

Dan shouts, 'You better scarper,
As I've called the law.' He clenches a fist.
He focuses harder as vision gets sharper,
As his face in anger, and tension twist.
Whilst barefoot, he stands outside,
On seeing a smashed window, he looks wide.
He walks to his car, as coldness erodes,
And to his head, a hard blow explodes.
He falls to the floor with an agonising shout,
And from his head, blood grows
As a machete chops, in rapid throws.
He lies dead, staring at death's route.
Diana's face at the window screams,
As a bearded man in neon light gleams.

11-15

Police surround and own the scene,
As an ambulance helps Diana
And detectives in white suits – clean,
As one calls out, 'Joanna.'
'Yes, gov,' as she approaches the DCI,
Trying to swallow from mouth, dry.
'This feels like a planned attack,
Not a spur-of-the-moment carjack.'
'I feel exactly the same, gov,
As no attempt was made to steal the car.
It's overkill, very bizarre,
Which Diane viewed from window above.'
Suddenly, a man addresses Joanna, 'DI Rhys!
I found a letter addressed to the police!'

11-16

Joanna puts on latex gloves,
Along with DCI Wallace
As he to Joanna, gently shoves
As morning birds sing in chorus.
She opens the envelope, in white,
As she attempts to read in dim light.
'Over here,' DCI Wallace directs
As the hallway light projects.
Joanna's cheeks redden,
As her thoughts sprout
As her words of doubt out.
'Could there be something in, to threaten?'
She opens and reads the poem aloud,
Letting words and rhyme to mind cloud.

11-17

Inside They Say

Inside, they say, I fell asleep,
Beneath the violence and the grief
Inside, they say, the flurries deep,
Beneath, I acted like a thief.

You had to drift inside to be,
Afloat in every day at dawn
Polite and placid man they see,
Hope pricks me hard, like a thorn.

Inside, I cried as currents gripped,
Beneath the river in my head
Inside, I cried as demons whipped,
In my cell, with the ghostly dead.

Upon my goals, my thoughts grew,
A garden gate of blood and splatter
So cold my conscience, the devil knew,
If caught, I'm back; it doesn't matter.

Inside I went a broken man
Romantic dreams had all been shattered,
Inside this man, there was a plan,
Bloodshed ruled; that's all that mattered.

Out I went, through the bloody gate,
The time had come, the time had come,
Cold, steel bars, had fuelled my hate,
The time had come, the time had come.

Yours sincerely,
The Mad Poet of London

11-18

Kram splashes water above the sink,
Rubbing his face wet
And to the mirror, a fluttering blink
To a feeling of slight regret.
Maybe he wasn't a pig?
As he imagines the machete dig.
Maybe he was a solicitor,
Or a police station visitor.
But he wasn't carrying a briefcase!
A solicitor would've done this.
And to the mirror he gives a kiss,
Then, in a towel, he buries his face.
And to the bright morning, he embraces,
Feeling alert and alive, as adrenalin races.

11-19

Kram is in a small room,
Talking to his probation officer, Iveta
Kram feels the office gloom,
But cheers on thinking of his vendetta.
'You're to see me once a week,'
In foreign tones, she does speak.
'As you're written down as high risk.'
To those words, his thoughts whisk.
'Why is my risk high? I live as a priest!
And with all the therapy I've done,
To a fresh start, I've begun.'
'It's standard, for all who've been released.'
Throughout the meeting, Kram carefully speaks,
And of the prison system, he jokingly critiques.

11-20

He puts his headphones on
As he walks back home
The rhythm plays upon
Through streets, he does comb.
On sighting police, he tightens sinews,
But still, casually, he continues.
Throughout the day his doubts flail,
But then relief to mind, assail.
As he reads the paper about the kill
But nothing about his poetry
Only focusing on the bloody body
But it was police blood I did spill!
Kram keeps focused, on his next kill,
As he feels in air, a slight chill.

11-21

'Si, d'you fancy gravy n' chips.'
'Nah, Mina, I need to lose weight.'
As Simon, with milk bottle, drips.
'I've put on four stone straight!'
'Is that why you walk to work,
Rather than drive the Merc?'
'Yeah, Mina, my weight's a major worry,
As I don't want to die in a hurry!'
Mina sits by him on the sofa,
As she studies the telly
Then, cuddles his belly,
As a noise outside alerts her.
'What's that, Si? It sounds like...'
'I'll go, Mina.' In stance, ready to strike.

11-22

Simon looks out the front door,
With a darting gaze to the night
With fists tensed, ready for war,
As he sees the Merc burning bright.
Simon walks out into his front garden,
Shouting angrily at the arson.
The fire flickers and takes hold,
In orange, red, and gold.
Out on the pavement on bare feet
He curls his arms over his head,
In peripheral vision, his sight does spread
As he scans carefully down the street.
Mina now joins Simon, and calls police,
As when together, their anger finds peace.

11-23

Then suddenly, they hear a rustle,
Near a thick, dense, dark hedge
Simon tenses to react to trouble,
As his anger on thoughts dredge.
Simon kicks the thick hedge row,
As he feels the heat from fires glow.
'It's probably teenagers getting their kicks,
Those fucking bastards, stupid pricks.'
Then suddenly, out the hedge darts a fox,
Mina screams, and Simons shouts,
As the car's flames, to sky, sprouts
And the fire, to the neighbourhood rocks.
Some neighbours come out to give support,
Saying they've seen no teenagers to report.

11-24

The police and fire brigade arrive,
As Simon and Mina sit on the pavement
Drinking in night's air to revive
As Simon prepares to make a statement.
He mutters to himself as police near,
And firemen with hosepipes, to fire's sphere.
The flames roar to smoky bellows,
Up towards the night, it goes.
Into the house, the police and all, blend
As Simon details the basics,
And Mina also adds to the mix
As her paranoia and suspicions ascend.
'I think…' A cigarette she then stubs,
'This is due to Simon's work at the Scrubs.'

11-25

'So, you work at Wormwood Scrub;
D'you think it's a revenge attack?
As the prison's full of nutters and thugs.'
'I doubt on me there's a contract!
It's probably teenagers fucking around,
Who, if I catch, I'll kick to the ground.
The prisoners I've met, aren't very bright,
Most can't barely read or write.
Besides, I get on with most
As the rules, I don't throw about
I don't either shout or flout
They're mostly mentally ill, undiagnosed.
No, I'm sure it's teenagers acting wildly.'
'Well, sir, that's probably highly likely.'

11-26

'Well, thank you, sir
We'll keep in touch,
To teenagers, we concur
We suspect as much.'
The police leave, past hosepipe jets,
As the car now, is doused wet.
'Mina, I'm tired; let's go to bed.'
'Yeah, Si, it's all been said.'
Within minutes after brushing their teeth,
They dress in night clothes,
As annoyance still flows
They then cuddle, under duvet beneath.
Soon, they drift, in sleep's claws,
Away from reality, they do pause.

11-27

Then, downstairs, Kram moves
Walking in shadowy darkness
Surveilling all, his sight improves,
In night vision sharpness.
Whilst they sleep upstairs in snores,
He creeps upstairs and explores.
As to dreams, they both greet,
A dark image they both meet.
A nightmarish demon in black
Who slowly approaches,
As unease encroaches
As they both awake under terror's flack.
Kram, in shadows, stands with axe,
Then suddenly to them, with force, he whacks.

11-28

Mina is knocked out immediately,
With the blunt edge of the axe
But, to Simon, he bleeds easily
As Kram's voice impacts.
'I crept in, when your backs were turned,
As to the fire, you were concerned.'
Kram then chops Simon in rapid fire,
As the axe reflects his murderous desire.
He pulls Simon at an angle,
Then decapitates him, in three blows,
Then picks up his head, and throws,
Together with a poem to rankle.
He walks out the room, and into the night,
Then towards home he takes flight.

11-29

Joanna Rhys is on the scene,
Dressed in a white paper suit,
She passes the letter from scene's obscene,
To DCI Wallace to compute.
'It's written, for sure, by the same killer,
This case is a real spine-tingling chiller!
And, Mina, might have seen his face.'
'That's if she recovers, in God's grace.
But I'm going to have to go and report,
That we're now hunting a serial killer,
Who writes poetry in mystery's river.
To the chief constable, as we need support.'
DCI Wallace to Rhys, reads aloud,
As the words and rhyme, to them, shroud.

Society's Rejected Evacuees

Standing like a dilapidated castle
Covered in pigeons and CCTV,
Black and white swaggering hassle
The nightmares began, *c'est la vie*.

Wearing an old, scratchy, grey tracksuit
Plus, an overboiled pale blue T-shirt
Feeling like some insignificant newt
Disguising with banter, all the hurt.

At night, I'm flooded in sodium light
As I pace the small graffitied cell
Vexed and angered by all this shite,
Whilst hearing the occasional crazed yell.

The cell is cold, sterile, and hard,
With a bed that creeks at every turn
Being spied on routinely by a guard
I'd love to see this whole place burn.

Clattering chaos from morning unlock,
With shouts, banging and rattling keys,
Misery swirls like some cold, dark loch
Were society's rejected evacuees.

The reality of jail seeps slowly in
Through the fabric of my mind
Now let the devil's work begin,
Creating this devilish mastermind.

The public thinks it's a holiday camp,
Television depicts it a blood bath,
In reality, it's more of a training camp
With explosive mixtures of wrath.

So here I am after all those years,
Society's creation I'm one of many,
A person now, that everyone fears,
A maniacal fiend, I'm ten-a-penny.

Good luck in the hunt!
Yours sincerely,
The Mad Poet of London

11-31

DCI Wallace is on his mobile talking,
As he uses fingernails, like dental floss
Suddenly, Joanna notices Kram jogging,
Dressed smartly in Hugo Boss.
Kram looks at Joanna and smiles,
With his hand through hair, he styles.
But she feels unease, as a thought cycles,
And as he passes, her unease spirals.
Why is that man flirting, at such a scene,
With forensics, and uniformed bodies
As to the seriousness the scene embodies.
This thought cuts through, like a ravine.
DCI Wallace waves Joanna over to convey.
'These murders are now being deemed a Cat-A!'

Kram continues jogging a bit further,
Then, he turns a corner to walk
As he hears a slight murmur
From Royce to his thoughts, talk.
Shit the bastard's coming back,
Was it because of the attack.
Or maybe a lack of sleep,
Or axing that body deep?
Kram gets the Tube to go back home,
As Royce's voice, still goes,
In low murmuring, it throws,
'You belong in the Colosseum in ancient Rome.'
Rome! Why did Royce say that?
Was it because of the bloody combat?

11-33

Kram talks deep with his CPN,
Community psychiatric nurse
He talks of the morning when,
Royce's voice did curse.
She asks if he's been stressed of late,
Or had any problems, laying heavy in weight.
'It could have been both,
As prison's memories increase in growth.'
Avoiding any hints of wrongdoing,
As the slight suggestion would restore
His life behind a locked cell door,
And suffer in anger, with mad eyes brooding.
But Kram's been worrying, that he's left DNA,
At that possibility his mind does play.

11-34

She suggests setting up a meeting,
With his psychiatrist Dr Suman
And also maybe, with Anne Kneeling,
'I think, Kram, that's the plan.
For Anne is a therapist,
And also, a specialist.
In helping with stress and PTSD
Which I think you have, to a high degree.'
Kram's CPN details Anne's success
In attacking tormenting thoughts
Which to minds, twists and haunts,
And how therapy could address.
Kram agrees eagerly, in feigning interest,
But must keep up, the pretence as best.

11-35

Metropolitan Police Operation HQ
In Grove Road, Romford, London
As top brass is doing a review,
In the middle of a luncheon.
DCI Wallace and DI Rhys,
Detail the crimes to their chiefs.
'This killer has a plan, and will go on and on,
And time and resources must be laid upon.'
'This killer is clever, and cunning,
And poetry is this killer's twist,
As he dances in mystery's mist,
And with death, he comes crushing.'
They decide to set up a special squad,
As they all secretly pray to God.

Joanna interjects about the poetry,
And explains it should be the focus,
'Despite it being vile and ugly,
It conveys his life and art, in symbiosis.
It should be made public,
And this must be done quick.
As the Mad Poet must be known,
As his life in rhyme is sown.
He must have a violent past,
And will also be known for his poetry,
As it has a certain worded grocery
Tinged with madness's mast.'
They all agree that it must get published,
As the killer's poetry's known, it's established.

CANTO 12

12-1

The media has a field day,
With the killer's poetry, they span,
And a profiler writes an essay,
Of the killer and type of man.
Through the media, the police warn,
Of the killer's M.O. and blood oath sworn.
Kram listens to the media in delight,
As he plans for another night.
Dozens he has planned,
And poetry is already written,
Within disguises hidden
From CCTV's Orwellian land.
In delusions of grandeur and eccentricity,
Kram basks in glory from the publicity.

12-2

Taking a deep, satisfied breath
Danny exits his bedroom,
As morning light gives breadth
In freshness, it does consume.
Then, into the kitchen, in an easy walk,
And to himself, he does talk.
'I must remember to finish my report,
As I could be questioned in open court.'
Suddenly, a blade flickers in light
Then, through his neck, it strikes,
And in spurting blood, it stripes,
As his vision turns ghostly white.
He lies dead beside the door,
As a poem's left upon the floor.

12-3

Kram sits in a local café,
On the following morning
Eating breakfast in full-fried array
As teenagers come in shouting.
'He's fucking struck again!
Another police officer slain.
His latest poem is in the papers.'
Kram's mind to those words, tapers.
Everybody stops and listens,
And Kram follows suit,
All but the reader goes mute,
As morning's light on Kram's tea glistens.
Loudly and clearly, the boy recites,
As words in rhyme take on new heights.

From Blood, Venom, and Fire

All those long, long, long nights
Of blood, venom, and fire
All those long, long, long days
Built a devil's deadly desire.

Inside the cold hard justice factory
Came endless rigid years of suffering,
But suffering had become my fuel,
In which my soul found fulfilling.

I'll never ever, ever, fucking be,
The bloody same ever again
Entrenching thoughts grew slowly,
Faraway dreams, faded in pain.

Finally, it happened, I was released,
I acted the simple subservient,
I smiled the big, goofy smile,
A cunning double-minded serpent.

Officially, now I'm a serial killer,
Happily, I've done at least three,
I love power drenched in blood,
You bastards will never catch me.

Now I've had no more nights,
Of blood, venom, or fire
Blissfully, I'm happy and fulfilled,
Due to soul's vengeful desire.

Mark me! What a great profession
What such an exhilarating story
Death relieves my earthly tension,
I'm revealing in my ghostly glory.

Yours sincerely,
The Mad Poet of London

12-5

Most of the customers look in awe,
As some show looks of disgust
At killing workers in law
As others, in excitement, fuss.
'He's just killing out of vengeance,
At a long inhuman sentence.'
'In another poem, you sense a lost love,
What other motive is better reason, thereof.'
'Nothing makes right – murder!
He's evil, twisted, and fucking sick,
And hopefully, the police catch him quick!'
Says the vexed café shop worker.
Kram leaves, from the buzz and excitement,
As he focuses on his next assignment.

Joanna Rhys storms in with the paper
Into the incident room
'He's changed his M.O. by an acre,
By killing in morning's bloom.'
DCI Wallace looks grumpy,
As Chief Constable Montgomery,
Shouts and hits the desk,
'This is fucking grotesque!
To kill a fellow officer like that
Like culling an animal
In a cut diagonal
He's an evil, diseased rat!
The media is working both ways,
And now he's killing in daylight's rays.'

'We must offer a huge reward,
I'm thinking half a million!
That will cut with a sword,
His war on any civilian.
Someone will be in the know,
And in the reward, he'll glow.'
'But, sir, will the tables turn to our side?
To a mass of crank calls, we'll be supplied!
Across the entire wretched country!'
'But, Rhys,' says Wallace, 'filtering will be easy,
By following our profile, you see.'
'It's the only way,' barks Montgomery.
All three eventually, wholeheartedly agree,
As the reward they felt, would guarantee.

12-8

Kram, in his room, watches telly,
Half asleep as his fantasy leads
Feeling his body weigh heavy,
As the six o'clock newsreader reads.
'The police are offering a reward,
Of half a million to record,
To police, the Mad Poet's name,
Or suspicions to end his game.'
Kram jolts up from his bed,
As fear in his imagination flows
An image of his capture grows
This reward will be my death's bed.
I'll be caught for sure, so must work quick,
And pile up the bodies high and thick.

12-9

An axe spirals through the air
With moonlit flickering upon
Then, into a man, hitting him square,
Into death's distant song.
Next day, cameras flash and glare,
As the police cordon off, within tape's snare.
Then, inside the police headquarters,
The world's press films in close quarters.
As Chief Constable Montgomery
With Rhys and Wallace
Discuss their hunt, flawless,
Giving a detailed, quick summary.
They then read aloud, the latest poem,
Hoping someone out there, might know him.

In the Prison Van

I sat in the prison van,
Watching the passing streets
People were walking free,
People were scorning me.

It was like a silent movie,
Behind dirty tinted plastic
Lost to me for years,
Lost within my tears.

My heart was now ablaze,
Twisted thoughts like a maze,
Cyclones of distant faces,
Cyclones of distant places.

I screwed up my fists,
I screwed up with tension,
I'm cattle cuffed in fright,
I'm cattle for the Isle of Wight.

Then, I had a vision
Of apathy and perdition
A horizon of expulsion
A horizon of ascension.

Calmness had engulfed me,
Peace of mind descended,
A smile radiated inside,
A smile of devilish pride.

Treated like cattle, I was,
Ordered by bellowing cogs,
Like an animal they made me,
Like an animal, I'll kill when free!

Yours sincerely,
The Mad Poet of London

12-11

They detail the info in slow burst,
Making sure they get it right.
'He probably went to Parkhurst,
Situated on the Isle of Wight.
Due to the details, we are sure,
He's been to prison before.
According to our profiler, Dr Destry,
He probably has a mental health history.
A history entwined with violence,
And is probably known for his poetry,
Inside and out, throughout the country.'
As the press and all listen in silence.
Then reporters shout aloud their questions,
As the murders increase, everyone's tensions.

12-12

'How many people have been killed?'
'That which we know of, four.'
To the reporters, it chilled.
'But, sir, aren't you sure?'
'No, we aren't sure of anything,
As this killer is a new being.
He's incredibly intelligent and cunning,
A legend he plans on becoming.
But his poetry is unique,
The Mad Poet of London is known,
To others, his awful poetry has sown
It's to them we want to speak.
With a half-a-million reward,
We're sure we'll strike a chord.'

12-13

'There's more to his profile!
He's between his mid-thirties.'
The reporters' cameras become hostile,
'Possibly up to his mid-forties.
He's most likely to be highly intelligent,
And of a criminal past, that's evident.
And probably suffers from mental illness,
Also, in the past, he has been fearless.
He's committed risky crimes, that we're sure,
A history of burglary,
A history of arson, in theory
And spent lengthy sentences behind the door.
He's definitely known for his love of poetry,
Especially by people who work in psychiatry.'

12-14

Kram sits with his psychiatrist,
The neatly dressed Dr Suman
As he listens with interest
To help Kram find a resolution.
'So, Kram, you struggle to sleep,
As to your past, it makes you weep.
What time do you take your medication?'
'About ten,' Kram lies under examination.
'But your mind is full of the past.'
'Yes, I still feel a lot of anger,
As my time in prison, does anchor.'
To this question, Kram's truth does cast.
'I'll up your meds, to see if it'll have effect,
And see if therapy to your memories can correct.'

12-15

Kram leaves the meeting deep in thought,
Hoping the meds decrease the voice,
Thankful for having so much support,
Wishing he could get hold of Royce.
I hope when the therapist is done,
I still have anger to carry on.
Shall I be truthful for once,
Or shall I lie and put on fronts?
At police HQ, Rhys to Wallace interrupts
'The tip lines, sir, have nonstop rang,
Thousands of names, so far, have sprang,
At which, to this investigation, it disrupts.
As we need tenfold, more in manpower,
As the tip lines, sir, names do shower.'

12-16

Kram's dark silhouette
Against the growing hallway fire
As he outwits the net,
To Royce's voice, like a town crier.
And within his memories, hated faces,
And to their deaths, he praises.
With a burning passion from his soul,
As he takes on the world by whole.
He disappears down a walkway,
As the house is now engulfed by fire
And to the darkness, smoke does spire,
As the shadows of death play.
Soon in the distance, sirens roar,
Of fire engines and the law.

12-17

Midday comes as the rain sweeps,
Kram leaves his room in gloom,
And down stairs he creeps
To frying bacon's rich perfume.
He outstretches a stiff posture,
As staff notices his departure.
'Hey, Kram, good morning or afternoon,
We see you've escaped your cocoon!'
Kram laughs and greets them all,
As he sees Henry cooking
And Sara, with a paper, smiling
With come-to-bed-eyes, like Lauren Bacall.
'Hey, Kram, the Mad Poet has struck again,
Listen to his latest poem; it's insane!'

The Schizophrenic

The world is raining down messages,
Around this graffitied bus stop
The air is gushing out memories,
As my wet hair, against face, flop.

As I tramp upon the ground
Leaning against the dirty plastic
Pushing against my weary, bent back
As my thoughts become speedily erratic.

Car pollution scents the air,
Like a force upon each lung
My ears turned down the noise,
As haunting voices to mind clung.

The world is endlessly saying,
The world's words do grimly bark,
I feel my time slowly coming,
As I wait for the cover of dark.

My killings repeat rain gossip,
My killings they laugh my name,
Even that breeze spells out death,
And even my tears glisten with pain.

Yours sincerely,
The Mad Poet of London

12-19

'It sounds like he needs meds,'
Says Kram. 'Like quick!'
As all staff laugh with nodding heads,
'He really sounds sick!'
Kram zips up his jacket, and leaves,
To the slanting rain, he receives.
As his calm demeanour is simply tiredness,
As to them, reading the poem, requires this.
They haven't a single clue?
Despite roughly knowing my past
And that mental illness has cast,
Across my past, all the way through.
Maybe they do, but can't believe,
Like, to this rain, I don't perceive.

12-20

Prison staff are sorting,
The parcels and numerous letters
And through all, exploring
For drugs or signs of criminal endeavours.
A sniffer dog goes over them all,
Across letters, it does crawl.
Before barking or pointing at some,
As a guard gives colleagues the thumb.
The morning is simply dull and ordinary,
At the X-ray machines shoot
Lighting up packages in pursuit
Hoping to find something out of the ordinary.
Then, to their surprise, the light goes red,
They open it up, and find a head.

12-21

'Dear Christ,' they shout out,
'It's the governor, Pete Edwardson.'
Their fears and anger sprout,
As they call for Officer Compton.
Wearing latex gloves, Compton nears,
And further confirms everyone's fears.
It is the prison governor's head,
Then, find a letter, in dread.
'This is the work of that psycho!
The Mad Poet of London,
From insanity's dungeon
He belongs in hell fires below,'
Compton says to the growing crowd,
As he opens the letter and reads aloud.

12-22

Solitary

You feel the cold, hard walls,
Slowly closing in
It fills your wiry veins,
With ice.

You hear your own heart,
Slowly beating
You feel the wasted years,
Slowly fleeting.

Routines always the same
You pace your cell,
You eat alone, you think alone,
You pace your cell.

Reality becomes blurred,
Erratic thoughts spiral,
You completely lose your mind,
Madness is viral.

In a state of delirium
You evoke the devil,
You curse all humanity,
And even your inner rebel.

Society's heading for oblivion,
Manufacturing people like me
My life's almost Dickensian
Murder's my *dernier cri*.

Yours sincerely,
The Mad Poet of London

Prison shocked by decapitated head,
Reads a newspaper headline,
Prison governor's body found in bed,
Spread out in a star-shaped design.
The article goes on,
As the world's eyes were fixed upon.
Terror runs through our streets,
The hunt for the killer heats.
The police up the reward to one million,
To all citizens' shock and surprise
Hoping it would lead to the demise,
Of the serial killer, reptilian.
As the world looks for the evil villain,
Kram keeps his chaos, and anger hidden.

12-24

One million reward has been made,
By the chief of police himself.
In front of cameras, as flashes cascade,
'Let's put this killer on the shelf.
As to all who knows him, he'll dread,
As to all loyalty, it will unthread.'
Kram switches off his television,
And snarls with deathly vision.
Back at HQ, Rhys pleads, 'It's too high,
We'll be inundated with cranks,
And to the chief, we'll owe thanks.'
As Rhys, in frustration, looks at the sky.
'I think, Rhys, it might just work,
And to the killer's friend, his mind might jerk.'

12-25

'Rhys, we have a suspect!
He's been named seventeen times,
And his past to the profile is correct,
With mental illness and past crimes.
We've sent a car to put him on surveillance,
Before interviewing, we must have patience.'
'At last, we have a name,
At last, we have someone in the frame.'
Kram, in his room, gets ready to leave,
As he's certain staff are asleep
And slowly breathes with breath deep,
He creeps out, into night's reprieve.
He unchains his mountain bike and rides,
And along London's roads, he glides.

12-26

After an hour and a half of cycling
Kram feels sweaty and hot,
But senses a car circling,
As he feels his stomach knot.
He feels unusually paranoid,
And feels aggressive, and annoyed.
But when Kram nears his target area,
He gets off bike, in sudden hysteria.
The car slows down near him,
And Kram gets ready to run,
As he handles his replica gun
As blood pumps to each limb.
The car stops as a man exits, with a girl,
And into a house, past Kram, they whirl.

12-27

Kram chains up his mountain bike,
And walks casually along,
As to paranoia, he manages to outpsych,
And to his plan, he feels strong.
At HQ, 'Rhys, we've picked the suspect up,
He was walking at night like a stray pup.
He's been arrested on suspicion of murder,
As he was seen with an axe, by an observer.'
The man paces the police cell,
Cursing and laughing aloud,
Shouting in posture proud,
'To Satan and hell, I dwell!'
Rhys watches him through the spyhole.
'Is he acting mad to outwit or control?'

12-28

The man freezes dead, in fright,
With an inner compulsion to flee
Kram stands in the light,
With a gun, towards the man's knee.
'I'll shoot you in the leg if you disobey.'
'I promise to do, what you say.'
Kram cuffs the man's hands behind his back.
'Your wife will be fine if you don't fight back,
Good, just keep calm, okay.'
They exit the house and into the man's car,
'Remember, do as I say, and you'll go far.'
Kram starts the engine and drives away.
'You're doing well, you'll be fine,
And maybe tonight, we'll drink wine.'

12-29

Wallace and Rhys stand by,
As a forensics officer approaches
Under the brightening sky
Tension to both encroaches.
The forensics officer hands Rhys a letter,
And to the crime's details, he feeds her.
'It looks like the killer, drove here to abuse,
The kidnapped victim, Mr Hughes.
Then decapitated him, before setting car alight,
The homeowners, the Andrews, they reacted,
To tackle the arsonist, in anger, they acted,
But were killed, too, all within one night.
He tied the Andrews uncomfortably tight,
Then, stabbed them both, with all his might.

12-30

'With all his might, you say?'
'Yes, I can see, their ribs were broken.'
The forensics officer then walks away,
As terror to Rhys's heart lay open.
'It looks like Mr Hughes worked in prison,
And both the Andrews were detectives risen.'
'Risen, sir?' she says in query.
'The Andrews were fast trackers in theory.
Simon Andrews had a degree in criminology,
From Nottingham University
And his wife Jane did study,
A master's degree in psychology.'
Wallace opens the letter in latex gloves,
And reads the poem, as words to air stubs.

The Killer's Song

I'm hunted by the law,
Through night's cold wind
To early frosty morn.

I'm the lost child of Cain,
Riding on the wave of revenge
Laughing with the dead.

I'm the maker of my soul,
Hell, crashes within, and
Silence and secrecy are my friends.

Yours sincerely,
The Mad Poet of London

12-32

With his head cocking to the side
Kram has a slight furrowing brow
With his legs outstretched wide
In thoughts, he does plough.
Should I go deep and express,
As my demons cause me distress.
For once in life, should I unload,
And how my enemy's faces glowed.
But I could slip and make a mistake,
And vent my urge to kill,
And to my killing spree, I could spill
Which would end my world and break.
Kram feels unease on catching a woman's eye,
Then lowers his head, as his thoughts fry.

12-33

Then, to Kram, a woman approaches alone,
'Hello, I'm the therapist; are you Kram?'
She says with a smile in a pleasant tone.
'Yes, I'm Kram.' He smiles. 'I'm the man.'
'Name's Anne; follow me please,' she replies,
And Kram follows with lowered eyes.
They enter a room calm and cool,
As he feels, like a pupil at school.
They sit in opposite chairs,
And they start off casually,
Both speaking naturally,
Before giving him some questionnaires.
'I do this before and after therapy,
It's to chart your progress with more clarity.'

12-34

Kram completes the questionnaires.
'Well finally we meet, at last.'
Kram, then firmly, declares,
'I'd like to discuss my past.
As I'm tormented by so much anger,
About prison, my curse, my cancer.
I was afraid to go in-depth inside,
As I feared my parole would be denied.
As inside, you have no confidentiality,
As everything you say gets reported
It's an unhelpful system distorted,
It wasn't therapy but a weird reality.
But now I'm on licence, mostly out the system,
I'm still walking in torment, like a victim.'

12-35

'I'm sorry you felt that way,
But with me, you can talk and get support
But I would like to convey,
That I have to write a report.
On summarising what we've discussed,
I hope to that you can adjust.'
'Who does the report go to?'
'To your psychiatrist to review.'
'But he could tell my probation officer!
To that, I feel nervous about
It could put my freedom in doubt,
I feel the fear, it would be sent to her.
And probation might cause me trouble,
I feel like I'm back in a bubble.'

12-36

'I shouldn't have come here, Anne,
I should've known,
I wish I were a tougher man,
As I fear prison's cyclone.
I feel I can't say what I want to say,
But I'm sure my memories will go away.'
'Maybe, Kram, we could work on a technique,
To make your memories weak.'
'Okay, I'll just focus on that,
As those faces make me depressed
Maybe working on that will be best,
I think to that, I'd like to chat.
You see, I want to live a happy life,
But I'm tormented by memory's knife.'

CANTO 13

13-1

Kram sits up, as night frights,
To the stars, he wonders
As World War One poetry ignites,
And war film's imagery, he plunders.
That within hell, only love does matter,
Despite machine guns' fiery clatter.
Across fields of blood red,
Across bodies cold and dead.
If only I could have someone to hold
Just for a moment
Christ, how potent
To my soul, so unloved and cold.
Damn, I must throw away, this feeling.
As he feels his soul screaming.

Christ, maybe I'll fall in love inside,
Sutcliff got loads of love letters,
When he was in Broadmoor's divide
Despite the law's fetters.
Yes, of course, I'll be adored,
With fame, I won't be ignored.
Kram laughs aloud as the ceiling spun,
As he reaches for his replica gun.
And points it up and smiles,
I will love again,
And avenge my pain.
Then, reaches over to his poetry files.
With a deep intensity, he reads through,
And picks out a poem to review.

Don't Let Your Soul Fall Like Rain

Don't let your soul fall like rain,
As laws and morals burn with hate
Fight, fight against the ball and chain.

The rich win again and again and again
As the poor suffer and cower in fear
Don't let your soul fall like rain.

Don't let your life be all in vain,
As life, obeying and praying is a waste
Fight, fight against the ball and chain.

From years inside, I was driven insane
As the rich fuckers fucked and played
Don't let your soul fall like rain.

Most are oppressed, whilst only a few reign,
So stop cowering but blaze up and rage
Fight, fight against the ball and chain.

Oppression and poverty are soul's reins,
That drives it along into the dust, so
Don't let your soul fall like rain,
Fight, fight against the ball and chain.

13-4

Christ, I was an idiot with Anne,
My growing fame is my cure,
I'll have everything I need to be a man,
As murder to soul does mature.
No more whimpering in loneliness,
As society, depriving me of love, was felonious.
My soul will blaze up and rage,
As my crimes on society are my stage.
Kram gets dressed for another kill,
Slips out of house, and to his bike,
And cycles fast, as thoughts strike
Then to a lower gear, up road's hill.
Idiot, I felt an urge to talk to Anne,
Stupid idiot. I must keep to my plan.

13-5

Rhys sits with DC Brook
Interviewing a nervous man
And to each question the man took
His fingers, through hair ran.
'Where were you on October the first?'
As the man drunk water in thirst.
'I was staying at my nan's,
Throughout night's hands.
Would you like her number,
As she's mostly at home, in low mood
I'm sure she'd remember as we ate food,
Then, on the settee, I did slumber.
But I do spend time, writing in rhyme,
After my release from doing time.'

13-6

Rhys, on mobile, talks to Wallace,
'He's definitely not our man,
And his alibi is flawless,
We've spoken to his nan.
And he received a takeaway late,
And the delivery driver, did also state.
As he remembered him from his photo,
As he looks strange, like Quasimodo.
He would've stood out a mile,
Especially with his limping gait
And all his poetry is about a snake,
It's in a completely different style.'
'I'm sorry, Rhys; come back straight,
I've just now heard, the killer struck late.'

'Christ, sir, it's only been four days after
The dreaded triple murders.'
As teenagers pass Rhys in laughter
As two eat huge burgers.
'Rhys, I feel these interviews are a waste,
As in the poem "The Killer's Song," he laced,
That silence and secrecy are his friends.'
'But maybe his feeling in poetry transcends.
His growing fear, of being grassed upon!'
'Maybe, Rhys, how many have you got today?'
'Interviews? About another two say,
I'll be finished by twelve or thereupon.'
'Good, Rhys, so this will conclude,
Nearly sixty suspects interviewed.'

13-8

Kram wakes up to midday's grace,
As he yawns and stretches
And to the cold, he does embrace
As his distant dream edges.
He gulps down a mug of milk,
Its coldness flowed down like silk.
He finishes off a cold, hard pizza,
Whilst doing squats as he completes a
Poem which bounced in his head
As words and style did rhyme
As he feels his heart's lost time
As a ballad in imagery spread.
In inspirational desire, he sits at his table,
And writes, a poem from mind's cradle.

Pearl

Through hell's fire, I pondered,
As thoughts spire.
Over black dust, and smoke
Red like rust.
Then to a nearby rock, on hearing
A ticking clock.
Then, a gentle tapping at my
Tired soul rapping.

I awoke to morning bleak, as
A voice did speak.
As to the dying embers, my
Dream distempers.
The voice was soul's beat, casting
Shadows in repeat.
Of a life in sorrow, entering,
Into the day hollow.

The bedsheets rustled, as I
Tossed and tussled.
I stretched my muscles, and
Cracked my knuckles.
Then a thought did soar, as
A vision thro' light bore.
Of a radiant girl, whom the
Fates named Pearl.

I knew her years ago, in
Memory's hazed plateau.
Like a ghost, washed upon
Heart's sandy coast.

Across the windswept beach, my
Pain dug like a leech.
Repeating as I grew sad, repeating,
As I grew mad.

Out of bed, I snapped, as the
Cold to body wrapped.
Into a life unloved, only memories,
Hold my beloved.
And into clock's hand, my future
Drifts like hourglass sand.
No pause of time, to hold my
Love in rhyme.

The day drifts to empty faces
Passing me as daylight races.
But as to my distant memories
My Pearl remedies.
Like a babbling brook, in
Nature's hook.
Surrounded by a cold city, which
To the suffering doesn't pity.

Then, into my deepest fears, I
Stood in tears.
My memories slide, and my
Thoughts dance wide.
As I picture the chasm, like
An evil phantom.
The years stolen, in one quick,
Courtroom motion.

Of the judges' gavel, smashing
On law's anvil.
Which propelled me, into a

Tormenting sea.
Where hope has vanished, and
Where love's been banished.
Decades gone and more, by
The unforgiving law.

Sitting here on a park bench,
Hiding in a trench.
From bullets of pain, as rats
Bite in a chain.
And water seeps thro', as I live in
The stagnant tableau.
Startled by park's stillness, I
Sit within my sickness.

But then a Pearl lit, lit up,
From a mind split.
Not the Pearl of yesteryear, but
The pearl of a devil's spear.
As of love's lost passion, to
Now, a different fashion.
To burn the world in fire, in
My hellish desire.

13-10

The man sleeps in night's arc,
Next to his dear wife
Kram stands in shadows dark,
With a kitchen knife.
The blade flickers off neon's kiss,
From a streetlight in night's abyss.
As his dream fades from sleep's grace,
The man awakes, and rubs his face.
Suddenly, he sits up in a jolt,
Resulting in Kram pouncing
With his knife announcing
As he punches Kram's head like a bolt.
Managing with force, to kick Kram off,
As his wife awakes, and also fought off.

13-11

They flick the bedside lights on
As Kram is taken aback
To Kram's face, the light glows upon
As Kram calls off the attack.
He runs out, from their home,
And into night's haunting dome.
'Call the fucking police, Christy,
As that man was no mystery.
It was the Mad Poet of London,
Who I'm sure, we've been faced,
And a million reward we'll be graced,
And to a hard day's work, we're done.
Keep in mind, every detail of his profile,
As his mug shot, should be on file.'

13-12

Kram runs hard to his stolen car,
Pulling off his wig and beard
He drives off with thoughts ajar,
As to his near capture, he feels weird.
Damn, they partially saw my face,
And to my mug shot, they could embrace.
Kram's disappointment echoes the night,
Of failing, and not leaving a poem to bite.
But cheers due to having on a disguise,
And layers of clothing to increase his size,
Which together will prevent his demise,
From a focused plan, careful and wise.
He creeps back home and into his bed,
To disappointment, fear and dread.

13-13

'Rhys, its Wallace; we've had a break!
The Mad Poet failed in an attack,
This is his first major mistake,
And two witnesses, in this case, might crack.'
'Brilliant, gov, I'll be in soon,
I felt something would occur, on this full moon.'
Rhys showers and dresses,
And to God she blesses.
The police headquarters has stirred,
As Rhys enters the incident room
As senior officers are in plume,
Talking about what has occurred.
'Rhys, Mr and Mrs Harvest,
Are working with our sketch artist.'

13-14

Kram studies the front page,
Of a newspaper with his sketched face
It looks of a much older age,
With beard, as long hair did lace.
Laced the edges of his features,
But as to his eyes, it reaches.
Which are near perfect, and his eyebrows,
As Kram's feelings of nervousness arouse.
Then, suddenly, a knock at his door
'Hi, Kram, the residence meeting is soon.'
'I thought, Miss, it was this afternoon?'
'That was the old time, please ignore.'
'I'll be down soon, Miss, okay.'
As Kram folds his newspaper away.

13-15

Kram sits within the residence meeting,
With four others and staff
Some on the sofa, others against the heating
Some stone-faced, as others laugh.
'Okay, everyone, today's agenda,' says Chris.
A senior member, holding his hand-written list.
'Firstly, we're starting a rota for,
For doing your washing machine chore.
So, everyone will have an equal access,
Instead of being left out.'
Mick defiantly growls throughout,
'Why should I follow what the rota says?'
'It's the new rules, I'm afraid, Mick!'
'It's bollocks, Chris; go on, then, be quick!'

13-16

'Secondly, as some of you are aware,
CCTV cameras will be fitted.'
Kram jolts up in a fixed stare.
'Linking to head office, it will be transmitted.'
'That, Chris, is fucking bollocks too!
Why do you all, have to view?'
'There's been many incidences,
Where the evidence is,
Involving unsigned-in, overnight visitors
And there's been violence,
We must have compliance,
This place, we must create safe perimeters,
And be a safe place for people to recover,
And not a place for people to suffer.'

13-17

Mick snarls, 'When will this happen?'
'Probably next month.'
Kram feels his plans blacken,
'One camera out back, one out front.
Also thirdly, staff will no longer sleep in,
As of next month, this will begin.
They'll be in the office working late,
This will benefit all,' Chris firmly does state.
The meeting ends, and everyone departs,
As Kram thinks of the composite sketch
And news of changes, to mind does etch,
As staff unknowingly to him, outsmarts.
I must increase my kills with more frequency,
As soon I must stop, due to zero privacy.

13-18

To kill at night in darkness's hand
Is so much easier,
I've killed once in light's expand,
It felt less superior.
As there were many people to see,
And could attack, and grab me.
As the noise breaking into a house,
Wouldn't at night stir a mouse.
But within daylight's breadth
A slight crack would alert,
And would be a dead cert,
To my capture and certain death.
Then to the hands, of prison's Third Reich,
Of vile guards, with hate and dislike.

13-19

People crowd around the newsagents,
To purchase a paper
Even the rough-sleeping vagrants
To the latest caper.
Of the Mad Poet of London's, latest crime,
Of a murder, and another poem in rhyme.
Even children in groups read aloud,
On buses, and in cafés, words shroud.
They read and repeat in delight,
Of the crime's horror and gore
And the killer's ease, at evading the law,
As the poem to raised voices takes flight.
A man by a wall reads to his friend,
As a poem to each, their minds transcend.

You Villains

So, who are the biggest villains,
From the David Cameron's Piggate scandal
Through history's death of millions
Vicious fucking governments, I can't handle.

Europeans were slaughtering all around,
On distant continents, in faraway land
From slavery, imperialism, or battleground
Decent Christian fellows, I can't understand.

Throughout history, the top reasons for war
Were economic gain and territory,
eager to earn a King's or God's awe,
legal terms for mass murder and robbery.

So why am I so hugely demonised,
A minor villain in all comparison
Society has hugely and deeply scrutinised,
Hypocrisy and apathy are my prison.

The definition of a criminal, you see,
Is not the act, for sure,
It's simply thinking yourself, you see,
Instead of obeying blindly society's law.

Thinking for yourself, they see as evil,
But free thought is what I adore,
Can't stand society's delusional drivel,
One day, I'll be knocking on your door.

Yours sincerely,
The Mad Poet of London

Five police killed in night of horror,
Reads the next day's headline.
A night of horrifying disorder
Reads the sub-headline.
Everyone is in complete shock,
Throughout society, the news does rock.
'How was that possible?' people say
As they listen to the news convey.
The crime is described in detail,
As the killer used a stolen car,
From his first victim, a Mr Nagar
Then, in his wake, a fiery bloody trail.
The newsreader reads, as the poem erupts,
With flustered looks, her voice thrusts.

My Time to Fight

I'll be written down in history,
The Mad Poet with venomous pride
You'll write the very worst,
You'll write like dirt,
But still, I fight.

As the moon clings to Earth
And stars to the night sky
I'll haunt the streets of London,
I'll haunt your fucking minds,
But still, I fight.

Does my arrogance upset you,
With my devilish mind collide
The police will try to break me,
And the laws aren't on my side,
But still, I fight.

Do you want to see me dead,
My body pumped full of lead,
Or when caught, bowing to authority,
With lowered, sorrowful eyes
No way, José, I will fight.

I've planned my magnum opus,
To shock the world to shreds
And cement my killing status,
Through lists of numbered dead.
I will fight.

Yours sincerely,
The Mad Poet of London

13-23

The incident room is bustling.
Wallace roars. 'We're upping night patrols,
In a number almost doubling
To stop this bastard's murderous goals.
And we're putting out composite sketch,
On television, every half-hour stretch.'
'Sir, he's probably upping his game,
Because he'll know, we'll have his name.'
'Right, Rhys, so it must closely resemble,
We must popularise the picture,
And with his poetry in the mixture
And, hopefully, this bastard will tremble.
As it should ring someone's memory bell,
So, we can kick this fucker, into a cell.'

13-24

The night draws in quick,
As roadblocks check all cars
Along main roads, thick
As anger and frustration scars.
Police ask for ID and question,
As car queues cause congestion.
Some cars, the police search thoroughly,
Resulting in many arrests of criminals, unholy.
The criminal community are enraged,
As their night activities are smoked out
As police stop and search if in doubt
Resulting in many criminals being caged.
But the Mad Poet remains free,
Within London's grey urban sea.

13-25

Throughout the daylight hours
Hundreds of interviews are undertaken,
As their notetaking overpowers
And names grow from tiplines, taken.
Many are released prisoners,
Whose names come from solicitors.
Many are ex-mental patients,
Some are even vagrants.
The police are getting nowhere,
As tension and urgency rise
And the panic is seen in the eyes,
Of senior police as they pull out hair.
Many active criminals hide and run,
As many are raided, in force by gun.

13-26

Pushing in rumpled, dirty clothes
Into the washing machine
In stooped posture, Kram loathes
His dull daily routine.
He switches it on, with a watery gaze,
As sunlight beams in dusty rays.
He clears his throat, and sips his tea,
As thoughts float, he rubs his knee.
Suddenly Kram hears loud knocks,
As staff member Tony answers
In nervousness, Kram's mind dances
As through his soul, anxiety rocks.
'Hello, sir. Could we speak to Mr Skyal,
I'm DC Allen.' 'I'm DS Abdel.'

13-27

The officers stand before Kram staring,
As storms lash Kram's sails
'They'd like to talk to you,' Tony says smiling,
As Kram's pleasant calm act, prevails.
Tony leaves and closes the door,
As their eyes, through Kram, bore.
'How can I help you?' Kram mutters,
Then DC Allen, speaks the line, that shudders.
'Your names come up in our enquiries!
And we'd like to ask you questions.'
'Well, that's fine; I've no objections.'
Kram replies, trying to act at ease.
Both detectives, on chairs, sit down,
As Kram fights back a worrying frown.

13-28

'Where were you on October 1st,
Between twelve to two in the morning?'
Kram replies, an answer rehearsed,
'I was here in bed sleeping.
I'm here almost all of the time,
As my drugs beckon sleep's climb.
You can speak to the night staff,
They'll help confirm on my behalf.'
'We'll check that out, sir.
Do you like writing poetry?'
'No, I'm more into my TV,
I did attempt writing whilst in stir.
But poetry isn't really my thing,
I'd rather listen to music and sing.'

13-29

'What size shoe d'you take?'
'My trainers are a size nine!'
As fear up Kram's back does snake,
In anxiety's design.
He told the truth as they could check,
As Kram does automatically expect.
'Can we check, please, sir.'
As Kram's anger does stir.
He slips off his well-used trainer,
'Excuse the smell. I go jogging,
It helps when thoughts need unblocking.'
As for this, being truthful is a no-brainer.
Because refusing would cause suspicion,
Plus, they don't need Kram's permission.

13-30

'Could we look at all your footwear?'
'Sure,' says Kram in unease,
As Kram puts his trainers on, in despair,
And twirls his chain of keys.
Upstairs they go, and enter Kram's room,
As Kram thanks God, he hid his costume.
Kram points to his Timberland boots,
And to newer trainers, Kram's finger shoots.
The officers examine his soles,
With an investigative stare
As Kram acts upright and square
And fears a room search, like hot coals.
As his smoky, hot disguise, lies under his bed,
And fear at that thought, rises in dread.

13-31

Kram bit into his lip
His gaze flits, as his tension balloons
He attempts a quip,
But panic in his mind consumes.
They put down his footwear,
And DC Neil gives Kram a stare.
'Could we have a handwriting sample?
Just a line will be ample.'
'Sure,' Kram replies and sits at his table,
As they give him an A4 sheet
For his pen to words greet
As Kram acts calm and stable.
'Write, *don't let your soul fall like rain,*
In capitals.' As Kram feels the strain.

13-32

Kram writes in his usual style,
As the poems, were in a blocked pace,
But still, he imagines his trial,
And in history books, he will grace.
On finishing the sentence,
He beckons acceptance.
By trying to look ordinary and sane,
As he returns the paper to their domain.
They thank Kram, with looks askew,
'You know this is really strange,
You haven't asked us to explain,
Why we're interested in you!'
'It did cross my mind, but I feel so tired,
As Olanzapine, to my mind, has rewired.

13-33

The police accept his reply,
And politely leave,
Kram gives out a deep sigh,
As thoughts weave.
I shouldn't have acted so casual,
Not questioning them was unnatural.
The police talk to Tony downstairs,
And soon they leave to Kram's stares.
Abdel remarks, 'I'm not happy with him!
To his name, we must mark
As further investigating, we must embark,
But today, we've more interviews to swim.'
'Next, we have a Mr Charles Anders,
Who online, the police and courts he slanders.'

13-34

From a draw, Kram grabs a knife,
Tonight, I'll do that judge,
And gut him with this knife,
And, finally, end, a lifetime's grudge.
He puts on latex gloves to find,
A prewritten poem, refined.
Hours pass as sky morphs to night,
As he leaves the house, in neon light.
He embraces the coldness on exit,
As he hears staff snore
Then, gently closes the door,
And to the dark streets, he does hit.
He makes his way to a stolen car,
And heads to London's suburbs far.

Kram, in the dark, clears his throat,
A man jolts up in bed
Fear and panic in him, float,
As the outside neon light fed.
'Hello, Judge, your Honourable Honour,
A true gentleman and scholar!'
'Are you the Mad Poet of London?'
'Yes, I've exited from your dungeon.'
'How did you enter my home?'
'Hammer and chisel at windows' edge,
As it makes the perfect wedge
To open sesame, which allows me in to roam.'
The judge stands up, 'Make it quick.'
'Like you did to me! You fucking prick!'

CANTO 14

14-1

Kram sits with fidgety hands,
In a downcast expression
And nearby, a thin man stands,
In the waiting room of probation.
'Have you read the newspaper?'
Says the thin man, as Kram's eyes' radar.
'About the murder of the judge,
Hanging from a window, in a bloody sludge.'
A woman pulls out a newspaper,
And starts reading the poem aloud,
As people visualise a haunting cloud
And in everyone's mind, emotion taper.
As her words bounce and jolts,
And imagery in madness, bolts.

The Cloud

Out of my cell window.

A cloud turns into a face,
In laughter, gently moving.

I answer it back with a laugh,
Back to its gentleness.

Its white, jolly bearded face,
Staring down at me.

My body embraces the cold,
A cold breeze from the window.

As autumn leaves flutter by,
Brushing sky, in beauty's haze.

But then I noticed it was not –
Not laughter, but a scream.

I screamed back.

Yours sincerely,
The Mad Poet of London

P.S. Enjoy the judge!

14-3

As the woman solemnly finishes,
Everyone falls into silence,
At the vivid poetic images
And the killer's steely defiance.
Suddenly, Iveta enters the room,
With a smile and gentle perfume.
Kram gets up, and walks towards,
To her office, through various doors.
'How've you been since last week,
Any problems or trouble?'
'No, as I live in a bubble,
And it's mostly to staff, I speak.'
'You got a visit from the police!'
As Kram's heart through his chest, beats.

14-4

'Yes, they questioned me for a while,
But I felt tired, lethargic, and dopey,
They were pleasant without a smile,
And checked my footwear, all three.
They asked for a sample of my writing,
And to a sentence, they stood reciting.
It felt like being peeled like an onion,
But they left in ease, job done.
I think it was about those murders,
By that psycho, the Mad Poet nut,
Who himself needs his freedom cut,
For his evil acts, in poetic murmurs.
As me, I'm a great fan of the police,
As I like security and living in peace.'

14-5

'It must have been a shock,
When they visited you.'
'Yes, as I was from dream's dock,
To the day, I just began to view.
As my meds make me sleep a lot,
It wasn't nice, being on the spot.
But that should be that,
I doubt again, they'd want to chat.'
'Let's hope not, as you're doing well,
Since being released
And you have ceased,
With crime, as you fear the cell.'
'Prison's a place for young men,
Never do I want that life again.'

14-6

As Kram's meeting is ending
They set a new date,
For next Wednesday, repeating
For again morning late.
He leaves the office to London's mouth,
As he senses, Iveta's fangs dig south.
Then, feels tension within his stomach,
But calms with his memories of Suffolk.
The many trees and empty fields
And gentle rivers flow
Flickering with light, slow
As the thick bushes shields.
From the vicious wind, as it invades,
On open fields, of cold green blades.

14-7

With narrowing eyes, he stares,
With iPod music on low
As sunlight to window glares
From the bus window.
He worries at the police's visit,
As it dampens his positive spirit.
But knows he's not high on their list,
As he killed that judge, in neon's mist.
In an adrenaline rush, he plans
To strike again hard
And to completely disregard
The nearing suspicions, of law's hands.
The judge's murder was a treat,
And tonight others, he will meet.

14-8

'Sir, I have an unsettling feeling,
That he'll strike tonight,
As a thick fog's been creeping
In this evening's light.'
'Yes, Rhys, it makes for a good cover,
And he'll be harder to discover.
I'll speak to the chief to further increase,
Patrols in cars and walking on beats.
There's not much more we can do,
All police, judges, and prison guards
Have been warned to make disregards,
To all noises outside, and not to pursue.
And make sure windows are locked,
And by bed, keep weapons propped.'

14-9

'Have you checked the windows?'
Dennis says with concern.
'Yes, that's twice you've asked,' Primrose,
She says, sounding very stern.
As they both get ready for bed,
They leave their fears, unsaid.
'Is your sister coming Tuesday?
As it's your mother's birthday.'
'Yes, Dennis, I spoke to her today,
This afternoon, is that okay?'
'Sure, I like your sister, Faye,
In the spare room, she can stay.'
By the bed, he lays his golf club,
As Primrose gives her hands a rub.

14-10

'Simon, is the bedroom door locked?
Jane asks sternly,
'Yeah, double bolted and blocked,'
And kisses her firmly.
'Don't worry, I've got the shotgun,
It's fully loaded; he won't outrun.'
'I hope that bastard chooses us,
And we'll kill him, without a fuss.'
'D'you think we'd get the reward?'
'I don't know; we should, Jane,
Christ, my anger, I won't contain,
Do you still have the sword?'
'Of course,' as she holds it overhead.
'Once you shoot, I'll make sure he's dead.'

14-11

'Mummy, why's Daddy saying we need
To move, at this time of night?'
'It's just temporary, sweety, for us to succeed,
It's a lovely night, for us to bite.
Your daddy has a new position at work,'
She shouts, 'Isn't that right, Kirk!'
'What's that, Sarah?' 'Your job change.'
'Err, yes, just a temporary exchange.
We'll be back in a month or so,
You'll see your friends again,
Please, sweety, don't complain,
I'll be making big money, you know!'
The little girl skips, away to her room,
As Kirk quickly walks out of the bathroom.

14-12

'Come, Kirk, it's getting late!
I'm not staying here another night,
Leaving our home, I really hate
But it's not safe, and I feel uptight.'
'They'll catch the Mad Poet soon,
And then to prison with my platoon.
For his time inside will be hell,
As us prison staff rule, and dwell.'
'I almost feel sorry for him, Kirk,
His days are numbered,
And then to a life doing bird,
Where prison staff seethe and lurk.'
'He'd be lucky to survive a year,
And no one will ever shed a tear.'

14-13

Kirk leaves the house with bags,
And piles them into the boot,
Whilst Sarah, with suitcase, drags
With their daughter in pursuit.
'The fog is really thick tonight.'
'Yes, Kirk, perfect to hide out of sight.'
'You're thinking what I'm thinking.'
As the world to them was shrinking.
They finally finish their packing,
And are sitting, tightly within
On feeling goosebumps, upon their skin
On hearing a man in distance, laughing.
'Come on, let's go,' as Kirk starts the engine,
They all drive away, with creeping tension.

14-14

Kram stands watching the car go,
As he tries controlling his laughter
Hiding in a garden's overflow
As he feels the fog rolling after.
In a blanket of cool mystery,
Feeling his destiny entwined with history.
Where his murderous ways define,
Of a true original, devilish design.
My whole life has come to this,
To kill in bloody rhyme
To define this modern time
And to revel in infamy's bliss.
For books and films, will be made about,
And my poems, through time, will shout.

Kram approaches the house casually,
And walks around the back,
Then, against the window, frantically
To window's edge he does attack.
Bang! Bang! With the hammer and chisel,
Then it opens without alarm or whistle.
If they, in fear, left this space,
Then this house I'll make my base.
Before entering, Kram looks around,
And sees nothing nor a dog's bark,
As he stands hidden in night's arc
As thick fog layers surround.
He crawls into the kitchen quickly,
As adrenalin makes him feel prickly.

He grabs a nearby knife,
And runs through house, high and low,
Being greeted by its empty life,
As he shouts to its comforting echo.
He puts the downstairs lights on,
And searches everywhere, thereupon.
He manages to find numerous keys,
With a seasoned burglar's ease.
And his breaths are relaxed and slow,
As slight paranoia, finally subsides,
He sits with confident and eager, vibes,
As his revengeful embers grow.
This house is my good fortune,
As I'll twist London in distortion.

14-17

He sees houses like a series of nests,
And within, sitting birds of law
And to set them on fire, the evil pests
In glee, with petrol through the front door.
He feels the second car lies in wait,
I think with fate, I have a date.
Thank God I've got its key,
And around London, I will flee.
In the hallway, Kram does go,
Twirling the keys with glee,
To the white Ford Capri,
Wow, that fucker can really go.
He also finds cash, in coins and notes,
And to a Shakespeare's sonnet, he invokes.

14-18

Then into the car, and to a garage, he drives
Buying petrol canisters, *red like the devil*
But he feels on him eyes,
As he fills them both, to top level.
He fills the car also, and pays,
As his slight nervousness, betrays.
He leaves with a feeling of suspicion,
But drives off to fulfil his mission.
Did my false beard give me away,
As up close it fails,
In its finer details
Of its glossy-coloured grey.
Well, what can they do? I paid in cash!
To houses I must dash, to burn down to ash.

14-19

The fire in the hallway roars,
Like some demonic spirit
Through several houses' front doors
Throughout London, Kram did visit.
People scream at the bellowing smoke,
Through upstairs windows, in fogs cloak.
Some immediately jumped from windows,
And from downstairs doorways, fire glows.
Dennis and Primrose panic,
As smoke creeps under the door
'Phone the fire brigade, and the law.'
As Dennis's eyes look quite manic.
'This fire could be the Mad Poet's bait,
As he hides quietly, outside in wait!'

14-20

'Jane, help throw the mattress out,
It'll soften our fall.'
'But the Mad Poet might be on scout,
In the foggy, shadowy shawl.'
'It's either him, or burn to death,
As soon the smoke, will be our breath.'
Jane and Simon push it out,
As the flames from stairs sprout.
They then jump one by one,
Landing in a gasp, hard
Whilst keeping on guard
As Simon still has the gun.
Simon shouts at the shadowy darkness,
'Come on, cunt; try and harm us.'

14-21

Kram rummages through the house
Taking all valuables
A Rolex watch and diamond mouse,
On a charm bracelet with animals.
He fills the car, bags high,
Then makes a coffee, to defy.
The beckoning claws of nearby sleep,
As aching muscles begin to creep.
He decides to cook a meal,
And switches the TV on
As fighters box upon
As bacon's smell, makes its appeal.
Then a lager from the fridge's light,
As thoughts of his fires, excite.

14-22

Rhys gets a call on her mobile,
And reaches for it quick,
'Rhys, it's Wallace; it's like Chernobyl,
Five arsons in fog thick.
Four have died, in a firestorm's laugh,
They were either police or prison staff.
He poured petrol through the letterbox,
And through our patrols, he did outfox.
All in one fucking night!
Four bloody murders
Six attempted murders
All in fog's dim light.
But a man witnessed, he drove a Capri,
As he heard a car start, and went to see.'

'Has a poem been found near?'
'Yes, Rhys, it's shite
That's why I was called to arson's sphere,
Of towering houses alight.'
'I'll be there, sir,' she gasps,
'What's the poem say,' Rhys asks.
'Wait a minute, it's in a bag.'
As Rhys waits, for seconds to drag.
'It's best to meet me at police HQ,
As each scene is clogged,
As the streets are logged.
By people and reporters anew.
Here we are, Rhys; are you listening?'
As Wallace reads with voice bristling.

14-24

Liquid Night Flowing

Liquid night flowing,
Into dark eternity.

Full moon glowing,
An ancient deity.

About my killing,
And building notoriety.

Blood I'm spilling,
I'm attacking society.

I'll continue killing,
During my liberty.

My soul's rising,
From prison's captivity.

Bastards are dying,
Into bloody infinity.

Liquid night flowing,
Into dark eternity.

Yours sincerely,
The Mad Poet of London

14-25

In the early morning
A garage gets a newspaper delivery,
As the customers start swarming
In early bird activity.
On the front-page cover,
The headlines smother.
Arsons rock the city,
And to another poem, gritty
The Mad Poet strikes again,
The garage attendant read,
As a thought storms his head
Of that suspicious man so plain.
'Shit, I've got to call the police,'
He says to his boss, a man obese.

14-26

'Gov, we received a panicked call,
He might have been caught on CCTV.
But a downturned hat did sprawl,
And to his face you can't see.
Also, gov, the man wrote down his number,
As he was suspicious, of that punter.
I've run it through already,
It belongs to a Sarah Manfredi.'
'Okay, Rhys, let's go there quick,
She could be another victim.'
'Yes, gov, she lives in Wyndham,
Christ, we're close! I feel sick!'
They head off, as sirens blare,
Through dozy traffic, in sunlight's glare.

14-27

Kram makes a fried breakfast,
And is eating it slow,
As his happiness has grasp
From night's fiery inferno.
The bacon and eggs melt in his mouth,
As a bottle of beer flows down south.
His excitement flutters in his belly,
As another poem falls like confetti.
He clears and cleans his plate,
And gets ready to leave,
And wipes his mouth on sleeve,
As morning time is getting late.
He needs to get home, before it's too late,
As he begins to fear, the prison gate.

14-28

Rhys and Wallace are driving,
Mentally replaying past events
With anger and frustration rising
As slow-moving traffic prevents.
Finally, they reach Wyndham,
To another possible victim.
'Shall I call forensics?
With their intricate technics.'
'Not yet, Rhys, until we investigate,
As it might be a false lead
As we're not guaranteed
Someone else, passed through heaven's gate.'
They arrive at the house and are lost for words,
As the house's still quietness, unnerves.

14-29

Kram drives back to his home,
As the car radio blares
With scanning eyes, he does comb,
As thoughts on mind flares.
Rhys notices the windows are open,
And waves of smoke, are in motion.
'Sir, he's set the house on fire.'
'Make the call to prevent a pyre.'
Wallace goes around back,
And sees a window open,
And enters in devotion,
To save someone from fire's flak.
The sofa downstairs was now ablaze,
As Wallace hunts round the smoky maze.

14-30

He sees no bodies about,
And coughs due to the smoke
Of that, he is of no doubt,
As he starts to choke.
He's unable to go downstairs,
As now, a fire upstairs blares.
He opens the bedroom windows,
And across the conservatory, he tiptoes.
Then jumps to the ground,
With a desperate gasp, he starts coughing
As he feels his head throbbing
Under the sky in rain surround.
'Rhys... there's... no... body to be... seen,
So... why burn... the... house?... Routine?'

14-31

Kram parks in a layby
Near his chained-up bike
He glances round in reply,
To the early morning strike.
A strike of faces in rainy air,
And women in beauty fair.
He leaves the car with a bag,
In hope today, of selling his swag.
He closes the car door behind
And walks back home,
To staff's watchful zone,
But knows to his activities they're blind.
He enters quick, looking smart,
And to his room, he does dart.

14-32

He lays his goods upon his bed,
And picks out the gold,
Then he hears footsteps in dread
As he feels icy cold.
Knock. Knock. Knock. At his door,
As he covers gold and clears floor.
He opens the door sheepishly,
As he in tone asks peevishly.
'Yes, can I help?' He grins.
'What time did you leave today?'
'After night staff left, okay.'
'So, you weren't out all night?' She spins.
'Oh no – as to the rules I am aware,
I just wanted some early morning air.'

14-33

'Kram, love, if you leave at night,
You must always inform staff.'
'Miss, I know that, alright!'
As Kram trickles out a laugh.
She walks away. He closes the door,
Feeling anger, as she lays down the law.
'Power corrupts,' he murmurs,
As he focusses on his murders.
He switches the TV on, and learns,
With open mouth to the news
To hear the reporters' reviews
As to the death list, he yearns.
Then feels annoyed on killing just four,
As he feels he deserves, a much higher score.

14-34

Firemen finally dowse the fire,
As smoke, from windows, to house, masks
And Rhys stares at the smoky spire,
As Wallace in ambulance, coughs and gasps.
'If… he uses… that car… again,
Then… soon… we'll end his… campaign.
Put… all… cars on alert… for the… Capri,
All… throughout London's urban sea.
As it's in a distinctive style
Which he… could use again
Maybe in North London's terrain
We could have him in a short while.'
'Christ, sir, I hope he uses it again.'
As she wipes her face within the rain.

14-35

Kram stares out the window,
As it's hit by rain
He feels a warm, comforting glow,
Like he's taken cocaine.
I've done over a dozen murders.
Which are only precursors.
To a bigger, more terrifying campaign,
Where pigs will die in poetry's domain.
He breathes slow, as memories take over,
Mixed with fantasies ablaze,
As to the sky, he does gaze,
As clouds in grey skies, rollover.
He then finds inspiration to write,
Another poem to shock and fright.

CANTO 15

15-1

2016, February the fourteenth
The night's wind howls outside,
To the moon's bequeath
An eeriness for ghosts to hide.
The shadowy figure of Kram stands
In black, to the night he commands.
An owl hoo-hoos,
As the wind to the night, brews.
As Mr and Mrs Stapleton sleep
A loud smash comes to their surprise,
The car alarm to night defies,
Mr Stapleton from his bed, makes a leap.
He stares out of the bedroom window,
As a mist of rain sweeps in neon glow.

15-2

'Emma, I'm sure it's him!'
As car lights in orange flashes
'I can feel his circling fin.'
Then, out of bedroom, he dashes.
He puts on a sweater, and slips on boots,
As fear to anger dilutes.
'Dean, be careful; he'll be armed!'
'But not with a gun, so don't be alarmed.'
He picks up a long-handled axe,
And walks outside in a violent show,
In shouts, beckoning his foe,
As night's cold hand to him smacks.
'Is that all you can do,' Dean lashes,
As rage and anger within him crashes.

15-3

Suddenly, he feels incredibly spooked,
Like a rabbit caught in a snare
His stomach churned and looped,
Noticing a cloud, a breath of air.
He grips the axe handle tight,
And steps further into the night.
Suddenly, a crossbow bolt enters his chest,
And he falls, dying, nearing death's rest.
Kram's dark figure stands in eerie pose,
As Emma's screams from window drown,
He drops a letter to shock the town,
Then, into night's blanket, he quickly goes.
Dean's eyes close, as death embraces,
Still, Emma screams, as terror races.

15-4

Emma grabs her mobile and calls,
To alert the police
And to the bedroom window, she falls
Still screaming to release.
'He's just struck seconds ago,
I live at fifteen Elm Lane, Walthamstow!
The Mad Poet of London struck again,
He must still be in North East's domain.'
The phone rings, 'Sir, Rhys, it's him!
He struck minutes ago,
In the heart of Walthamstow.
I've called patrol cars to search within.'
'Good, Rhys, thanks for letting me know,
Where abouts in Walthamstow?'

15-5

Kram drives along the A503,
With the window down
As the radio blares Paganini
As he exits, Walthamstow's town.
He feels the heat of capture entrench,
As the knots in his stomach, clench.
The wind pricks his eyes in tears,
As aloud, he curses, whilst changing gears.
Suddenly, blue lights, flash behind
From an unmarked police car
Peddle down, he accelerates far,
And skids around a corner blind.
The high-speed chase is on,
As Kram's nerves grapple upon.

15-6

He heads on the A406,
As neon flickers off, rain-drizzled roads,
And swallows saliva like little bricks
As fear and anger within a shout, explodes.
He sets fire to the passenger seat,
And crashes purposely in the street.
He bails out the car and sprints,
Hoping the fire, will burn his prints.
Then, fast across Forest Road
As his determination hardens
He darts into back gardens,
As to his nerve, sirens erode.
Kram bolts over walls, and crosses lawns,
As police strategically place their pawns.

15-7

With increased blood flow
And a pounding in his ears
He runs through night's plateau,
As finally, his thinking clears.
I must hide within a home,
As the police in this area will comb
Under a car is no good
Nor in a tree in some wood.
Suddenly, he sees a small window open,
And nears it slow, as sirens harass,
Walking across neatly cut grass,
As he looks upon, night's dark ocean.
Kram picks up, a nearby patio chair,
And places it under, window's glare.

15-8

Suddenly, he fears a barking dog,
As his hand reaches through
The house is drenched in mystery's fog,
As its stillness swirls like stew.
Could there be a family, or old lady,
Or a young mother with a baby?
He manages to open the larger window,
Opening carefully and extremely slow.
He moves objects from the windowsill,
And quietly crawls in
As goosebumps crawl upon skin
And finally, he's in with great skill.
And closes the windows quick,
Each window with a click.

15-9

He stares outside for any signs,
Of heads above walls
Or any movement which defines,
Nature's outlined halls.
The house is in unnatural silence,
As he walks through in defiance.
Still no sound of a large dog's bark
As to the police, it will mark.
He enters the living room slow,
With clenched, grinding teeth
As his heart pounds beneath
In the uncharted plateau.
Then, a sight catches Kram's eyes,
As he looks toward it, in surprise.

15-10

In minutes, police swarm the streets,
As the Capri, lies in a fiery blaze,
At his near capture, the tension heats,
'He's within this urban maze,
He's here! We've got him, gov!'
As Wallace hears a helicopter above.
The burning Capri, which lights the night,
Is doused to smoke, from firemen's fight.
More police descend around,
As Wallace gives an icy stare
And directs in order, to snare,
As the stress and urgency compound.
Dozens of police climb over walls,
As dawn to night, slowly crawls.

15-11

Rhys arrives with a positive gaze,
As she searches for Wallace
As hundreds of police scour the maze,
The results of a plan, flawless.
She sees Wallace and nears,
As the helicopter circles its spheres.
'Sir, are we sure it's him?'
'Yes, but like a fox, he did swim,
Into the urban jungle
A brick-blocked maze
Where his cunning does blaze
As we, outside, struggle.'
'Sir, shall we search everyone's home?'
'Yes, Rhys, every inch, we must comb.'

15-12

The dawn pushes further forward,
As night fades, goodbye
And the stars behind clouds orchard
Fizzle out and die.
'Let's start searching houses thoroughly,
Slowly, carefully, and meticulously.'
'Great, sir, as he couldn't have escaped,
But must work fast, or he'll create,
More death, pain, and bloodshed
As he's nothing else to lose
As he heads for prison's abuse
By guards holding a grudge, with faces red.'
They begin searching houses in five,
With full determination, will, and drive.

15-13

Police knock the door loudly,
As a frazzled old man
Who stands facing them proudly,
In blurry-eyed scan.
'Why are you banging so?'
'Sir, we need to undergo!'
'Why do you force me to emerge?'
'Sir, we need to conduct a search.'
'It's not even fucking six!'
'Sir, please let us in.
A search we must begin.'
The old man, to his ear, picks.
'Can you tell me why?'
Then in force police push by.

15-14

Other police teams knock on doors,
Then, stand still and wait,
As a cold breeze gives pause
To bemused residents hate.
'Sir, we need to go in hard,
With battering ram's shard.
And along with armed police,
To cut this morning's peace.'
'I know, I'm going to make that call,
As it's extremely vital
We can't stand by idle,
As death on people might fall.'
Police on doors, continue to bang,
As some enter within, like in a gang.

15-15

A nearby resident enters their car
And drives off slowly,
Towards a roadblock, as police bar
The police look closely.
The car stops and is searched by three,
As a police officer asks for ID.
'We need to search your house,
As we're looking for a louse.'
The man hands over his keys
'Please let yourself in,
But my wife's asleep within
As she works trimming trees.
And I must dash to work, as I'm late,
As I'm the one that unlocks the gate.'

15-16

Then suddenly, another car approaches,
And goes through the same procedure,
As their desperation encroaches,
As Rhys almost has a seizure.
She orders on radio in a voice coarse,
'Just fucking break in and use force!
We can't approach this soft-hearted,
As the killer for months has outsmarted!'
Nearby, a motorbike slowly glides,
When, suddenly, a man runs in haste
And desperately, the police give chase,
And within seconds, the man collides.
Slam-bang, he runs straight into a trap,
As the many police, close in the gap.

15-17

Rhys breathes a sigh of relief,
'Sir, we've bloody got him!'
In delight to her chief
As many police to the man, swim.
Rhys looks up at the road block,
As all the police cheered in shock.
And notices the motorbike speed away,
Towards the crisp brightness, of a new day.
Rhys and Wallace go to view,
Their tired breathless prisoner
Who in gasps asks for a solicitor,
As police cars surround, in flashing blue.
The prisoner growls and shouts abuse,
Until he goes silent, running out of juice.

15-18

The man sits handcuffed in the car,
And shouts in defiance
As Wallace stands by door, ajar,
Giving the man guidance.
'It'll be better if you simply confess,
As to your crimes, you must address.'
'I'm not saying a bloody thing,
And I want a solicitor to ring.'
Wallace slams the car door,
And turns in concern, to Rhys,
As her tension decreased
'To his hideout, we must explore!'
'He came out from number sixteen,
Over there from the door, dark green.'

15-19

Wallace and Rhys cautiously enter,
With a team following behind
As Rhys's hand in anxiety does tremor,
On expecting dead bodies to find.
Rhys enters a small bedroom,
As her vision focuses on zoom.
To a girl looking at her in terror,
As Rhys's staring eyes, scare her.
'You've arrested my Ricky!
I can't live without him,
As our hearts together swim.'
As Rhys's head spun. 'Ricky?'
'Ricky! The man you arrested.'
Suddenly, terror to Rhys has nested.

15-20

'Sir, we might have trouble!' Rhys shouts,
'The man arrested, might not be our man!
That numpty is this girl's spouse.'
'Quick, we must surround and scan.'
'Look, Miss, how long has Ricky been living here?'
'Why, what's he done; is it severe?'
Wallace approaches the terrified girl,
And requestions her, in terror's whirl.
'He's my loving loyal partner,
He jumped bail ten months ago,
And we've been hiding here, you know,
He's been working as a freelance gardner.'
'And last night was Ricky with you?'
'Yes, like always, as he wants to stay out of view!'

15-21

Rhys thinks back to the biker,
In fear and growing dread
Gliding by like a strolling tiger,
Through the net, he had thread.
'What house did the biker come from?'
As her words struck like a bomb.
'I think number thirty-six,'
Says eagerly, PC Wicks.
They all run to that house, in crushing fear.
And smashed down the door, with kicks,
And enter fast, as unease picks,
Towards gurgling moans, they all can hear.
Within seconds, things quickly take shape,
On finding two people, tied with tape.

15-22

The biker speeds through traffic,
And down a quiet road
Then, in jolts, stops in panic,
As adrenalin to heart rode.
He gets off, feeling slightly weird,
As Kram laughs, through his beard.
He pulls off his helmet very slowly,
As the camera-free street feels cosy.
He puts on his baseball cap,
And carries the helmet under arm,
And walks casually, as not to alarm,
As to his whereabouts, he tries to map.
He walks for an hour before stopping,
Then, on the buses, he goes hopping.

15-23

With a need to jump and scream
With a build-up of energy,
From an intense moment extreme,
Of being in dire jeopardy.
He discards the helmet in an alley,
And walks down homelessness valley.
Then discards his biker jacket,
To someone with a drug habit.
With his beard and wig, now in bag
He takes the Tube home,
And styles his hair with comb,
And walks the street with a swag.
He finally enters his home, silently,
And walks his room, stridently.

15-24

But in his room, in a dizzy spell,
Due to the close near miss
And how close he was to a cell,
Where madness does kiss.
He stares at the sky, to a thick cloud,
As his inner tension's shroud.
I want everlasting fame,
And need more kills to gain.
I need my crimes, in the halls of infamy,
Where the world will sit and wonder
As terror and fame will thunder
So, history will sing my symphony.
And the system will get the blame,
For prison guard's abuse, driving me insane.

15-25

He undresses and sleeps,
To dream's twisted game,
Where cupid weeps
And energy to muscles regain.
Five hours later, he awakes trembling,
As in his thoughts, he's wrestling.
I'd easily give up fame for love,
In a flash, like hand to glove.
He sieves through memory's ark,
As he thinks of his Gloria
And of love, and sexual euphoria
His pot of gold, at the end of rainbow's arc.
If only I could turn back time,
I'd happily surrender my life of crime.

In a know not what, feeling,
He rummages through his papers,
And as he sits kneeling,
His mind to prison tapers.
He finds his old address book, in tatters,
And through his memories, he scatters.
But amazingly finds details of Pete,
As to whom he'd like to meet.
He reads Pete's brother's address,
In the suburbs of Hackney
I could get a taxi,
Smack bang, within London's mess.
In eagerness, he picks up his phone,
And in fear, that Pete might disown.

Rubbing the back of his neck
He holds his phone,
As to the number he does check,
As thoughts cyclone.
Was it just prison patter, prison chatter,
Or was Pete a nutter, on prison's platter?
Was Pete really a friend?
Or was Pete all pretend?
Kram ignores his thoughts and dials,
And within seconds, a familiar voice
To the cockney accent he does rejoice,
'Hi, Pete, mate, how's it going.' Kram smiles.
Pete cheers, 'Alright, Kram, are you on the out?'
'Yeah, to the new me, they weren't in doubt!'

15-28

Pete laughs. 'When d'you get out?'
'Twenty-fifteen,
I went through the mental health route,
Done twelve years clean.
How about you, Pete?'
'Four years, before hitting the street.'
'Christ, four years on a recall,
That's a long way to fall!'
'D'you want to meet up, Kram,
Sometime this week
So, we can speak,
Or maybe sniff a gram?'
'I don't do drugs, Pete, anymore,
As I'm blood tested, regularly by law.'

15-29

After arranging a time to meet
Kram lies back and relaxes.
Finally, he has a friend to greet,
But emotionally, he collapses.
He screws up his face at his near demise,
Then, an image of Gloria, in light does rise.
For days, he ignores the media coverage,
Regularly drinking for Dutch courage.
Finally, the day comes, to meet Pete in the park,
And, on meeting, they both hug,
As prison memories to both did tug
And they quickly regain friendship's spark.
'Christ, Kram, it's good to see you; been a while!'
Kram nods with a huge Cheshire cat smile.

15-30

They both spoke in-depth,
About their pasts
And to future's breadth
As darkness casts.
'Kram, I want to be remembered,
Not to die old, looking weathered.
I'm a fragile old man to passers-by,
I want to end my life on a high!'
'Don't you fear dying inside?
In a dark, dank cell.'
'No, for I'm a rebel,
Inside, I have respect and pride!
Outside, I'm seen as a coffin dodger,
An old nineteen-seventies rocker.'

15-31

The talk turns to Kram's true love,
His girl in Kent, the beautiful Gloria
And in advice, Pete does shove
In him becoming more of a warrior.
'As no faint heart won fair maid,
And to your crimes, Kram, you've paid.
So, to Kent, you must find her,
Don't let life go by in a blur.'
'I've been thinking about hiring,
A private detective
A person effective
In spying and finding.
As I need to know if she's single,
To see whether I should try and rekindle.'

'Do you have money?' asks Pete,
'I'm on high disability allowance,
And after each payment, I secrete
In bank, soon I'll have thousands.
I'm planning on taking driving lessons,
In probably fortnightly sessions.
And to pass my motorbike CBT,
So, legally, I can venture London's Sea.
But I still have plans to make money,
As I'll never get a job,
As I'm also a snob
And ambitious, I know that sounds funny.
But I need to get rich, so peace will fall,
And around my life, I can build a wall.'

15-33

Kram leaves Pete feeling upbeat,
And of Gloria, his mind lights
In which he'd love to meet,
But the urge to kill, he fights.
After a week, he goes to see,
A private investigator for a fee.
To find Gloria, his lost love,
As he feels fate pull, and shove.
The P.I. asks him question after question,
'Gloria Seth, she's of Irish descent,
And of meeting her again, I have dreamt,
No, I've no photos in possession.
Yes, she worked and lived in Kent,
But before, she lived and worked in Ghent.'

15-34

The meeting ends quick,
And after paying the fee
He thanks the P.I. named Mick,
And is told there's no guarantee.
But Kram feels hopeful,
And left the office thoughtful.
He unbuttons his top shirt button,
As he enters the city's oven.
He phones Pete, telling him of the news,
And listens to Pete's encouragement steer,
Then, suddenly, police, in Kram's vision, appear,
Kram steps back while paranoia stews.
They soon pass Kram, without a stare,
As Kram recites Keats, like one would a prayer.

15-35

As the days pass by, he rests,
Watching DVDs and TV
No poetry or murder infests,
His mind's clear and free.
Only thoughts of love and passion,
And to himself, he has compassion.
To give himself a chance to be loved,
Without baying for revenge in blood.
He talks to staff and laughs,
And meets up with Pete,
In cafés, and walking the street
And in positive thoughts, he baths.
Then, suddenly, midday, he gets a call,
From P.I. Mick, in Kent's sprawl.

'I've found her, it wasn't too hard,
As she has an unusual surname.'
To Kram's mind, memories bombard
As he wonders if she looks the same.
'Meet me at the office tomorrow.'
As Kram feels, to his past, sorrow.
'Will about eleven be okay?'
Kram agrees, as he feels himself sway.
The phone goes silent,
As he stares outside his window
Listening to birds' crescendo
In tweets and coos defiant.
Kram suddenly feels himself cry,
But soon realises, his eyes are dry.

CANTO 16

Kram finishes a hand-rolled cigarette,
Then heads inside into the P.I.'s office.
As bad news to mind, does threat
That Gloria had a wedding chorus.
Or a boyfriend big and ugly,
Photo'd beside her smugly.
He makes odd noises in his throat,
As he feels his stomach float.
He knocks and enters civilly,
As he's motioned to a chair
Kram looks at him, square,
As the investigator reads out her activity.
After he finishes, he passes him a photo,
Of Gloria, standing next to a shop logo.

324

16-2

'Is that where she works?'
'From my studies. Yes.'
'And she's not with any jerks?'
'Not that I can assess.
As she lives alone in a flat,
She has a child and a cat.
And works at that very store,
And finishes work by four.'
Stiffening hair at the nape of Kram's neck
He begins to feel a light-headedness,
At the investigator's success
As he keeps his uncertainty in check.
Unsure, if to meet her or not,
As to him, she might have forgot.

16-3

Kram pays him and leaves,
With Gloria's details and photo in hand
Through the street, he weaves
As thoughts jammed.
I've planned my revenge for so long,
In murder, on poetry's song.
But I can't take revenge, and be in love,
As I need hatred, to myself shove.
To shove me into a killing ferocity,
And to write my dark poetry
From my memory's tree.
But if I fall deep in love, it's gonna be,
The destruction and end of my killing spirit,
And remove my life's meaning, in a minute.

16-4

As fame, my life's meaning
It's my essence,
As Satre put it, in being –
And nothingness lessons.
Without poetry and murder,
I'm like an insignificant searcher.
Lost in normal everyday life,
And coping with everyday strife.
Love couldn't be, my life's meaning,
It doesn't make sense,
As my experiences condense
Into turning me into a killer scheming.
Could I have both? Love and murder?
Could there really be, such a merger?

16-5

Or is life and meaning absurd,
As Camus puts it
In The Stranger, *blurred,*
As reality split.
Am I fighting against nothing,
In my cunning and cutting?
Should I simply give up, on life?
Or simply end it all, with a knife?
But fame has become my friend,
History will know me,
Forever to eternity
And without fame. My life will end.
As fame, turns mortals into gods,
And unknowns, are simply frogs.

16-6

Fame is the ultimate meaning of life,
Throughout our history
From good acts to bad, using a knife,
It's in our genetic victory.
Either to have children, so genes live on,
Or by doing a deed or creating upon.
From hand paintings in a cave,
Or in churches to God, people pray.
Even a gravestone's etched name
To social media
It covers the encyclopaedia,
Our strong urge to scream or proclaim.
That I was here, world! Remember!
Hoping our existence will ripple or tremor.

16-7

Kram pockets the small photo,
And walks home in a daze,
As he creates a moto
To the world and history, I'll blaze,
Loves for the hoi polloi,
And in poetry to the world, I'll toy.
He finally enters his house,
And upstairs quietly like a mouse.
He puts on his stereo, to Ella Fitzgerald
And puts the photo on show.
As words and rhymes grow
Then texts Pete, as his thoughts had settled.
He pulls out a pad, and fountain pen,
As another poem marks its way again.

Text if You Must

Text if you must, but to talk is better,
As words to soul do enter
Like food from a simple seed
Or becoming high from simple weed.

Text if you must, but life is short,
And conversations do transport,
Passions and treasured memories
As others have through the centuries.

Text if you must, but feelings are hidden,
As they're short and poorly written
Not expressing much, only the profane
As you restrain your better brain.

Text if you must, but keep in mind,
Your lives aren't designed,
To be expressed so small and quick
Save it for epitaphs on gravestones thick.

Suddenly his mobile phone rings
And he could see it's Pete,
To his phone, he quickly swings
Brilliant, what a treat.
'Kram, what the hell are you doing?
To give up on Gloria, and end pursuing.
If you give up, forever, you'll wonder,
And your head on lonely nights will thunder.
You've got to speak to Gloria,
Life's short and quick
If you don't you're thick
And you'll endlessly suffer in dysphoria.
As love, is life's precious gemstone,
Where your heart, and soul, cyclone.'

'You think, Pete, I should…'
'Kram, go after her!
It's for your own good,
Go after her!'
'Okay, Pete, I'll write her a letter,
I think that will be better.'
'No, Kram, speak to her face to face,
In Kent, at her workplace.'
'Okay, I'll leave tomorrow,
But if she's not interested, that's it!'
'Right, Kram. Only then end it,
As long as you've tried. Go tomorrow.'
Pete hangs up, and Kram feels different,
More stirred up and belligerent.

16-11

The rain pours down in Kent,
As Kram walks the streets
Thinking of words to represent
His feelings when he meets.
Shall I be open and outright,
To speak straight to ignite.
But she might panic and run,
But so, what! I've neither lost nor won.
He presses his lips together,
With tightening fists
As repeating sentences twists
And curses the wet weather.
He stands still, outside the store,
As to his anxiety, he does ignore.

16-12

Suddenly, he sees Gloria leaving,
Umbrella against the rain
He follows in street, weaving,
In composure, he tries to maintain.
Then he feels his moment's come,
And feels his heavy heart drum.
He runs up behind, then walks beside,
As her expression, of hurt and shock collide.
'Fuck! It's you! Kram!' (pause) 'It's been so long.'
'Hello, Gloria, I've been inside,
But I never forgot you, in prison's divide
I made a mistake; I got it wrong.'
'What do you want after all this time,
Do you live nearby, in Kent's chime?'

16-13

'No, I don't live in Kent,
I'm here to meet you,
For years inside, I've spent
Thinking about you.
You're the only girl I ever loved.'
She smiles as memories flood.
'I was wondering in Kent's terrain,
If we could get to know each other again.'
'You haven't changed much, Kram,
Just more grey hair
And that intense stare.'
Kram feels her presence slam.
'I don't want to go out with a criminal,
I have troubles; I don't want additional.'

16-14

'I've gone straight, and on life licence,
Living in London city
And to the law, I'm in compliance,
In city's pollution, stark and gritty.
I'd love to move down here,
To Kent's coastal frontier.
And breathe air from Kent's fresh sea,
And walking the long sandy beach, free.'
'I don't know, Kram; you hurt me,
You just upped and left
For years, I felt bereft.'
'Sorry, look, let's talk over tea,
Would you like to talk, in a café?'
'Sorry, I need to collect my daughter, May.'

16-15

'Oh,' Kram replies in sadness.
'But we could talk along the way,
And share my umbrella from sky's badness,
Come on, Kram, I can't delay.'
Kram smiles, and ducks umbrella's gauze,
As the rain taps upon in applause.
They laugh and break the tension,
As they reminisce and make a connection.
'The school's near; you better leave
As it'll confuse May;
Kram, is that okay?'
'Sure.' As Kram feels a reprieve.
'Can I have your number, to talk more?
As I think we both have issues, to explore.'

16-16

'Christ, Kram, it's been years, people change!'
'We had something, Gloria, time can't break,
And time can't break or rearrange –
Our fate. And departing forever will be a mistake.'
Gloria reluctantly and in an uncertain voice
Tells Kram, her number making his soul rejoice.
Then he presses the dial to make sure,
So, it's fixed in his phone, secure.
Kram quickly kisses her cheek,
To Gloria surprise
As he caught her eyes
In delight, as she is unable to speak.
'I'll call tonight, when I get back.'
As he slips phone into pocket's crack.

Kram sits on the train, packed,
To empty oval faces
As meeting Gloria makes impact
As his heart laces.
I want to give up my war,
I don't want to fight the law.
I want to feel love again,
No more bad memories and crying in pain.
Kram's phone lights up, and rings
And he recognises it's Pete.
'Pete, I'm truly complete,
I feel true happiness in cupid's strings.'
'Brilliant, Kram, let's meet up again,
As it'll be the last time, I'll explain.'

16-18

'Okay, Pete, how about tonight?
Come to my place,
You've got the address, right?
And to your news I'll embrace.'
'Okay, Kram, I'll be there by eight,
But I don't want a debate.'
Suddenly, the phone goes dead,
As he sees a new future ahead.
After pocketing the phone
He rubs his forearms,
As he remembers her charms
He no longer feels alone.
But what's wrong with Pete,
Is he in legal trouble, feeling heat?

Kram walks home smiling,
As people look at him oddly
As a poem in mind is compiling
In happiness, it does embody.
No more killing
And blood spilling.
I'm going to move down to Kent,
And live in peace, 100%.
He enters his home to frying vapour,
As he, in turn, greets,
Then, to his room, he fleets,
And pulls out sheets of lined paper.
He closes his door, and writes,
As to a poem, his pen fights.

My Soul Took Flight

The clouds kissed the sky,
In love, they drifted
By a wind that doesn't reply
But still committed.

I fell asleep in a forest,
Listening to nature's songs
Early in the month of August
It's where my heart belongs.

I dreamt of my lost love,
Like a wild, flying bird,
Who glided from above,
As my lonely soul stirred.

I awoke to hope fulfilled,
As stars talked at night
The tale they told drilled,
And my soul took flight.

16-21

Kram's lying half asleep, on his bed,
When rapid knocks to mind, recall
Kram jolts up, as the fear spread,
As he felt police on skin crawl.
'Your friend Pete is here.'
'Thanks, Sara, I'll soon appear.'
Kram quickly hides his poetry,
And tidies his bed in symmetry.
He then jogs in joy downstairs,
And beckons Pete up to his room
And closes the door to resume,
As Kram looks at Pete, and prepares.
Kram cuts straight to the chase,
'What's happening with you? What awaits?'

16-22

'I'm sick of this normal life,
People just see me as an old man,
Not a street fighter with a knife
Or a cunning criminal with a plan.
I want to be an infamous villain,
As I miss my real home: in prison.
I've spent over thirty-five years inside,
And inside, I felt huge pride.
But now I'm nothing, a nobody,
I want one last glorious stand,
A shootout from a bank job planned,
And in cunning and gallantry, I'll embody.
I've already got an automatic gun,
And bullets for the police to succumb.'

16-23

Kram fell silent and in awe,
As he understood completely
As both their lives had been raw,
By a system that routinely.
Destroys lives and condemns,
To inhuman sentences, it stems.
Then, to rough, brutal places,
Locked in small coffin spaces.
Which feeds frustrations and anger,
Until you're released
And brutality ceased,
But forever attached to prison's anchor.
As society will always shun you,
Apart from other criminals, with jobs to do.

'I have a solution that will blast,
You into eternal infamy
And regarding your plan, fame won't last,
Despite a gunfight symphony.
I trust you more than anyone I've known,
So, I'll confess the seed I've sown.
Have you heard of the Mad Poet,
Who kills serpents of the lowest?'
'Yes, of course, a fucking star, a legend.'
'Well, Pete, it's me,
Killing in London's Sea
And I'm being hunted by all, every second.'
'Wow, Kram, fucking hell!
You've grown far from prison's cell.'

'What's your plan, Kram? Please tell.
D'you want a partner?
To kill and bid scum farewell,
For I'm much smarter.
Much smarter than a normal villain,
And I don't follow religion.
And so, I don't fear hell or the devil,
Or laws or prison's vessel.'
'No, after meeting Gloria, I'm giving up,
My beloved murder spree
As with Gloria, I want to be,
But your plans, I want to disrupt.
As we could set you up to true infamy,
And you'll be talked about for infinity.'

'For you can wear my bloody crown,
And I, the reward
As the police are starting to surround
I feel their sword.'
'Christ, yes, I'll admit to being the poet,
But we need evidence to show it.
I love it, Kram, as I'm sixty-seven,
I've not long for villainy's heaven.'
'We'll plan for your arrest to be dramatic,
And fulfil that planned shootout,
For your lovely bullets to sprout
You must get more guns, a semi-automatic.'
'Fuck, Kram, I'll have everlasting fame,
And throughout history, they'll know my name.'

16-27

'How much is the reward, Kram?'
'An unbelievable, one million!'
'Holy shit, Kram, damn,
A golden ticket, a fucking million!
There's one thing for it to be perfect,
For you to send me money direct.
Yearly, so I can live like a king,
On the high-security wing.'
'Sure thing Pete, that's a deal
But I'm going to have to kill again,
And this time, I need to obtain,
Your mobile to start the wheel.
But first, Pete, are you totally sure?
Will worldwide infamy really cure?'

16-28

'I've never been so sure, mate,
All my life, I've wanted fame,
That thought keeps me up late,
For all of history, knowing my name.
I'd love to be remembered like the Krays,
Or like Charles Bronson in prison's craze.
To have films made about me,
And books, TV programmes for all to see.
It's always been my dream, mate,
Like you, too, Kram
Before love to you, swam,
Besides living on a pension, by the state,
Is the worst thing to happen to me,
After my colourful life, don't you see?'

16-29

'But what about you, mate?
This is your shout!
As this name carries such weight
In prison, you'll have such clout.
I remember you're interested in fame,
Like me, we're both the same!'
'I know it's early days with her,
But I feel the spark, as it were.
It's love, I want more than anything,
And maybe children, too
It's Gloria I need to pursue,
I can't explain it, but she's everything.'
'Kram, you're an old romantic,
And a legend, this plan's fucking fantastic.'

16-30

'First, Pete, we must leave evidence,
That you're the killer,
That will make huge resonance,
For police to trigger.
A deep and larger investigation,
From their city-wide operation.
As a confession won't be good enough,
We must work hard to bluff.
Your mobile I'll take with me,
And leave it on
For signal masts to zone upon
Which is great evidence for them to see.
As forensic digital evidence, is highly regarded,
And your confession, they'll believe wholehearted.'

16-31

'Handwriting too, we could use,
As to the poems I write.
I carefully to each letter produce,
A style that isn't quite right.
I'll teach you how to write,
As each letter, I keep tight.
Also, at the end of my next poem,
You can write a message to show them.
Something in your natural style,
Something cheeky
Something freaky
Something evil, creepy and hostile.
Plus, what size shoes do you fill,
I'm a nine, but wear a size ten when I kill.'

'Wearing a larger shoe when you kill is clever!'
Most criminals don't plan in so much detail,
I'm an eight, which works, however –
They might test my poetry skills, which will derail!'
'No, Pete, as you will also write out, my poems,
Etched with vexed emotions.
As some haven't been published at all,
And the unpublished will install.
The belief you're the Mad Poet –
Of London.
It'll be like a smoking gun,
And having my disguises will prove it.
Here's a poem, write a message below.'
As Pete dons gloves for handwriting's show.

Revenge Yourself

Revenge yourself
For everything they did
When you were inside.

Let the storm of pain,
Burn through,
Every atom, ablaze.

Let your rage beat,
Your heart
And fire your blood.

Let memory's rivers,
Fuel your mind,
And aim your focus.

As to kill takes everything,
Your all, in order to
Revenge yourself.

Yours sincerely,
The Mad Poet of London

P.S. *You bastards will never come close to capturing me!*
As I'm just beginning my murderous game.
Xxx

16-34

'Tomorrow night, I'll strike,
As tonight I need to rest,
And need to plan and outpsych,
As I'm still shaken from near arrest.'
'Has anyone seen your face?
Or heard your voice embrace?'
'To most who've seen me, I've killed,
Others were in terror, when blood was spilled.
Plus, I always wore my fake beard,
And long-haired wig.
Careful of CCTV's jig
To purposely look terrifying and weird.
To make it harder for police to capture,
And enabling me to enter infamy's rapture.'

16-35

'Fuck, Kram, this is unbelievable,
That the killer is you!
You seem so normal and agreeable,
Not the man I knew.'
'The system turned me into this man,
But now it's ending, as love I've planned.
If you meet me, tomorrow night,
And bring your mobile, for them to sight.
In signal mast's bite
At victims' home
Or near that zone
Meet me at seven, alright.'
'Okay, where shall we meet here?'
'No, on airplane mode, near park's sphere.'

CANTO 17

17-1

Pete enters the Metropolitan HQ,
And asks to speak to DCI Wallace
'As I've got information anew,
About the Mad Poet, which is flawless.
I want my info and details recorded,
As after his arrest, I want to be rewarded.'
Soon, Wallace and Rhys walk out,
And greet Pete with smiles and doubt.
Pete is sitting in a side room office,
And tells all, whilst being recorded,
After two hours, they're all exhausted
And upstairs, police break out in chorus.
'We've got the bastard, we've got the poet,
We must carefully arrest him, and not blow it.'

17-2

Armed response surrounds Kram's home,
And outside his bedroom window
As Kram naps in dream's dome
Whilst the police go upstairs on tiptoe.
Suddenly, Kram awakes to a smash,
As the police through his door crash.
Kram shouts in complete shock,
As desperate thoughts flock.
'It was Pete, wasn't it, who grassed,
That fucking rat!' Kram shouts,
As a violent thought sprouts,
Kram looks around, aghast.
His legs go weak, and he sinks through bed,
As the world in light, turns to red.

17-3

Suddenly Kram awakes to knocks,
Into reality, he enters
As he realises, he was in dream's box,
As the knocks to Kram, ventures.
'Kram, are you okay? We heard shouting.'
As Kram felt he was drowning.
'I'm okay, Sara, I was having a nightmare,
I was dreaming of being chased by a bear.'
Sara laughs and walks away,
As Kram feels clammy and sticky
Realising, telling Pete was risky,
Especially with a large reward at play.
He pulls shoulders back to a straight posture,
As doubts and betrayal to mind, foster.

17-4

With a fluttering feeling in his chest
Muscles tighten in readiness,
He stares out the window, feeling stressed,
Akin to a leafless tree's emptiness.
He decides to give Gloria a call,
They chatter as feelings sprawl.
Laughing over good faraway memories,
As laughter to Kram's stress, remedies.
He finishes the call and drinks coffee,
As his nightmare beckons near
Could Pete grass, and end love's sphere?
As Kram chews several pieces of toffee.
He feels the darkness encroaching,
As the time to meet Pete, is approaching.

17-5

Seven o'clock nears, and Kram leaves,
Towards the nearby park
His heart beats, as his focus weaves,
As he quickly walks in the dark.
He inhales deeply, then gently sneezes,
Then on seeing Pete, he instantly freezes.
And glances the streets for police on obs,
Or a suspicious character walking dogs.
Kram calls Pete, 'Alright.'
Pete replies the same,
As Kram feels he's in the frame,
And prepares to fight.
But still, no police running eagerly towards,
And against his ears, the wind's rough cords.

17-6

He walks up to Pete, close,
And studies for nervous ticks
Or anything to diagnose,
Signs of betrayal or tricks.
Could the police strike now,
In armed rage to me, plough.
Or will they follow me tonight,
Catching me, in red-handed spite.
'Here in this bag, is my phone and gun,
As the gun, I thought you'd like!
Where in London will you strike?'
As Kram feels wary, of the words he spun.
'I don't know, Pete, I haven't decided yet,
As I must be clever, to outwit the net.'

17-7

Pete continues with small talk,
Before Kram returns back home
In a long-strided, determined walk
Carrying the bag, with the gun and phone.
He feels them tight in his pocket,
As sudden tension does rocket.
He makes his way to his room,
And stands still within the gloom.
He waits for police to enter like thunder,
Pointing towards him, with machine guns,
He feels the pressure, weigh in tonnes,
As images of prison, swallow him under.
Seconds turn to minutes turn to hours,
As dread to excitement towers.

17-8

Two o'clock in the morning comes
As Kram exudes excitement and focus
As he feels the night's distant drums
While fantasising of murder ferocious.
I feel better to keep it simple,
But in my heart, I want a triple.
If Pete went to the police
It's now to my plans; they'd cease.
As I'm disguised and carrying
My poem and murder kit,
Which the courts would commit,
Me to a whole life-term, entwining.
He stares at the eerie neon-lit street,
And heads towards a stolen car's retreat.

17-9

He sits in the driver's seat,
As he wipes his forehead
Still no movement on booted feet
As he drives off, focusing ahead.
Does Pete really want such infamy,
And die in prison's cemetery.
And to give up pocketing a million,
And live comfortably as a civilian.
Kram's unease rises and falls,
As thoughts intermix
As memories kicks
Of life in a cell, where madness calls.
The police don't know. I'm in luck,
As I'm sure, they would've struck.

17-10

Kram pulls up on a quiet street,
And looks behind for movement,
Then, relaxes back into his seat,
And smiles in amusement.
He smokes calmly, whilst eyeing the target,
As his mind rolls, in fantasies carpet.
A noise suddenly pounds his heart,
As he crouches down, his eyes dart.
He then sees a cat clawing a bin bag,
And to that, he deeply sighs
As his world nearly dies
Then switches Pete's phone on to flag.
He then slips it into his coat pocket,
And into hell, he plans to make a deposit.

17-11

Dan awakes to the dog barking,
Along with his wife, Drew.
Dan shouts, 'Stop fucking barking!'
As his wife throws a pillow, too.
Dan stumbles downstairs tiredly
As the dog continues barking defiantly.
He makes an uncomfortable swallow,
As he enters darkness, cold and hollow.
The dog barks toward outside
As Dan hears cats fighting
And exits back door like lightning,
As feelings of tension and anger slide.
Like cascading rocks, from high on up,
On seeing a stereo, playing near a cup.

17-12

The stereo's music is of cats fighting,
Feeling anxiety, he switches it off.
And suddenly, a dark vision striking,
With an axe, lobbing Dan's head off.
Blood spurts like an erupting volcano,
Then, to the dog, Kram kicks low.
And enters the house sprightly,
And up to the bedroom precisely.
He puts the bedroom light on
So, Drew could see his face,
And in aghast, her thoughts lace
'It's you, Skyal, that mad con!'
Kram laughs. 'That's right, Miss D,
And finally, to you, I'm glad to see.'

17-13

'Gov, he took out two prison
Officers, from Wormwood Scrubs,
And I have an idea, listen.'
As Wallace, in tiredness, shrugs.
'Let's stop probing suspects, from all directions,
Just suspects from certain, prison connections.
I feel he targets staff, from prisons he's been in,
I feel this strongly, beneath my skin.'
'Okay, Rhys, that's good; move on it,
As his poetry, to prison, does reminisce,
But remember, he might have foreseen this,
He's bright despite a mind unfit.
Also, the time between murders is shortening.'
'I know, sir; it's incredibly alarming.'

17-14

Kram's in Pete's flat, watching TV,
As the newsreader reads
Of the latest poem and killing spree,
And pleading the public for leads.
'Christ, Kram, you're a fucking star,
Two screws dead in a world bizarre.'
'Well, Pete, you'll be the star soon,
And your life and trial, will balloon.'
They slurp their tea and dunk a biscuit,
While going over their careful plan
As ideas, strategies, and poetry ran,
As Kram focuses, on the million-pound ticket.
Nearing the evening, Kram walks home,
Together with Pete's mobile phone.

17-15

Kram lies on his bed in rest,
To jazz and classical music
Lying in boxers and a vest
As he sees murder, as therapeutic.
He listens to Rimsky-Korsakov on CD,
Humming to the "Flight of the Bumblebee".
It excites Kram with its rhythm,
As he squints light, like a prism.
He then closes his door, and writes,
As words and rhythm take flight
As anger and passion ignite
With the music in heights delights.
He crosses words out, and rewrites
As he feels, Kent's windswept beach, bites.

Coup de Grace

The death blow came,
As I hit him with my hammer
I had become insane,
As he laughed at my stammer.

He cowered with fear,
The stupid little street punk
As I stole his gear
His mind-blowing strong skunk.

The rain soon came,
As I decided to walk it off
Murder was my game,
As I listened to Rimsky-Korsakov.

It soon became night,
To the "Flight of the Bumblebee"
As my chest felt tight
As I reached the moonlit sea.

But then I started feeling guilt
But why? He was such a pest,
I stared at the sea's quilt,
Deep in thought, *interemptus est.*

I stayed awake till day,
As I felt like a mad beast
So, off to church to pray,
Before confessing to a priest.

17-17

Kram studies the poem up close,
And quickly tears it up,
'No, it's stupid and morose.'
As he sips tea from a cup.
He crosses his arms and studies the sky,
Almost expectantly waiting for a reply.
As clouds try covering the stars' light,
Distant freckles on a cold night.
Kram breathes deeply, through his nose,
Audibly, like wind through a tunnel,
As he sits proud, daring for trouble,
Then gets dressed in clean clothes.
He sits on his bed for time to pass,
Waiting to kill, on dew-tipped grass.

17-18

Suddenly, a poem springs to mind
As he needs to leave clues
Towards Pete, the criminal mastermind
To cement the ruse.
Pete is London, born and bred,
This must be clear; it must be said.
He has a slight cockney accent,
This must be in a poem's content.
He sits at his desk and writes,
As ideas beckon, and feelings supply
To a poem, with words that fly,
And soon finishes as time bites.
He reads the poem again and again,
Making changes as ideas rain.

To Hell, I'm Falling

I dashed with fire,
I danced in flames,
In poetry's spire
I broke my chains.

I kill the police,
Like a farmer culling
Disrupting all peace
A legend becoming.

The devil I kissed,
To feel complete
In whisky's mist
On London's Street.

From prison's choir
You did select,
A hymn of fire
In cockney dialect.

I love my work,
It's my calling,
A life berserk
To hell, I'm falling.

Yours sincerely,
The Mad Poet of London

17-20

A sudden thrust and cut went,
As the man lay dying
The sword flickered flames hell-bent,
As he feels revenge, smiling.
He leaves a letter and walks away,
Scanning the streets in survey.
He drives off in a stolen car,
As he lights up his Havana cigar.
He makes his way to the next target,
And parks in wait,
In a housing estate
Near a dirty yellow skip, holding carpet.
Kram waits for his target's shift to end,
In anticipation for bullets to send.

17-21

Finally, the red Escort came,
With his target inside
Kram exits his car to claim,
Another life denied.
In creating more misery in prison,
Where Kram's anger had risen.
Kram runs across the car park,
As his target exits to morning's arc.
Suddenly, he shoots the target dead,
The shot loudly echoes,
And attention arrows
Of the bullet straight to his head.
Kram drops the letter in haste,
Then, back to his car, no time to waste.

Wallace and Rhys are on the scene,
As they're terrified at the news
That a gun was used by the machine
A killing machine's night, of targeting screws.
'When is this madness going to end,
And how can citizens defend.'
'I agree, Rhys, these killings are demoralising,
Two prison officers are completely horrifying.'
A forensics officer approaches Wallace
With a sealed bag
As Wallace smokes a fag
For nicotine's rush and solace.
With latex gloves, he opens the bag,
And reads the letter, as he takes a drag.

17-23

I'm a Type of Man

I'm a type of man, who can't fit in
A type that can't sit still,
I play with death and always win,
As I travel this city at will.

I soar the streets, in trails of blood,
And blaze my name in red,
I think I'm cursed with gypsy blood,
As the judge sentenced me dead.

If I'd gone straight, I would've died,
As your prisons had broken my will
And if I had died, it would've been suicide,
As all I wanted, was to kill.

Yours sincerely,
The Mad Poet of London

17-24

Pete and Kram were in talks deep,
Discussing cleaning out Pete's flat
So, no natural writing of Pete would creep,
As on all papers, poems' styled writing must splat.
With only Pete's fingerprints upon,
As the police must be convinced on
That Pete is the true writer of the poetry,
That has terrified an entire country.
And that Pete, without doubt, is the killer,
As ballistics will match Pete's gun
To nights of terror, he has spun,
And in blood, London flows like a river.
And to a legend, soaked and drenched in blood,
A man from prison the devil has loved.

17-25

Kram also advises Pete, to fire the gun,
Quietly alone, at night in the park
So, he's touched by gunpowder spun,
As it's essential, he must embark.
Also, maybe he could do a bank robbery,
An elite crime in criminal snobbery.
Where he could engage in a shootout,
From the bank's door or hideout.
Kram then washes with petrol,
To clean himself of gunpowder residue
And to all the evidence, he wishes adieu
So, no evidence from flat will unroll.
To spoil their carefully worked out plan,
Which through history, Pete's name will span.

17-26

'I've changed my mind, about the banks,
As I'd love to kill some police,
As killing police, to robbery outranks
And to my name, infamy would increase.'
'Okay, so when I go to police HQ,
You must live elsewhere without leaving a clue.'
'I'll sleep at my brother's flat,
And kill police like swatting flies, flat.
They both laugh in joy and delight,
As both were on the same page
Like performers on a stage
Engaged in a historical, glorious fight.
Pete, with cunning, mischievous eyes,
'I'm going to leave the police a nice surprise!'

17-27

A week passes by, for Kram and Pete
Carefully sorting, their living spaces out.
No more killing in London's heat,
The reward for Kram, is what it's all about.
Kram thinks carefully of what to say,
As doubt and fear of imprisonment sway.
But beams at the idea of being a millionaire,
As a life, full of peace and love, will repair.
Kram feels close to the perfect life,
A sunny, flowery seafront home
With birdsong around his loving dome
No more pain, loneliness, or strife.
Kram nears the bustling police headquarters,
Surrounded by police and CCTV recorders.

17-28

Kram walks into the crowded building,
And heads towards reception
Which he found funny and thrilling
As he focuses on the deception.
He lines up in a suited queue,
As tension and nervousness begins to stew.
Before he knew it, he was face to face,
With a woman smiling, in pleasant grace.
'Hello, I'd like to talk to DCI Wallace.'
'Okay, sir, can I take your name?'
'Kram Skyal. I know the Mad Poet's name!
Could I talk quietly, in a side room office.'
'If you care to take a seat, sir, please.'
Kram nods, as people stare, in murmuring seas.

17-29

'Hello, sir, I'm DC Pascal.'
The suited officer says as he approaches.
'Hello, I'm Kram Skyal.'
As great nervousness to Kram encroaches.
'Follow me, please; we can speak in private.
There's much chaos here, in this current climate.'
Kram feels a twitching in the extremities,
To be in such a building, with his enemies.
They enter a small room with CCTV,
And they sit opposite ends at a table,
As Kram focuses on remaining stable
With deep breaths, picturing a Kent's sea.
'I'm here not just about the reward,
As too much blood has been poured.'

17-30

'The man you're looking for is called,
Pete Townsend.
He showed me in poetry scrawled.
He was my friend.'
'You say he was your friend?'
'Yes, but now that's at an end!
He's such an evil, horrible man,
With such an evil, horrible plan.
He showed me the gun, an automatic,
Which he said he used last week,
In a drunken state, he let leak,
And showed me a poem, quite dramatic.
I heard it all in the news, which confirmed,
As he has hatred for his sentences, deserved.'

17-31

'All he does is piss and moan,
Every fucking day!
He's like a child, he hasn't grown,
And you know what they say!
If you can't do the time,
Don't do the crime.
He still hasn't learnt that lesson,
He's constantly in depression and aggression!'
'What's his address please?'
'Twenty-five, Artillery Way, Hackney
Also, the fact that he
Has no other friends to breeze.
To breeze the days in casual chatter,
And to talk of poetry, in bloody splatter.'

17-32

'Here! I've written down my details.'
Kram to Pascal, passes a piece of paper,
In unfamiliar writing trails
As DC Pascal's mind does taper.
'So, this, Kram, is your mobile,
I see also you're a London local.'
'Yes, also, could my identity be hidden,
As there are nutters out there in Britain.
Who'd view me as a grass or such,
And see this maniac as a hero,
Fucking numpties with IQs near zero
Who'd love to kick me in the crotch.'
'Of course, Mr Skyal, that's not a problem,
No journalist will name you, in their column.'

17-33

DC Pascal questions Kram further
As Kram speaks in a sincere tone
Pretending to fear another murder,
Worried his pretence has blown.
But after a good full hour,
His confidence does flower.
He shakes Pascal's hand and leaves,
Back to the free air he breathes.
DC Pascal runs to the incident room,
And shares the news with all,
As he stretches posture tall,
To a good suspect, they can zoom.
The incident room buzzes with excitement,
On reading Pete's record of confinement.

17-34

'Pascal, isn't he too old to be our man?
As our killer is fit and strong!'
'I was told he exercises, all he can,
Even inside with sentences long.'
'We need to brief armed response,
We must act quick, as kills he wants!
Maybe tonight he plans to kill,
Maybe tonight, I feel that chill.'
Kram sits in his room, quiet and still,
Watching the film *Zodiac*
As he stretches his back
Wondering how many police Pete will kill.
What did Pete mean by surprise?
What was behind those mischievous eyes?

CANTO 18

18-1

Armed police block off the street,
And surround Pete's flat
Then, with a ram, they beat,
Against the door, to wall flat.
'Armed police!' they shout on entry,
'Show yourself to us, gently!'
They head towards the bedroom,
But everything's tidy, like a hotel room.
After five minutes of searching high and low
They announce Pete isn't here,
Then, plainclothes police soon appear,
And to a detailed search, they go.
DC Andrews approaches a wooden chest,
Hoping for poetry, he unlocks it with zest.

Suddenly, on opening, an explosion rocks,
Ripping DC Andrews' head off,
And to all around, the blast shocks
In smoke, they all cough.
Others are wounded by shrapnel,
Whilst wrapped in a cordite smell.
Rhys stumbles out into the air,
And shouts on radio, in despair.
'Get ambulances now, officers down!
And the bomb squad fast
As another bomb might blast
And clear residents from all around.'
DCI Wallace runs straight to Rhys.
'Pete's name and photo we must release.'

18-3

Kram and Gloria walk, as happiness shows,
The busy streets of Margate,
As their comfort, with each other grows,
In their casual date.
Kram glances at his watch,
As he steps up a notch.
And expresses to Gloria his intentions,
That he has strong romantic inclinations.
Gloria blushes and explains outright,
That honesty is love's key,
And to unlock it, he'll be free,
And without it, love won't take flight.
Kram looks solemnly, as his heart pounds,
As those words dance, like devilish clowns.

18-4

Pete sits in his brother's flat,
Watching the television,
And suddenly, whilst they both chat
Pete talks of his killing mission.
Suddenly, a photo of Pete is on screen,
As Pete's blood is full of caffeine.
Which heightens his focus to kill,
Feeling an urge with an unbreakable will.
Pete looks at his watch and leaves,
As his brother is left in shock
And unable to quite take stock,
In a daze, he rapidly breathes.
In a baseball hat, Pete storms the street,
As he feels the hunt, burn with heat.

18-5

A forensic officer approaches Rhys,
And passes her a letter,
Which is addressed to the police,
As she feels slightly better.
She approaches DCI Wallace,
As he, in kind, gives solace.
With an arm across her shoulder,
As he fights the urge, to enfold her.
'Rhys, this is coming to an end.'
As they put on gloves tight,
As anger and tension fight
'Soon, we'll either kill, or apprehend.'
She opens the letter and reads,
As the words to their mind, recedes.

The Absurd

Where is my rehabilitation?
As I'm scowled at by a guard
Dressed like Gestapo, unfriendly.
Cold. Cruel.
Where is my rehabilitation?
As my neighbour screams at night
Before falling asleep to sobs.
Where is my rehabilitation?
As the blood pours from my nose
From a punch, as my eyes water,
And my stomach curls into a ball.
Where is my rehabilitation?
As years pass me like hourglass sand,
As I, in another dimension, watch.
Fast, like water dripping.
Where is my rehabilitation?
As I stare at the freckled, starlit night
As its cold wind slips through,
Into my empty, heartless cell.
Where is my rehabilitation?
As a man pushes in front of me,
In the bustling dinner queue.
Then, giving me crazed, hard looks,
As if to say, he's more entitled than me.
Where is my rehabilitation?
When prisoners rush into my cell,
To rob me of my canteen.
Where is my rehabilitation?
After I'm nicked by a screw
For arguing my rights.
For speaking my mind.

Where is my rehabilitation?
When I'm contemplating suicide,
With thoughts of a lost love.
Where is my rehabilitation?
When I'm released with nothing!
Where is true justice?
Where's your peace of mind,
After my release?
Where is my rehabilitation?

18-7

Pete catches a bus to Bethnal Green,
And sits quietly,
Feeling like Michael Myers from *Halloween*,
With slight anxiety.
Not through the fear of capture,
With fear, he won't grow in stature.
In not increasing the kill count,
As he needs a larger amount.
The bus stops, and Pete gets off,
Near a parked patrol car,
As a busker plays guitar,
With a loud, rough, smoker's cough.
Pete grabs the gun from his rucksack,
And waits patiently to attack.

18-8

Kram cast his eyes downwards,
As they walked slow
And around them, blackbirds
Swirling in urban flow.
'One thing, Kram, you should know,
I'm a free thinker, not with the status quo.'
Kram listens and remains in deep silence,
Desperate to escape his life of violence.
'Kram, there's good and bad in all of us,
And to which one, we project
Depends on an outer object,
Upbringing, school, prison and thus.
Everyone is a product of outer forces,
But people can change as love enforces –'

18-9

'But love can't bloom without trust.'
Kram looks at her, then away.
'Let your past fall away like dust,
And to a future, we'll play.'
Kram realises that will be impossible,
For many murders, he's been responsible.
In an expression that appears painful,
Kram now feels strangely shameful.
To be near someone so kind
And beautiful and deep
Maybe Gloria is not a sheep,
Obeying society's laws, blind.
Kram rubs his cold red nose,
Wondering if to his life, he could expose.

18-10

A police officer nears, then stops,
Fumbling keys, as Pete takes aim.
But suddenly to the floor, Pete drops,
Under huge weight and pain.
The busker is struggling on top of him,
The gun fires, as they struggle and swim.
The police officer kicks the gun away,
And handcuffs Pete in complete dismay.
'He was seconds from shooting you,
You were lucky I was here,
It would've been severe.'
'Thanks, mate, I truly owe you!'
The officer bundles Pete in the car,
As a letter falls, near the busker's guitar.

18-11

The busker picks up the letter,
And hands it to the officer
'Here, it's his; hope you're feeling better.'
As the busker's limbs feel like rubber.
The officer takes the busker's name,
And picks up the gun, with mind aflame.
He notices the letter's addressed to the police,
As both men stand, with curiosity apiece.
Adrenalin rushes, as reality overpowers,
The officer opens the letter quick,
On scanning, he feels sick
As to each word, his mind devours.
'My God, mate, d'you know who this is?
It's the Mad Poet of London! Listen to this!

The Wasps

I stare from my cell window,
Waiting for your visit
Like winter waiting for spring.

I wrap my fingers around the bars,
Its coolness never changed,
Like white enamelled teeth.

I had many missed opportunities,
To tell you to forget me,
As I've got a life sentence to serve.

But I couldn't bring myself to say,
Those dreaded words like wasps
Hovering around me, waiting to sting.

I thought money brought happiness,
But I chased it too far,
Across laws and behind bars.

And now I stand in no man's land,
Between life and death,
And in my dreams, I hold you tight.

Yours sincerely,
The Mad Poet of London

18-13

Kram sits in his bedroom,
As the TV screen flashes
And shouts of people consume,
As Pete's photo crashes.
Kram's stomach twists into a knot,
That police would uncover the plot.
As life for Kram has turned,
As Gloria, to his mind, churned.
He makes an uncomfortable swallow,
At how near he came
For the world to know his name
Forever in a prison cell hollow.
He makes a coffee, and holds mug's heat,
Between two palms, as these thoughts repeat.

18-14

Pete sits in a police cell,
As the door opens
A doctor and police personnel
Examines him, with stirring emotions.
Whilst touching his bruised and battered ribs,
From the busker, Andy Hibbs.
The doctor shines a light in his eyes,
As Pete, in annoyance, deeply sighs.
'I'm fine, Doc; besides I've given much worse.'
Pete gives a frozen smile,
'Put that in your file,
As I've sent dozens of yous to hell's hearse.'
The doctor looks with lips pressed tight,
And exits the cell, with a look of fright.

18-15

Pete sits in an interview room,
Opposite two detectives
As Pete's murderous boasts consume,
To the detectives' objectives.
'Could we have a handwriting sample,
Write these lines down, will be ample.'
'Look, I can't be fucked to write,
My flat's full of samples, alright!'
Pete sits back and folds his arms,
Taunting the detectives with a smile
'I can't wait for my glorious trial,
Where I'll display in court, my charms.'
Pete laughs loudly as detectives look vexed,
And Pete's solicitor's face, looks perplexed.

18-16

'Look, I was caught red-handed!
What more do you want?
Let me be straight and candid,
I'm a serial-killing savant.
I admit to all the bloody killings,
And admit so in my courtroom hearings.
I can't make it any clearer,
I am the fucking killer!
Now, I refuse to say any more,
Take me back to my cell!
Your glorious fucking hotel
And kindly close the fucking door.
As I'm going to refuse to talk upon,
As in sleep, I'll dream of police gone.'

18-17

They escort Pete to his cell,
Without saying a word
As Pete's ego does swell
To infamy, submerged.
To his mattress, he lies down,
Lying smiling in infamy's crown.
The evidence from Pete's flat, mushrooms,
As it fills a couple of rooms.
'Gov, we've matched all the writing,
From the poems to quotes
Are experts saying it matches his notes,
It's him, sir; the similarity is striking!'
'Thank God, Rhys, we've got the fucker,'
As Rhys's feelings of relief, strike her.

18-18

A forensics officer approaches Wallace.
'We found the wig and beard.'
'Thank God and good old Horace!
To us, you've really cheered.
If it wasn't for DC Andrews' death,
I would've gone home with drunken breath.
But to his wife and family, I must meet
In sad reflection, I do retreat.'
'Sir, would you like me to go along?
As it might be easier for you,
As I knew him, quite well too,
As we both can sing the same song.
That he was a good and kind man.'
'Thanks so much, Rhys; I mean Joanne.'

18-19

Wallace and Rhys are driving along,
Towards DC Andrews' house
As they're psyching themselves up strong,
To talk to DC Andrews' spouse.
'Thank God, this nightmare's over,
But the amount of lives he's run over.
It's not something to celebrate,
As the suffering is hard to calibrate.'
They pull up outside, by the road,
And solemnly exit the car
From working a case bizarre
To now talking to the widowed.
They walk slowly towards the door,
Their emotions heightened and raw.

18-20

They press the bell and wait,
As voices stir inside
At the gravity and weight
In stress, beside.
The door opens to a woman,
With Slavic looks uncommon.
She immediately senses it's bad news,
Immediately sensing from their cues.
'Mrs Andrews, I'm DCI Wallace,
We...' The woman, in anguish, breaks down
'Is he?' As her voice in tears drown
'Was it? Was it due to behaviour lawless?'
She falls to the floor in discomfort,
As Rhys and Wallace give comfort.

18-21

They're all sitting in the living room,
Whilst Wallace explains
The details of the bomb's plumb
And to his death, it pains.
'He was a good and funny bloke,
And to gallows humour, he did joke.
The suspect name is Pete Townsend,
To a whole life tariff, he'll be condemned.'
They all drink tea and ate cake,
As Andrews' wife talks through memory's mist
'He loved his job, and getting pissed,
Oh, God, my heart does ache.'
After nearly an hour, they both left,
Leaving a widow, alone and bereft.

18-22

In the car, they speed away
With music on low
In the car, Rhys does display,
Her anger on show.
'Life imprisonment for Pete, in any event,
Will mean hero-worshipping upon descent.
As cop killers are the elite inside,
And to a reputation, it does provide.
His time will be cool and sweet,
Until he dies, which won't be long,
As he's nearly seventy years gone
Barely ten years he might complete.'
'I know, Rhys, you're right,
And from his capture, a legend will take flight.'

18-23

'Also, we have a reward to pay,
To a Mr Kram Skyal
To a friendship, he did betray
Directing us to Pete's locale.
He's a criminal with a record long,
Not just sentences, but section's song.
I read he's a schizophrenic,
And that he's changed, that's authentic.'
'I wish we could split the reward,
And give to families who've lost,
And to people who've crossed
As they're also victims ignored.'
'Life, I'm afraid, Joanne, isn't fair,
And money won't cure their despair.'

18-24

Kram stands nervously outside,
The Metropolitan HQ
As his paranoia is far and wide
That his real identity, they may view.
After psyching himself up, he walks in,
Breathing deeply, as thoughts spin.
He approaches a woman receptionist,
And gives details. She checks her list.
'Please take a seat, sir,
Someone will be with you soon.'
Kram pretends he's immune,
That a possible arrest may occur.
Pete would never reveal the truth,
As he's far too long in the tooth.

18-25

A woman walks up to Kram, confidently,
'Mr Skyal?' Kram nods.
'Hello, pleased to meet you, follow me.'
Kram responds.
'It was you who led the police to Townsend.'
'Yeah, he was an evil bastard, I encountered.'
'Where did you meet that monster?'
'In prison, is where our relationship did foster.'
They walk in silence the rest of the way,
Then, into an office, crowded,
As Kram's paranoia, sprouted,
'Hello, Kram. Pleased to meet you today.
It's good to put a face to a name,
And it's good you ended, Townsend's game.'

18-26

All the detectives shake Kram's hand,
In smiles and laughter
As photos were taken with high command
To end this bloody chapter.
Kram talks about Pete in detail,
As Kram felt his plan prevail.
Then was handed a million-pound cheque,
With photos marking his growing respect.
Suddenly, the door opens to Wallace and Rhys
As Kram instantly recognises her face,
As he remembers jogging, in slow pace,
At a crime scene one morning, full of police.
Anxiety, to Kram soars, as he walks toward,
Whilst putting in his wallet, the reward.

18-27

He shakes hands with Wallace and Rhys
As Rhys gives him a look, askew
Which wasn't picked up by other police,
But Kram's heart, in that instant flew.
'Have we met somewhere before?'
As Kram feels himself, sink into the floor.
'I don't think so; I would've remembered,
As you have a look, that would've entered.'
Kram laughs in fear and dread,
Thanking himself for not shaving
And kicking himself for passing her jogging,
As now, his life, hangs by a thread.
With more askew looks, from Rhys,
Kram acts calm, as tensions increase.

18-28

After a short while, Kram leaves
And is escorted out,
As tension and success interweaves
As his future, is left in doubt.
It's going to keep bugging her!
As his intelligence and gut concur.
She's bound to remember in time,
Her memory will connect to rhyme.
Kram gets a taxi to his bank,
To deposit the cheque
As he rubs his neck,
As his thoughts to his heart, outflank.
The taxi stops, and he pays with tip,
As tension mounts, he bites his lip.

18-29

After he deposits the cheque
He sits in a café, in thought.
There's no evidence, not a speck,
And with Pete confessing in court.
But so what, if Rhys remembers!
I could say the scene sent embers,
Burning through me in curiosity,
At such an awful atrocity.
But how do I explain the smile?
It was a strange thing to do,
Strange through and through
I should've kept clear by a mile.
Maybe now I should grow a beard,
But keep it trim, so I won't look weird.

18-30

Kram's in a pub drinking
A cold pint of ale
Whilst constantly ruminating
With sweaty face pale.
I'm so close to pure happiness,
But for that moment of craftiness.
Running past a crime scene smiling,
Attempting to be beguiling.
That moment has destroyed my life,
Why did I think I was so smart,
That moment could rip my dreams apart,
And away from a possible wife.
Kram bangs his pint glass, loudly down,
And walks out the pub, with a frown.

18-31

Walking through London's bustling street
Kram starts to take a different view,
Pounding the pavement with heavy feet
As positive thoughts grew.
So, what if she recognises me,
So, what? That's no guarantee.
Of an immediate arrest,
I'll just be spoken to at best.
It's not a fucking smoking gun,
Most people are curious at crime scenes,
And smiling at women are in men's genes,
It's where the world begun.
Kram laughs aloud, as people stare,
And heads back home, to the house share.

18-32

Kram gets home in a relaxed posture,
Nodding to others in greeting
To staff in happiness, he does foster,
Then, to his room, retreating.
He jumps on his bed and stretches,
Demolishing past vestiges of stresses.
Leaving him totally relaxed and at ease,
To an image of Gloria, he sees.
He pulls out his mobile and dials,
And listens to the ringtone,
Whilst imaging buying a home
A piece of heaven from life's trials.
He finally hears Gloria speak,
And rests the phone upon his cheek.

18-33

'Hi, Kram, how are you doing?'
Kram gives an enrapturing laugh.
'Oh, Gloria, how am I doing!
I'm in happiness, and in riches I bath.
I've just received a cheque for a million,
Just for being a good civilian.
I gave details to police, about a friend,
Who I suspected they wanted, to apprehend.
And he'll be inside for natural life,
For killing innocent people
Christ, this man was lethal,
He used an axe, gun, and knife.
This man was cold, hard, and cruel,
Heartless and devilishly brutal.'

18-34

'So how do you feel; are you proud,
Of little old me?
And is your head in the cloud,
Happy and free?'
'Oh, wow, Kram, you've finally risen!
Where did you meet him, prison?'
'Yes, Gloria, I met all kinds there,
It was an awful place with stale air.
I'm going to speak to probation,
About buying a place in Kent
I'm moving there 100%,
As I'm tired of this polluted location.
And, hopefully, we could start again,
As I am no longer, living in pain.'

They talk more and he cries in laughter,
Reminiscing from years back
As Gloria explains, this is their new chapter,
And to past sufferings he must rack.
'As Lennon said, all you need is love!'
But Kram replies, 'Money is my dove,
Like in the bible, finding land,
As poverty and suffering is in sea's hand.
Money is happiness; on island green,
Without it, you're dead,
Drifting with a soul of lead
Living as a cog in society's machine.'
The conversation soon tapers, and ends,
And Kram writes a poem, as a thought descends.

I Walk in Lifetimes Gone

I left my house to electrified air as
The thunder drums the sky and lightning
Bolts scorch air in purple. A car nears,
And passes, as its engine is amplified by,
The stillness between the thunder. There is a
Familiarity to the scene which I've experienced,
Before. I closed the door,
Behind me and walk the empty streets,
Passing Edwardian detached houses,
With their years etched in stone.

I see myself as a small boy, barefoot,
Playing on cobbled roads to the sound of
Horse-drawn carriages. Then, thinking back to the
News hours ago, about the war in Afghanistan.
It brought images to mind of a war I fought,
With long single-shot rifles and sabres drawn.
I lean against a tree,
And have the sense of meeting a woman there,
Carefully planning each word and waiting.
Waiting for her reply in electrified air.

Waiting patiently for the bolt.

18-37

After writing, Kram looks aghast.
Shit, what am I doing?
Poetry must remain in my past!
To a new life, I'm now pursuing.
Kram rips the poem up,
And to the toilet, he gives up.
To a flushing water cascade,
As droplets of water sprayed.
Maybe in time, I could write,
In the safety, of my home
In an alarmed dome
Where security is tight.
But for now, I must be very careful,
And to security and love, I must be prayerful.

18-38

Kram's talking with probation,
In a small office
To which he has a good relation
Whilst being cautious.
'So, Kram, what's your plan?'
'Buying a house if I can,
Down in beautiful Kent,
I hope you consent.
As I'm rekindling a relationship there
With an old flame
Gloria is her name,
And she's beautiful and fair.'
'When d'you think you'll move?'
'Weeks yet, I hope you approve.'

18-39

'Yes. I'll simply pass your case over
To the Kent team.
Just be sure to make disclosure,
With your next team.'
'Sure, I've been online with an estate agent,
I've seen a perfect house, now vacant.
It's a mile from the coast,
And in a style, I'm engrossed.
With beams and an open fireplace
And three acres of land
And planning permission to expand,
It's in a world of beauty, I embrace.'
'Sounds great! When are you viewing?'
'Wednesday! But not viewing, I'm buying.'

CANTO 19

Kram walks Gloria through his home.
In smiles and laughter
'My own palace, my own dome
In life's new chapter.
And with you, Gloria, happiness will rain,
Happiness more lasting than cocaine.'
'It's amazing, Kram, it truly is,
Living with you here, will be bliss.'
'So, Gloria, you're moving in?'
'Yes, Kram, as life is short.
And in these months, I've thought.
To a relationship, we should begin.
As, from our past, love was born,
And throughout my life, it had never worn.'

19-2

'You mentioned about honesty,
How it's an important piece,
For a relationship to flourish, free
As honesty is soul's release.
But my past is too awful to mention,
And it would ruin love's tension.
And not to mention living in bliss,
And to me, you might even dismiss.
Dismiss me totally, from your life,
As my past is a fright
Which now has taken flight,
As now I want you for a wife.'
'But, Kram, I'm so intrigued by your past,
I'm sure it's in complete contrast!'

19-3

'You've seen the *Shawshank Redemption*,
Well, I was like Andy Dufresne
But my life was a much worse conception,
Where I became insane.
As I also crawled through a pipe,
A dark sewer pipe, from years of shite.
But you and money have brought me freedom,
From where it escalated back in Needham.
And with you, happiness will reign,
Like with Dufresne
Washing away his pain
From a sewer pipe in a torrent of rain.'
'Okay, Kram, the past is the past,
But a line's now been drawn, for honesty's mast.'

19-4

'So, from now on, we have total honesty,
From today!'
'Okay, Gloria, and vice versa, you promise me.'
'I promise, okay.'
'There's something else I need to say,
I want a dog, a chow chow today!'
'Yes, I'd love that' they're so adorable,
Also, May will love it. Is it affordable?'
'I'm rich, remember!' And in laughter, they kiss,
As they enter the living room from garden
As the TV blares, the opera *Carmen*
As Don Jose and Carmen kiss.
From her enticing, seductive song,
Where she escapes from a prison strong.

19-5

Belmarsh top-security wing is alight.
As Pete is escorted to his trial
To cheers, as his case burns bright
And to a legend, there's no denial.
And through the rigmaroles of reception,
He's dressed in a suit of perfection.
As he walks towards the prison van,
A group of prison officers scan.
He sits in the van's cubicle quietly.
For the grand Old Bailey
With its blindfolded lady
As Pete bathes in his notoriety.
Basking bright in a world infamy,
Knowing his legend will last to infinity.

19-6

News reporters and cameras surround,
The front of the Old Bailey
As the cameras to prison van hound
With camera flashes going crazy.
Pete, with bright glowing eyes,
Into the Old Bailey, he proudly sighs.
And is escorted from the van to the cells,
As guards stare, his ego swells.
He sits reading the cell's graffiti.
Too excited to think straight,
Then, to a packed lunch, he ate,
Whilst drinking cheap tea.
I wonder which actor will play me,
As Michael Caine's past eighty.

19-7

Ray Winstone would be great!
He was perfect in Sexy Beast,
And his fame would carry weight,
To my fury unleashed.
And as my cunning had outwit,
Even the police must admit.
That I'm the crème de la crème,
A real legendry criminal gem.
A fame, beating the Axeman of New Orleans
And even the Boston Strangler
As in poetry, I showed my anger,
As all will agree, from my fans to historians.
Christ, I owe Kram so much!
And hope to happiness, he will touch.

19-8

Kram is suited with a trimmed beard,
In the witness room
Next to the busker, who also appeared,
But in an ill-fitting suited costume.
'Hi, I'm the busker Andy Hibbs,
It was me who punched Pete's ribs.'
'You're a real hero!' Kram blurts,
As the busker to death flirts.
'We must go for a drink sometime,
As I'd love to hear you sing
As I've seen you on TV, swing
With your guitar, in musical rhyme.'
'That's a deal, here's my details.'
As Andy writes down, in scribbled trails.

19-9

'I don't believe he's pleading not guilty,
He was caught red-handed!'
Says Andy, drinking machine-made tea.
'I think it's standard,'
Replied Kram. 'All criminals do that,
As their defence teams try to combat,
A life sentence in an A-Cat prison,
To a softer life in a hospital condition.
He's not mad, he's only bad,
As the psychiatrist will say
Probably even today
Which I think Pete will be glad.
As life in Broadmoor would be hell,
He'd much prefer, life in a prison cell.'

The courtroom was bustling with electricity,
As the reporters pine, for a shocking trial,
To mark Pete's existence, in total infamy
Hoping their newspaper sales, will spiral.
The trial starts with the defence's statement.
'The crimes were Pete's repayment.
Of a prison system that makes the sane, insane,
Where man's inhumanity's to man, is it's game!'
The prosecution stands up and slams,
'Blaming the prison is a weak excuse,
As prison's aim is not to torture or abuse!
Pete's mind was already twisted,' he rams.
Then Kram walks in, and eagerly takes the stand,
With head held high, he gives command.

19-11

The defence council approaches.
'So, Mr Kram Skyal.'
As to the jury, the defence poses.
'Pete was your pal!'
'Yes, we were good friends,
As inside friendship, transcends.
But I had to put a stop to him,
As his crimes in evil, did swim.'
'From your experience, Kram, in the system,
How does prison affect or change people?'
'What goes on inside should be illegal!
But it still goes on, in society's skewed wisdom.
As Oscar Wilde wrote, "The bad get badder,
And the mad get madder!"'

19-12

'How so?'
'Well, it depends if you're singled out.'
'That so!'
'Yeah, as with me, I was tortured throughout.
Until I went mad and got sectioned,
I was lost and had no sense of direction.
I was twisted, angry and in pain,
The guards tortured me, until I went insane.
That's probably what happened to Pete,
In madness, he lost himself
Like I lost myself
But I got help, before hitting the street.
It wasn't Pete's fault, for the awful murders,
As a cell can twist you, with it's solitary murmurs.'

19-13

'Thank you, Mr Skyal, that's all.'
Prosecution counsel stands.
'But, Kram, you hadn't killed at all,
You had no murderous plans!'
'No, well, I had lots of help, and support,
But my soul does harbour, hatred of a sort.'
'No more questions, Your Honour.'
As Kram had his say, he feels calmer.
A forensic psychiatrist stands in the dock,
And explains the McNaughton rules for insanity,
'That it's a person who doesn't know nature or quality,
Of the act he was doing, when running amok.'
'Was Pete unaware of what he was doing,
Hunting in London, with death and poetry pursuing?'

19-14

'Yes! He definitely was aware,
With the poetry and detailed planning
He was careful, cunning, and did prepare,
And a steely focus when out hunting.'
'Thank you, no further questions.'
The defence stands on Judge's expressions.
'So, poetry and planning prove his sanity?
The bloody poetry and all! You see no abnormality?'
'Yes, I feel he's insane, that I see,
But not regarding McNaughton rules for insanity
As I don't feel he realises the gravity
That I'm certain, it's plain to see.'
'No more questions, Your Honour.'
As the psychiatrist leaves, people holler.

19-15

The judge, in anger, bangs his gavel.
'Any more shouting, and you all go out!'
Then, the counsels continue their battle
As Pete stares, sitting devout.
The busker, Andy Hibbs, says his piece,
Then wishes the world, could live in peace.
And at that moment, Pete in rage shouts,
As the court's security to Pete, sprouts.
Days flew into weeks, and the jury retires,
As Pete's fame in the news goes viral
And crowds around the court spiral
As his story to disenfranchised men, inspires.
Pete walks in a circle, within his cell,
As again he feels his fame, and ego swell.

19-16

Kram listens to the busker Andy,
Talking off society's troubled existence
And his love of Mahatma Gandhi
And of his nonviolent resistance.
'Kram, I'd love to end society's pain.'
As Kram imagines pushing him under a train.
'And with my music, I could solve.'
As Kram imagines him in acid, dissolve.
'We must celebrate Pete's conviction,
And see the end of that devil.'
'Your words, Andy, hit at a level,
As living in peace is my ambition.
Maybe something good can come from this,
Maybe goodness could escape, courtroom's abyss.'

19-17

Suddenly, a voice shouts out,
'Hey, everyone, the jury is in!'
As people storm about,
To get a theatre seat within.
Kram and Andy are unable to enter,
As in Court One, everyone wants to venture.
Kram and Andy stand in the hallway,
With others in expressions of dismay.
Suddenly, cheers can be heard by all
'He's not going to the comfort of a hospital ward,
He'll piss and shit with the devil's horde!'
While Kram sees laughter and dancing, like at a ball.
'He's been found guilty of twenty-four murders,
And several attempted,' from rumbling murmurs.

19-18

The judge with anger, from a deep breath forced,
'I'm sentencing you to a whole life order.'
As Pete, to life, already felt divorced,
Feeling perfectly happy in prison's quarter.
'There's nothing, Judge, you bastards can do,
As I'm perfectly happy, in prison's zoo!'
Said Pete with anger, and is escorted away,
Whilst sticking up a finger, in a defiant display.
He walks proudly to his cell,
Then within minutes into a prison van
Giving the streets a final scan
Whilst basking in infamy's spell.
I suppose I must write an autobiography,
To help make the film and documentary.

19-19

Pete enters back onto the wing,
As prisoners line up to shake his hand
He feels grand, like a king,
As prison staff feel hate, as prisoners band.
'Join the club, mate; I'm doing a whole life.'
'Alright, Pete, I hoped you gave them strife!'
Pete laughs and makes jokes,
As comments to his ego strokes.
But the guard's look with contempt,
Watching him revel in glory,
From his well-known story
In his historical stand, hell-bent.
Angered that he'll be remembered,
And all his victims, to dust, have surrendered.

19-20

Months go by, then one night,
Guards tell Pete he's going to the block,
Pete tries putting up a fight,
But to unconsciousness guards to him knock.
He awakes, as he's dragged past cells,
Finding himself naked, as coldness propels.
In a stress lock, he's dragged through,
As prisoners through door gaps, view.
Finally, into the block, to a dirty cell
He curls up alone, cold, bruised.
As he looks around, totally confused
'Hello, Pete – welcome to hell!'
'Why? What's happening, for fucksake?'
'We hear you're planning, an escape!'

19-21

'That's rubbish,' he yells as two guards laugh.
'We knew one of your victims, a good mate,
You're much hated amongst us staff!
And also, that prison governor was great.'
'So, this is about revenge –
To your friend, you must avenge!'
'Now you've got the picture, cunt!
And now to a new life, you must confront.'
Throughout the days, weeks and months
Pete's tortured with fear and fists,
Tied on the floor by his wrists,
As most guards to Pete, confronts.
Pete's lying rambling in the dark,
As his life is cold, painful, and stark.

19-22

One cold night, Pete jumps awake,
To see a razor blade slide under his door,
Is this on purpose or by mistake?
As Pete crawls, too, across the floor.
He grabs it tight, in his palm,
As he, for the first time, feels calm.
Finally, this torture can come to an end,
And into death, my dearest friend.
Suddenly, in vigour, he cuts his throat,
Then, to each wrist,
He cuts swift,
As he feels blood around him, coat.
Soon, Pete's body, drifts from night,
As Pete's soul moves, towards the light.

19-23

Warmth radiates throughout Kram's body,
As he awakes in bed with Gloria
As happiness and love, she does embody
As he draws curtains to sun's euphoria.
The phone suddenly rings downstairs,
And in a dressing gown he casually wears.
He descends down, to the kitchen phone,
He picks it up, as he stands on stone.
'This is Governor Hadley, and
I'm calling from Belmarsh; is this Mr Skyal?'
Kram panics. 'Yes, Mr Hadley, I'm Skyal!'
'You're down as next of kin to Pete Townsend.
I'm afraid last night he committed suicide.'
'That's crazy; he… he couldn't be… he really died?'

Kram drops the phone and cries,
As he struggles to take on board
In anguish, he wipes his eyes,
And curses the million-pound reward.
It doesn't make sense; he gained infamy!
And there must have been prisoner solidarity!
He became a legend, his dream,
And it couldn't be the prison regime?
As he's done more porridge than Goldilocks!
He can do bird on his head,
As through decades, he's bled,
He had it all! But now, to heaven, he knocks.
Kram grabs a small pad and writes,
And to his bottom lip, he bites.

In Moments of Despair

In moments of despair, I cast my nets,
I cast them far and wide.

I catch sometimes sympathy, sometimes –
Company, sometimes unwanted.

But sometimes I cast no nets, and I –
Catch inner growth and strength.

And sometimes, in these moments, I –
Catch the thought of suicide.

19-26

Rhys and DC Neil enter Belmarsh,
As they were greeted by Mr Hadley
A prison well known for being harsh,
As the governor stands, quite proudly.
'I'm surprised to read your name,
Weren't you the Rhys who chased his game?'
'Yes, Mr Hadley, that's why they phoned me,
To investigate his death, in prison's sea.
As we were all in complete shock
As Pete committing suicide is bizarre
We all felt inside, he would've been a star,
It's quite hard to take stock.'
'He went downhill fast, always fighting staff,
And harassing all, with his maddening laugh.'

19-27

'They took his body away at six.'
'Could we visit his cell?'
'Okay, but it's covered in blood-streak whips,
It looks like darkest hell.'
'Did you inform his next of kin?'
'Yes, a Mr Kram Skyal,' he says with a grin.
'Kram Skyal?! Are you sure?'
'Yes, as that name sounds strange and obscure.
Let's go to my office to check,
I think they corresponded frequently,
And Mr Skyal sent money recently,
A three-thousand-pound cheque!
Imagine sending an animal like that cash,
As Pete Townsend was complete trash.'

19-28

They all sat in the governor's office,
As Mr Hadley read the books
As Rhys feels hot and nauseous
As she gave DC Neil suspicious looks.
Rhys checks Pete's security file,
Finding they've been in contact, since the trial.
And yes, Kram sent Pete cheques,
As Rhys repeatedly checks.
'This is really weird!
What the hell is going on?
Why's Kram laying cash upon?
As it was Kram's evidence that steered!
Steered Pete to a whole life-term,
In prison deep, like Earth to worm.'

19-29

Both Rhys and DC Neil are escorted
To Pete's double-locked cell
As it reveals a world distorted
A dirty, grimy bloody hell.
Rhys spots fades of dried blood,
And shit, lightly scrubbed.
One looks like a bloody boot print,
As she places in her mouth, a mint.
'Neil, I want this sealed as a crime scene,
I want forensics in here quick.'
'Crime scene? Don't be thick,
As we need to get this cell clean!
We need the space, for Christ's sake,
You're making a stupid fucking mistake!'

19-30

'I'm sorry, Mr Hadley, it looks suspicious,
With varying layers of dried blood, and shit
And for Pete to kill himself, sounds fictitious
As him to prison, was like pig to shit.
Also, his crimes of killing prison staff,
I bet in revenge, you all had a laugh!'
Mr Hadley shouts, 'What are you saying?
I obey the laws! Me! To laws obeying.
Is that fucking clear, Rhys!'
'That's very clear, sir, I obey laws, too,
And anyone who breaks them, I'll pursue!
Is that clear, sir? I'm police! –
Also, I want the names of all block staff.'
As Mr Hadley begins to laugh.

19-31

The mortuary is stark and bleak,
Clean and clinical
As Rhys and the pathologist speak
About the noted criminal.
'On examining, the cuts were self-inflicted,
But on saying that, he was also tortured.
His ribs had been broken several times,
And recently healed, and there other signs.
Both his testicles have been ruptured
And has bruising on his back,
By boots from an attack
And his left ear drum has been punctured
His right eye socket, has been fractured by a blow,
I think you've a manslaughter case, to throw.'

Rhys steps outside, into the air
As she makes a call on her phone,
'Gov, we have a manslaughter case to chair,
Pete Townsend's, in Belmarsh's zone.
It looks like he was tortured,
For months, and it may have been ordered!
By the governor, Mr Hadley,
Who to me earlier laughed madly.'
'Look, Rhys, I've had a call from upstairs,
We're to sweep it under the carpet,
As he was the devil incarnate
And really, regarding Pete, who cares?'
'But, sir, a serious crime has occurred!'
'Rhys, forget it, that's my final word!'

19-33

Rhys pockets her phone,
And mixes within the crowded street
As she feels annoyed and alone
As her boss's words to her thoughts beat.
She goes into a nearby café,
And orders coffee as she looks at the display.
But she ignores the cakes and treats,
And eases to the rhythm beats.
From a surround sound speaker system
Playing Rihanna's, "We found love",
As a man past Rhys does shove
As she maintains calm, through wisdom.
She finds a table with coffee to relax,
As Pete and Kram's letters lay cracks.

19-34

Why were Pete and Kram corresponding?
Why did Kram give Pete money?
From the reward money! I must go prodding.
Christ! The reward money, stun me!
What if Kram knew all along
And was waiting for reward's highest song!
Rhys returns to work to get information,
Of where Kram resides, his location.
She jumps in her car,
And drives away, from London's grey,
Heading for Kent's beautiful display
To solve a case bizarre.
With window down, the wind does rush,
In mental Olympics, her thoughts gush.

19-35

'Gloria, I feel much better after the shave,
I didn't like that beard,
As ten years younger, it did save,
And it felt a bit weird.'
'You look much better, love,
It's more like you, like hand to glove.'
'I'm going out for a long jog,
And I'll also take the dog.'
'Good, it'll help clear your head,
And release uplifting endorphins
And bury bad feelings into coffins,
And lay them completely to bed.'
Kram puts the lead onto the dog,
And starts off upon his jog.

CANTO 20

20-1

Kram jogs round his extensive grounds
Past manicured hedges, and shrubs
With birdsong and rustling leaf sounds
As life, to creeping sadness snubs.
He notices sunshine glancing off leaves,
As there, tussled by a gentle breeze.
And bursts of colour surround him bright,
As good-natured thoughts, take flight.
He repeats to himself, *this is amazing.*
As he stretches arms up in victory.
Pete and my past are history,
And to my new life, I'm embracing.
Warmth radiates throughout his body,
As his soul to nature, does embody.

Rhys hits the multi-lane traffic,
In the centre of Canterbury
To pavements packed with people erratic
As she rubs the stress in her belly.
A delivery van stalls, and police sirens blare,
As people play on their phones, without care.
Rhys feels mentally bumped and jarred,
As to her professionalism, they disregard.
She drinks water from her bottle,
As it dribbles down her chin
As she remembers Mr Hadley's grin
As to him and others, she could throttle.
Car exhausts gust, and cloud the air,
And through the streets, she does tear.

20-3

Kram slows to a gentle walk,
As he takes the dog off the lead
To the Earth, he does talk
Did I, to all, really mislead?
He notices bees crawling on flower petals,
And over hidden stepping stones, nettles.
He notices a skittering squirrel dice,
Up a tree, as the branches to sky entice.
As if to say, 'Shower me, sky, gently,
As my leaves are starting to wilt
Gently spray this Earth's quilt
Be kind, dear sky, be friendly.'
Kram sits hunched upon the grass,
Feeling lucky to escape, crime's impasse.

20-4

Kram gets up and walks to a tree,
And sits leaning against it,
As he sees, around him, pinecone debris,
He picks one up, and holds it.
Dandelion fluff floats in the air,
As Kram's eyes upon, fixed their stare.
His thoughts float far and wide,
Realising without Pete, he would've died.
He owed Pete his life,
For his advice on chasing Gloria
Which led to him leaving infamy's euphoria,
As to now, he has a wife.
Kram reminisces over their wedding day,
As memories flowed like a ballet.

20-5

Tapping a loose fist against his heart
With a feeling of expansion
And upon his wedding day, his life did start
With feelings of serenity and compassion.
As these feelings he thought he'd never had,
As through his soul, love has grabbed.
And through his soul, destiny has steered,
And to a new life, his past has cleared.
He closes his eyes,
As sunlight touches his lids
In red, as vision skids
He lets out a gentle sigh.
Listening to the rustling of the leaves,
And in gentle breaths, he breathes.

20-6

The wind flutters a plastic bag,
Caught in a nearby bush,
As Rhys takes a break with a fag
Smoking heavily, as her lungs push.
A scrap of newspaper slides by,
As the sun on pavement, heats it dry.
With distant, rough voices shouting,
And to her suspicions, she's doubting.
Maybe he gave money out of guilt,
And that's why he wrote as well.
As she smells a familiar smell
Of a nearby spliff being built.
On noticing teenagers approaching,
She quickly feels unease encroaching.

20-7

Rhys drives out from Canterbury city,
As trees and quiet roads greet
And thinks of Pete with slight pity
As conflicting thoughts meet.
No one has the right to torture and kill,
Or cause pain or to blood, spill.
As prisons are created, to create stability,
To stop and cure criminal activity.
She notices thick brambles,
And bright berry bushes
Against the grey, it pushes,
As the cold grey road tramples.
Like a scar from a fight,
Reminding always of fate's plight.

20-8

Rhys is reaching her destination,
According to her sat nav's voice,
As she feels stress's elevation
But feels she has no other choice.
As her detective instincts have kicked in,
As she must understand, thro' thick and thin.
She hears slicing lawnmower blades,
As colourful gardens sit like parades.
She rolls her window down, to sprinklers hissing,
And a tinkling of wind chimes
And to birdsongs in rhymes.
And sees bees on flower petals, kissing.
Finally, she reaches her destination,
And drives up the driveway, brazen.

20-9

Rhys parks outside the house
As she sees a dog run past
Then, on seeing Kram, her heart shouts,
As he comes running past.
My God, he was that jogger in Hugo Boss,
Who ran past me, at crime scene's box.
This is too much of a coincidence,
And has incredible significance.
She quickly exits the car,
As Kram reaches the house door,
His mouth hits the floor,
As Rhys's presence to him jar.
'Hello, Mr Skyal, can we speak?'
As Kram tenses up, his slim physique.

20-10

'Erm, yes, come in.'
Kram replies with a thickening voice,
As he walks within
Knowing he had no choice.
His Adam's apple bobs in thick swallows,
As Rhys to Kram, closely follows.
'Let's go into the living room,
As I'm sure it's about Pete, I presume.'
They both enter the room,
To the scent of a lavender lit candle
As the stress he can barely handle
As tension in thoughts, consume.
'Sit down, please.' Kram motions,
As they both hide their emotions.

20-11

'How long again did you know Pete?'
As Rhys sits in an armchair
As to her real question, she does keep,
As her skin pricks with hair.
'I met him years ago in prison...'
As Kram goes on, in fixed vision.
Rhys vision focuses to writing, on a pad,
As adrenalin scorches through her like mad.
She picks it up and reads aloud,
'In moments of despair...'
As Kram fixes his stare
As her suspicions of Kram shroud.
Kram, in nervousness, looks for a weapon,
As he twitches with a growing aggression.

20-12

She finishes the poem and smiles,
'You like poetry also!
As well as Pete.' She beguiles,
As a question rises in flow.
'I know you from that morning,
Smiling at me in Hugo Boss, jogging!
You know Pete. You write poetry.
It's all coming together in perfect symmetry.'
Kram panics and charges at Rhys
As she kicks him in the head
Directly upon his forehead
As he falls beside her on sofa's fleece.
Rhys darts out the room quick,
As Kram recovers in dizziness thick.

20-13

Rhys darts from the house, feeling edgy,
As Kram grabs her fiercely
And falls on her heavy
As Rhys kicks Kram again, severely.
Rhys gets in her car, and locks herself in,
And starts her engine to wheels' spin.
Kram also gets in his car,
As he sees his life's dreams, drift far.
With a dry throat from rushed breathing
She focuses with wide eyes,
As Kram's attack implies
That he was complicit in every killing.
The cars shoot through the country lanes,
As both their thoughts, burn with flames.

20-14

With occasional passing of cars
They increase speed,
As Kram sees years behind bars
Guaranteed.
Kram's soul at prison does shudder,
As his life in the world does flutter.
If she manages to get clean away,
To a noose, I'll promise I'll sway.
Rhys feels her life flutter,
In her desperation to get away
As in her mirror, Kram's car does sway,
As at the truth, she does shudder.
They both head out onto the main road,
As their thoughts, in desperation, explode.

20-15

Rhys works her gearstick forcefully,
As the engine roars
Her suspicions hit with enormity,
As to the pedal, she floors.
Fuck, he's still on my tail!
As her face goes ghostly pale.
To her mobile, she tries to reach,
And past a lorry, she does screech.
But it falls, on the passenger-side floor,
As she realises, it's her only hope
As to all police, it would rope,
So, she decides to quickly explore.
She sees the road is clear ahead,
And tries reaching it, with fingers spread.

20-16

She manages to grab the phone,
And sits upright,
When suddenly she's thrown,
Crashing into wall's bite.
Smashed and crumpled,
Dazed and puzzled.
With blood dripping from her head,
All she can see is red.
Kram's car jolts to a stop
Before leaping out, proud
On seeing the smoke cloud,
From the car's bonnet top.
Suddenly, the engine bursts into flames,
As Kram stands, in stoic domains.

20-17

He sees Rhys's head moving,
As she frantically gasps,
As the fire spreads, with smoke shooting
And near her door, the fire clasps.
Kram jumps to, as thoughts restore,
And desperately tries to open her door.
Rhys looks at him in fear,
As Kram steps up a gear.
Kram grabs a nearby brick,
And rapidly strikes,
As the heat gripes
To, suddenly, glass breaking thick.
He grabs Rhys, pulling her through the door,
And lays her faraway, as flames roar.

20-18

Rhys coughs and gasps for air
And by her, he kneels
As his end, he is aware,
And to her suspicions, he reveals.
'Are you okay? You're not burnt?
As I panicked at what you learnt!
But your suspicions are slightly off.'
As Rhys rubs her eyes, to a smoky cough.
'Pete only killed that once,
As I'm the real Mad Poet of London,
Who got revenge in abundance,
As I cunningly escaped the hunt for months.
The deal was he got the notoriety,
And I got rich and lived quietly.'

20-19

'Look, don't tell Gloria about me!
I don't want her to know.'
'Sorry, I can't keep quiet, at any degree,
Plus, the papers will blow!'
Rhys sits up as Kram stands,
As the heat in wind, around them fans.
'It was because of Gloria I stopped,
As her love to my murderous rage, mopped.'
Suddenly Kram runs into the flames,
As Rhys shouts out
And flames sprout
'Don't say a word...' As Kram's run aims.
Through the fiery car's window, he dives clean,
Whilst letting out, a blood-curdling scream.

A marked police car stops,
As Rhys stands in shock
Then, onto her knees, she drops,
As people and police around her flock.
The police drag her away from the heat,
As people gather in the street.
Suddenly, the car explodes,
As it's engulfed in fiery robes.
The thick smoke in sky, towers
As police try talking to Rhys
She tells them she's police,
But Kram's death, overpowers.
'Was it an accident? What had happen?'
Rhys goes silent, as thoughts blacken.

20-21

Rhys sits in an interview room,
As she's questioned by police
Remembering the fiery plume
As she feels tension increase.
'I don't know why he flipped,
As I remembered to him, I kicked.
The next thing I knew, he was chasing me,
In his car, whilst I'm trying to get free.'
'What did you say? Had you argued?'
'I was talking about his friend Pete,
As he blamed his death on guards' mistreat
Then, in aggression, he then moved.'
'Pete – Pete Townsend, the serial killer!'
'Yes, Kram grassed, and to us, he did deliver.'

20-22

'So why was he so upset?'
'I think he felt responsible,
Look, have you a cigarette,
And a Coke, if possible?'
'Sure, anyway, this interview's over,
We're just crossing T's, moreover.'
'Would you like a lift back home?
Or maybe to use a phone?'
'I'd love a lift, and to phone a mate,
Either Kate or Louise,
As I don't even have any keys.
Time's ticking, and it's getting late.
But first, I need to speak to his wife,
And explain how, Kram lost his life.'

20-23

Rhys sits with Gloria in the kitchen,
As she retells the story.
'He was,' says Gloria, '…in a depressed condition.'
But in anger, she throws on Rhys her coffee.
'Why did you come here?
Why did you bloody appear?'
'I'm sorry, Gloria, I didn't want this to happen,
I was just talking about Pete; I didn't imagine.'
Gloria stares with glazed eyes,
As her voice chokes with emotion
As she visualises the explosion
And in disbelief, she cries,
'No! No! This couldn't have happened,
As to a life together, we both imagined.'

20-24

'There's something you're not saying!
He wouldn't have suddenly snapped like that!
What is it? You're not explaining!
What is it, Rhys,' as Gloria's voice falls flat.
Rhys pauses for a moment,
As she remembers Kram in that moment.
It was the reason he wanted to die,
For me to keep the secret and lie.
For in that moment, he saved me,
As Gloria had changed him,
No more was he able to sin,
Ending the terror, within London's sea.
'That's everything, Gloria, I give you my word,
I promise you, that's exactly what occurred.'

20-25

Gloria falls to the floor,
Sobbing in tears
No more could she endure,
Whilst covering her ears.
Rhys crouches down and holds her tight,
Whilst Gloria, in grief, does fight.
'He was my soulmate, it was meant to be,
And to my heart, he had the key.
I'd like to be left alone,
I can't…
I just can't…'
'It's okay. Here's my number for my phone.
Ring me at any time when darkness grips,
As I relate, as grief to soul whips!'

20-26

Rhys parks for the funeral by a church,
As her thoughts cascade,
Through Kram's file, she did research
Of how a killer was made.
With parental abuse to prison,
With years inside, he had risen.
Over half his life, he was inside,
Before being released, to a killer's pride.
What was society expecting?
To release someone from prison's abuse
And from asylums, before letting loose
Wasn't anyone suspecting?
But was the solution so very simple?
That love could change a violent criminal!

20-27

Love was something he never had,
Which led to a blackened soul,
Resulting in a character violent and bad
That no one in this world could control.
He could easily have left me dead,
To burn in that fiery bed.
And drove away to a happy life,
To comfort, security, and a loving wife.
But he wasn't able to kill me,
He tried but failed,
As decency prevailed
And now I hope his soul is free.
And not in a world of fiery shadows,
But to a world of light, where love echoes.

Rhys sees Gloria with some people,
As she exits the car
Then, glancing to a cross on the steeple,
A workman smoking a cigar.
Rhys walks down the narrow path,
And into Gloria's smile, she does bath.
Gloria approaches in a dark blue dress,
And nearby a photographer with press.
The light dazzles in Rhys's eyes,
As Rhys shakes Gloria's hand, blushing,
'Thanks, Rhys, for coming.'
As Rhys smiles and sighs.
'You're welcome, as I had to say goodbye,
For him rescuing me, I can't deny.'

20-29

Polished wooden pews in neat rows,
Either side of the aisle
With light from stained-glass windows
To a dozen walking single file.
A stereo is playing Lana Del Rey,
As the priest stands, on altar grey.
Rhys's eyes fix on the burning candles,
Then thinks of Kram, as fire entangles.
She closes her eyes at the awful cry,
As the priest switches the stereo off
And does purposely cough
To gain full attention to, say goodbye.
'Family and friends, welcome to this gathering.'
As the priest's words fly in sober scattering.

20-30

Gloria stands to all, in eulogy's embrace,
Recounting how they met
'We'd go to the beach, to picnic and race,
Running barefoot, from a sea, wet.
And I will always remember...'
As Gloria falls to a nervous tremor.
'And I will always remember,
His love for December.
As he told me, it made him feel cosy,
Wrapped in a blanket on the sofa,
And his great love for icy cold cola,
With his chubby cheeks, red and rosy.'
Gloria holds a notepad and reads,
And through goodness, her love bleeds.

20-31

'Most of you are my family,
And barely knew him,
But he is also your family,
As in our future, he will swim.
As of a week ago, I discovered I was pregnant,
And his DNA, in my baby, is remnant.
Of a hugely kind and loving man,
Who through our child, in lifetime's span.
Will, I'll make sure, be remembered,
Not just his troubled past,
Not just of schizophrenic's cast
But of his love and poetry rendered.
Years ago, when we met for the first time,
He showed his love for poetry and rhyme –'

'And everything he wrote I kept,
In a folder neat,
And to a particular poem, I wept
It hit me hard like concrete.
I'll read it to you in a minute,
As it reflects his deep, soulful spirit.
But I'd like to tell him now, he's wrong,
He's made his mark, in DNA strong.
And will be with us, in our family,
To his love, strong
And in his poetry's song
As he is, and always will be, family.
This poem is called 'Temporary'.
And its imagery is exemplary.'

20-33

Temporary

The sky in dark shrouds
Is only temporary, as
The stormy wind howls,
Is only temporary, as
Rain hits from clouds,
Is only temporary, against
Our windows in tapping sounds,
Are all temporary, like
Our lives not leaving a mark.

20-34

Gloria finishes and sits down,
As the priest gives the final prayer
With a fixed stone-faced frown
Gloria's emotions flare.
As she sobs, in a childlike whimpering,
Rhys sees near, a candle flickering.
Could that flickering be Kram's soul,
Who felt Gloria's emotions lose control.
Could he be here looking over,
From that candle flame flickering wild
In happiness, as she's having his child,
And that his DNA and poetry won over.
The service finishes, and people file out,
As Rhys follows quietly, looking about.

20-35

Rhys decides not to go to the burial,
As she imagines smoke drifting
Of Kram's fiery crimes, his acts of evil
Stopping twenty-three lives from existing.
Twenty-three people, stone-cold dead,
And a city on fire, in terror and dread.
But who's to blame? Kram the weapon?
Or society's penal system's depression.
The hand of justice!
Culling blindly without emotion,
Throwing coldly into prison's ocean
Creating waves of injustice.
'Those to whom evil is done,
Do evil in return.' W. H. Auden.

Rhys closes her eyes to sun's rays,
As the wind caresses her ears
Listening to birds in nature's praise
Filling her soul with tears.
Suddenly, her mobile goes off,
As she answers with a cough.
'Rhys, it's Wallace; we need you quick,
To a new case in mystery thick!
Three women were found naked,
Covered in gold paint,
For the faint-hearted, it ain't
By a diseased mind, it was created.'
'I'll be at the station by two,
Do you have a suspect or clue?'